Stages, volume 20

SERIES EDITORS
General Editor: Gerald Prince,
University of Pennsylvania

Michael Holquist,
Yale University

Warren Motte,
University of Colorado at Boulder

Patricia Meyer Spacks,
University of Virginia

Essays in Aesthetics

Gérard Genette

TRANSLATED BY Dorrit Cohn

University of Nebraska Press · Lincoln and London

Chapter 10, "A Logic of Literature," previously
appeared in Käte Hamburger, The Logic of Literature, 2d rev. ed., trans. Marilynn J. Rose,
published by Indiana University Press (1993).

LC Control Number 2004063769

ISBN 0-8032-2197-5 (cloth: alkaline paper)
ISBN 0-8032-7110-7 (paper: alkaline paper)

Set in Quadraat and Quadraat Sans by Bob Reitz.
Printed by Edwards Brothers, Inc.

Contents

Translator's Acknowledgment

All the translated essays in this volume were published by Gérard Genette as *Figures IV* (Paris: Editions du Seuil, 1999). Seven pieces from this publication have been omitted, either because they were of minor interest to American readers or because they were too much focused on the French language.

I wish to thank Ingeborg Hoesterey, an expert on modern art, for help with the translation of the essay "The Two Kinds of Abstraction," and Richard Cohn, a music theorist, for help with the translation of the essays "Songs without Words" and "The Other of the Same."

The essay "A Logic of Literature" is reprinted here by permission of Indiana University Press; it first appeared in the second printing by that press of *The Logic of Literature* by Käte Hamburger (1993).

Essays in Aesthetics

1

From Text to Work

If I try, in answer to an invitation, to examine a little the intellectual development that separates me from, or attaches me to, the first text that I published in 1959 (in the literary and aesthetic field, which interests us here), and that I later included in my first volume, I will do so without going back to the motives and circumstances that led to this apparent point of departure.[1] This exercise in pre-posthumous self-diction, it seems to me, can take on two quite distinct forms, which I will try to combine. The first consists in simultaneously measuring and defining the possible theoretical coherence of this body of work—if one can call it that. I am not certain that I am the best to do this with precision, but I can make the effort, hoping not to give in to the rationalizing illusion that often pushes us to impose a false unity on items assembled by the chance that rules us. The second consists in reconstructing, as faithfully as possible, the true diachronic movement that led me from one object to another. I don't know whether this reconstruction would be accessible to an interested external observer, but I think I can give some information on this subject that—useful or not—is at least, as one says, from the horse's mouth.

A first, very obvious statement shows that, starting from literary "criticism," in the sense we have understood it for more than a century, I passed rather quickly to "poetics," a word we have used for a little less long, even though it stems from classical times. These two words, whose present transparency is perhaps deceptive, call for a number of clarifications. I call "criticism" the internal, formal and/or interpretive, analysis of single texts or works or of the entire work of a writer considered in his singularity. University study, at least in France, has only recently, and rather weakly, devoted itself to this type of research; after Lanson, in a clearly positivistic spirit, it has remained centered on an essentially historical and philological approach and, as Péguy already reproached Taine in attributing to him the famous "method of the large belt," has preferred giving attention to what is peripheral to the works themselves. When I began working in this field—on the way to reconversion, at the end of "advanced," less than exciting studies and of an absolutely disastrous political and ideological engagement—the divorce between these two orientations, which was about to explode in the quarrel of the so-called *nouvelle critique*, was still latent. The first was still more or less reserved, as it had been at the time of Proust, of Gide, of Valéry, of Du Bos, of Rivière, of Paulhan, of Thibaudet,[2] and of Jean Prévost, to authors that did not (or no longer) belong to the university, like Sartre or Blanchot; or who were on the margin of the university, like Roland Barthes; or who were teaching in foreign universities, like Auerbach, Spitzer, Béguin, Raymond, Poulet, Starobinski, Rousset, Bénichou, de Man, and, at that time, Jean-Pierre Richard; or who were in other disciplines, like Gaston Bachelard and Gilbert Durand. I have just named most of those who were then, for one reason or another, at least in this field, my own teachers. Between 1956 and 1963 I myself taught, with full freedom concerning the objects and the methods, in a very discreet provincial *hypokhâgne*,[3] where (almost) no one took himself very seriously—and thus outside the university, in the strict sense of the term. I was not attracted by teaching at the so-called advanced level, which I had experienced as a student in a rather dissuasive manner and for which I basically felt no great affinity. I keep no memory at all of the four much less happy years (1963–67) that I then spent as junior lecturer, teaching improbable "recitations," at the Sorbonne, except that one day I met there, in a dark corridor, a young Bulgarian named Tzvetan Todorov, who, seemingly not well directed, was looking for a ray of light in that gloom. A seminar of the École des Hautes Études,[4] which oddly met on a highly elevated floor of this same Sorbonne, quickly became our common light: the seminar of none other than Roland Barthes,[5] who was then, for a few years, something like my mentor-despite-himself and to whom I owe, among other things, that I left the university a little later for this same école. Chance, as we know, writes in a straight line *por linhas tortas*.[6]

My first articles, all quite brief, written, for the reasons I have just stated, more as a moderately enlightened "amateur" than as a professional, later collected in *Figures*,[7] were concerned with French baroque poetry,[8] then with Proust, with Robbe-Grillet, with Flaubert, then with Barthes himself as semiologist, and with Valéry and Borges as critics. These last three and a few others (on Thibaudet, Richard, and Mauron) were clearly of a metacritical type that made them into a kind of stepping stone toward literary theory, the more so since I interpreted these works in the direction of my own theoretical biases—but at least one can't deny that Valéry refounded modern poetics nor that Borges had a panoptic vision of the universal Library, a vision to which

I perhaps owe the essential of my conception of literature and a little beyond that. I'll never forget that spring morning of 1959 when—a late "discovery" when all is said—I bought at a bookseller's of the Quartier Latin *Fictions* and *Enquêtes* and began reading them, [9] as it were, at the same time, forgetting to have lunch, with, all other things being equal, an analogous "transport" to the one of Malebranche discovering Descartes's *Treatise on Man*—at a time, I mean my own, when one could still stroll down the Boulevard Saint-Michel reading. And those two were really suited to common reading, with one eye on each, for inquest and fiction interchange and transfuse each other, in a manner never yet imagined, by way of the idea that all books are but one book and that this infinite book is the world. What was to be read, or at least to be thought together, was—and this faculty, if we believe Thibaudet, was already attributed by Jules Lemaitre to Ferdinand Brunetière—"all the books that have been written since the beginning of the world." [10] A vast program, but let us not anticipate too much.

A moment ago I spoke of the quarrel of the "nouvelle critique"; in the 1950s and 1960s this expression seemed natural: as I reminded the reader, this criticism was "new" in the sense it opposed itself to the discipline that was literary history, by contrast considered as "old," though it went back no farther than the late nineteenth century. With hindsight it does not seem to me today that the method of this *nouvelle critique* was as new as one then thought, for in many ways it only extended the critical activity of the 1930s, of which the manifesto is Proust's *Against Sainte-Beuve*—published posthumously, to be sure, in 1954. As we know, "Against Sainte-Beuve" signifies primarily "against" a biographizing idea, which seeks an external explication of the works in the life, in what Taine called the "race," the "milieu," and the "moment" of their author, and "for" a more immanent reading, one more concerned with the internal relations of the text. The French *nouvelle critique*, like the American New Criticism before it, thus wanted an essentially immanent criticism, deliberately, though perhaps provisionally, enclosed in what some (but not I) willfully called the "closure of the text." It did not take long for it to split up into two interactive branches: a so-called thematic criticism, inspired by psychology and psychoanalysis, even if Sartre and his group referred to a very heterodox "existential psychoanalysis"; and a so-called structural criticism, which concerned itself more closely with the formal configurations of the works. My first essays concerned themselves a little with the first, but I basically felt more attracted by the second, never having liked individual psychology too much. It is on this basis that I wrote for an issue of *L'Arc* devoted to Claude Lévi-Strauss in 1965—a highly symbolic patronage—an article with a militant appearance and a naïvely programmatic intention entitled "Structuralisme et critique littéraire." As a good neophyte, I tried to cover there the entire domain evoked by its title, envisaging a kind of even divide between the two branches of the *nouvelle critique*. But it rather quickly seemed to me that the (in my eyes) most pertinent investment of the "structural method" in literary studies was not so much the formal criticism of specific works— emblematically illustrated by the famous analysis of Baudelaire's "Les Chats" by Jakobson and Lévi-Strauss himself[11]—as the general theory of the "literary field," itself considered as a vaster system, in the way structural anthropology studies each society by way of the whole of its practices and institutions,[12] and in the way structural linguistics studies the whole of the internal relations that constitute the system of language. After which it was no longer a matter of dealing with the immanence of the work but, rather, the contrary: a vaster exploration, one for which the term *criticism* was no longer suited and for which a few of us proposed, before long, the synonymous terms of *literary theory* and of *poetics*. The first came to us at the same time from Wellek and Warren's famous textbook and from various texts by the Russian Formalists; the second, of course, via Valéry from Aristotle's fundamental book; and it was evidently the latter that was to give its common title to the magazine and to the collection that, a little later, in the innovative momentum of 1968,[13] we were to devote to the defense and illustration of this discipline—at the same time new and very ancient in its distinguished philosophical origin. This double or triple reference clearly made us leave the properly French tradition, for the benefit of a more stimulating opening to an apparently universal current of thought. In sum there was much immanence to be transcended, but I was only later to formulate in these terms (immanence and transcendence) a conceptual opposition that, little by little and in diverse respects, was to dominate the whole of my theoretical work.

This overly ambitious program was reiterated in September 1966 in a presentation to the famous Décade de Cerisy on *Les Chemins actuels de la critique*, under the provocative title "Raisons de la critique pure"[14] and in honor of the cherished Thibaudet, from whom stems the expression *critique pure*, referred by him to Valéry and defined as "criticism which bears on essences, not on beings or on works." In my mind it was precisely a matter of poetics, which Valéry himself, in his 1936 teaching program for the Collège de France, described as a history of literature without names of authors, which was something Wölfflin had already imagined for the history of art: *Kunst-geschichte ohne Namen*. [15] We know that this idea of anonymous history, "without the names of men and even without the names of nations," was already present in Auguste Comte, [16] and I do not think it is entirely alien to Hegel. Nor to be sure, and closer to us, to the school of the Annales and to the history of "long duration," which, unconcerned with individuals and circumstantial incidents, was defended and illustrated by Fernand Braudel. It was Tocqueville, not Marx, who said: "I speak of classes, they alone should occupy history," [17] and it seems to me that one can take the word *class* here in its largest, which is also its most logical, sense: the most pertinent objects of the historian are not individuals but categories that transcend them and that quite often survive them. The essence of history is transhistorical, that is to say, customs and institutions—in literature genres, themes, types, and forms—as long as they last and become transformed; "to last is to change," said the still cherished Thibaudet, [18] as a good Bergsonian; what changes is evidently only what lasts. [19] In a later publication I mentioned, [20] no doubt too briefly, the affinity between structural history—the history of the things that last—and poetics as analysis of (more or less) lasting traits of the literary fact. This was to oppose poetics, not to history in general but only to the anecdotal and sometimes pointless shortsightedness of what, after some "renunciations," [21] literary history had become by then—and that it would have been more correct to call "event-oriented history of literary life": after the too large "belt," the very little one, which, as Proust showed, is not always closer to the works. In my eyes this affinity makes less absurd than might otherwise appear my membership during a good quarter-century in the school founded in 1947 by Lucien Febvre: at the time a place of exemplary marginality, at least where literary and artistic studies were concerned, and which was, by this very fact, an incomparable center of research and intellectual invention for some of us; I say this without retrospective "institutional patriotism"—"of the anteroom," as Stendhal meanly said—which is not in my nature.

An effort at reinterpreting classical rhetoric was my first application of the said program, with a certain underground debt to Jean Paulhan. Several essays of this period bear witness to this, including the one that gave its name to my first collection, [22] then to the two following ones. My intention at the time was to look in rhetoric, and actually more specifically in the theory of figures, for a sort of ancestor of semiology, or at least of modern semantics and stylistics. I was to realize later that rhetoric could not be reduced to this sole aspect, [23] that this kind of restriction showed a somewhat narrow perspective and was no doubt biased by this rather too partial relationship. But I do not regret the attention I drew, thanks to this semi-misunderstanding, to texts as significant as those of Dumarsais and Fontanier nor that I contributed, afterward and with others, to reintroducing this method of analysis (for it is one) into our thinking about language.

The second investment was the analysis of narrative, which Todorov soon called "narratology." I should specify that this object was first suggested to me by Roland Barthes, who had taken the initiative, for a reason I still do not know, of a special issue on this theme for the review *Communications*.[24] I backed into this field, which did not especially attract me, having always, till then and probably a little beyond, considered narrative mechanics the least appealing function of literature. This included the novel, as is sufficiently attested by my 1965 essay "Silences de Flaubert,"[25] which is a justification for the non-narrative, even anti-narrative, aspects of this paradoxical novelist, for whom narrative was "a very tedious thing." When I voiced this disgust—which still leads me sometimes, in contrast to the more usual practice and in scorn of all good sense, to "skip" the narrative pages in favor of the descriptive ones in the novels I happen to read—Barthes, not very surprised, answered me just about as I should have expected: "But that's a very good subject, explain yourself on it." Which became the article entitled "Frontières du récit,"[26] in which I tried to limit the territory of this cumbersome practice as much as possible, by relativizing it. In the times that followed I got a little more involved, in 1968 trying my hand at the narrative pace of a baroque epic, Saint-Amant's *Moyse sauvé*, and of the Stendhalian novel. It was at the beginning of 1969, in New Haven, during my first stay on this continent, that I started an analysis of the *Remembrance of Things Past* as a whole, which served as touchstone, or rather as experience of the terrain (as ethnologists say), for a general theoretical essay on narrative structures. After diverse partial and experimental presentations, this essay was finally published in my 1972 volume *Figures III* under the title "Discours du récit."[27] I said "narrative structures," but I should add that it is here a matter precisely of formal structures, those that deal with *modes of narration* (treatment of time, management of point of view, status and function of the narrator), and not of logical or thematic "profound" structures concerning the represented action, which authors like Greimas and Claude Bremond have explored on their side. Narratology, as a properly literary discipline, devoted itself primarily to the former, so that the term is today spontaneously understood in this sense; but in principle this restriction is no more justified than the restriction of rhetoric to the study of figures, or the one that has for a long time focalized the attention of narratologists on fictional narrative, leaving historical and other types of nonfictional narrative to others, generally to philosophers like Danto and Ricoeur. I will not insist on these matters, to which I have returned later in Nouveau discours du récit[28] and in Fiction et diction,[29] except to say that such an implicit assimilation, of narrative to fiction and of fiction to narrative, equally injures each of these genres—which by the way aren't genres.

In the course of the same semester at Yale, then at Johns Hopkins in 1970 and at New York University in 1971—the first episode of a happy New York series—I had opened up a new path, which concerned another essential aspect of poetics: the one that one then called "poetic language." My purpose was apparently, in all modesty, to cover the two principal continents of the literary universe (or, as I would say now, of fiction and diction). The very notion of poetic language, the detailed history of which remains to be written in all our cultural traditions, came to us at the time in France essentially from Mallarmé, then from Valéry, and the analyses of Jakobson had, in their manner, put it back on the rails. The idea, at its basis post-Romantic and "Symbolist," correlated with a rejection, or at least a weakening, of the classical conception—in its way a formalist conception—according to which the essential criterion of poetic discourse is the presence of versification. This criterion once abandoned or relativized by the poets themselves—together with the thematic criteria that completed it (to regard certain subjects as more poetic than others)—what remained was only the specific semantic treatment of language, the principal aspect of which would be, according to the Mallarméan formula, to "remunerate the defect of languages," that is, their conventional or—according to the controversial qualification of Saussure—their "arbitrary" character. Poetry, by various means, would bestow, or would at least give the impression of bestowing, on language a mimetic motivation that it ordinarily lacks—and, it seems, sorely lacks—in its common usage. This hypothesis inevitably asked the question (not a literary question but a linguistic one and perhaps one belonging to the philosophy of language): what is it, or, more modestly, what can we know about the character, motivated or not, or of the arbitrary and motivated parts of human languages? This question itself led to an inquiry about the diverse theories held since antiquity on this subject. Starting in 1969, I thus threw myself, with more or less availability, into this on principle preliminary inquiry, focusing on it exclusively in 1972, after the conclusion of *Figures III*. But I soon discovered that the debate—since debate there is, at least since the *Cratylus* of Plato—between the adherents of mimetic motivation and those of the convention was of unequal aesthetic interest: the latter, like the Hermogenes of the *Cratylus*, only offered to their opponents a refutation, or at least a laconic skepticism, whereas the former, like Cratylus himself, supported and illustrated their thesis with a speculative arsenal of great imaginative power. This is how a project on the theory of poetic language was gradually changed into a (cavalier) history and theory, or at least an essay in typological classification, of the different variants of the Cratylian fantasy in our literary, linguistic, and Western philosophic tradition; whence the double title *Mimologiques, Voyage en Cratylie* of the book that resulted from it,[30] on the whole rather Bachelardian in spirit, since it testifies at the same time to a critical distance and to an aesthetic sympathy toward the reveries it treats, those "seductions that falsify the inductions" and which would "benefit the pedagogy of the scientific spirit if it were made explicit."[31] At the same time, the theoretical intention was accompanied by a sort of genre study, for it is rather clear that mimological speculation through the centuries, from Plato to Francis Ponge and beyond, makes up a kind of unrecognized literary genre. One can study this genre in its diverse states and in the historical evolution that leads it from one to another, not without bifurcations, omissions, and resurgences, since this tradition most often ignores and constantly reinvents itself without noticing its repetitions and contradictions. Once again, at the same time, I finally came to consider the very notion of poetic language as a version, no matter how fertile, of the Cratylian myth.

I had thus entered the field of poetics by the study of a transgeneric stylistic procedure (even though it is more typically invested in poetic discourse): the figure; then of a mode: narrative, which is not, properly speaking, a genre, since it includes several of them (epic, history, novel, fable, tale, novella . . .); then of a subliminal and quasi-covert genre: mimological reverie. This situation called for a larger reflection on the status of the kind of generic, parageneric, and metageneric categories that divide the literary field in all directions. A figure is clearly a formal category; a narrative as well, since it is defined by the act of telling an event or an action, whatever its content. Mimologism is quite as clearly a thematic category, since it is the content of its position in the metalinguistic discussion that defines as mimological a reflection or a speculation on the nature of language. There was thus a reason to inquire into the relations between these general categories, some of which had their source in a formal definition, others in a thematic definition, and most of them perhaps in a crossing of these two criteria. Thus, we know that tragedy can be defined as a noble action in the mode of a dramatic representation, epic as a noble action in the narrative mode, comedy as a familiar action in the dramatic mode, which leaves an empty compartment for the familiar action in the narrative mode; it is this empty compartment that Aristotle, in his *Poetics*, filled with a somewhat ghostly genre, or a genre whose classical manifestations did not reach us, which he named "parody" but which one tends to find illustrated today in the *novel*, in the English sense of the word, "a comic epic in prose," according to Fielding—*romance* being in our eyes closer to a sort of epic in serious prose: heroic or sentimental. There is in this picture— certainly rudimentary and incomplete but fundamental, implicitly proposed by Aristotle and adaptable to the later evolution of literature—something of a beginning of a general system of past, present, and future literary genres, a system that has fascinated and excited the theoretical libido of all periods. It has led certain scholars to attempt to complete it in that sense—in particular by the addition, next to the dramatic and narrative modes, of a third mode, sufficiently indefinite to include and federate everything the other two were lacking but which it is difficult to see in coherence with them: the mode called "lyric." It is to this complex, even confused, or at least shaky situation that I devoted a long article in 1976, "Genre, types, modes," which appeared in *Poétique* in 1977 and became two years later, with a few additions, *Introduction à l'architexte*.[32] This little book did not try for an exhaustive theory of literary genres—like Northrop Frye's *Anatomy of Criticism*—but, rather, a historical and critical examination of all sorts of problems and difficulties that this kind of proposition meets. The problematic left unresolved in this fashion will return a little later in *Fiction and Diction* and in the new perspective of an interrogation on the modes and the regimes of literarity.

The picture of the four fundamental genres treated or evoked by Aristotle had thus unexpectedly confronted me with this "minor" genre of parody, which Aristotle defined in the terms that I have recalled, but the rare examples of which he cites make one rather think of diverse literary (and other) practices that are "parodic" in the modern—that is to say, enlarged—sense of this term: among others the heroic-comic poem, of which Boileau's *Lutrin* is one of the classic accomplishments (farcical action treated in heroic style), or the distortion of Scarronian type (*Énéide travestie*), which in reverse treats in a farcical style a heroic action borrowed from a great anterior text. In relation to Aristotelian categories it was not a matter of searching, like Fielding, for the modern genre that can occupy the place assigned to parody by Aristotle but, rather, to ask oneself how to define and classify together the whole set of genres that we still commonly, and sometimes confusedly, qualify as parodic. This is the work I undertook in 1979 and which was to produce, three years later, *Palimpsestes*, subtitled *La Littérature au second degré*.[33] It is, in fact, their secondarity that as a whole characterizes these diverse works, from the pseudo-homeric *Batrachomyomachie* to Giraudoux's *Électre* or Tournier's *Vendredi*, and that all have as their common trait that they arise as it were from one or more anterior texts, of which they borrow either the theme, to work some sort of mode of transformation on it, or the manner (the "style"), to apply it to another subject. These two fundamental practices of transformation and imitation combined with the three cardinal functions that are the ludic, the satirical, and the serious regimes provided me again with the framework of a picture with double entries, dividing up and regrouping the innumerable manifestations of what I chose then to call "hypertextuality." A somewhat unfortunate name, among other reasons because the term *hypertext* was to receive (had perhaps already received) a rather different meaning (though not without some relationship) that quite clearly wins over mine and opens the door to diverse misunderstandings. I will still add, by way of self-criticism, that my entire definition of the hypertext, "text arising from an anterior text in a manner that is not that of commentary," was not very satisfactory, since it consisted of a purely negative criterion that was liable not to set up a sufficient condition of application, if one discovered one or several sorts of derived texts that were neither commentaries nor hypertexts. The positive criterion that my definition, but fortunately not my description, was regrettably lacking is that, in contrast to commentary, the hypertext is not *about* but *derived from* its hypotext, always resulting from modifying the latter, directly or indirectly: modification by a change of style (as in distortions), by a change of subject (as in pastiches) or else parodies in the strict sense, as when Giraudoux has one of his characters say: "You are missing a single being and everything is re-populated."[34] I should therefore have said, more positively: "a hypertext is a text that derives from another by a formal and/or thematic process of transformation." It is true that, as a result, this amended definition applies also to translations, which I did not consider at the time but which I was to remember a little later: the fact is that translations are in their own way hypertexts, whose principle of transformation is, or wants to be, of a purely linguistic order.

The exploration of the hypertextual continent had alerted me to the existence of a vaster object, namely the set of ways in which a text can transcend its "closure," or immanence, and enter into relationships with other texts. It is this textual transcendence of the text that I at the time named "transtextuality": explicit and massive hypertextuality is one of its forms; punctual quotation and allusion—generally implicit, qualified at that time as "intertextuality"—is another; commentary, already mentioned and renamed "metatext," is a third form; the "architextual" relations between texts and the genres to which one assigns them more or less legitimately are a fourth; and I had just met a fifth form of it in studying the first. The fact is that hypertexts almost always draw up a kind of *contract of hypertextuality* with their readers that permits them to make their point known and thus to give it all its effectiveness; if you write a parody of the *Iliad* or a pastiche of Balzac, you have every interest in *declaring* your intention, which would otherwise greatly risk remaining unnoticed, and thus missing its purpose, similarly to the way, according to Austin's theory of speech acts, a question must first make itself recognized in its illocutionary status as a question if it wants to reach its perlocutory aim, which is to get an answer. A literary work is also a speech act, and we know, at least since Philippe Lejeune's studies on autobiography, the importance of this type of "pact" for the understanding of its generic status and thus for the relevance of its reception. Hypertextual works hardly ever fail to proclaim themselves as such by means of a more or less developed self-commentary, of which the title is the briefest and often the most effective form, without prejudice against what can be indicated by a preface, a dedication, an epigraph, a note, a dust jacket, a letter, a declaration to the press, etc. In sum hypertextual works, like others but no doubt more than others, necessarily resort to the options of that set of practices called "paratextual," to which I was to devote in 1987 a book entitled—with a doubly paratextual wink—*Seuils*.[35] A perspicacious journalist (they all are) asked me on this occasion if I realized that I gave to this book a title that was the name of my publisher; I answered him that I evidently did not and that he had just revealed to me a stupefying coincidence; there was then much talk of Freud, of Freudian slips, and of revealing lapses.

It is thus a detail of one book that supplied the entire subject of the next, and this as it were oblique genetic process seems to me fairly constant in my work—as it is perhaps in everyone's, but each person can, in this domain, only testify to his personal experience. It is at any rate again this same kind of collateral filiation that was to lead me from the study of the paratext to what is, as of today, the last stage of my theoretical course.

To take things in their most concrete relation, it seems to me that the sequence was roughly the following. I had written in *Seuils* that the paratext—which includes, to be more precise, the whole of the editorial practices, or at least their readable traces—is on the whole *what makes a text into a book*. I don't in the least disavow this quick formula; I will, rather, say that I did not perceive until later its theoretical implications, or—to use a more specific term that I strip here (as elsewhere that of *transcendence*) of any kind of metaphysical meaning—its *ontological* implications, that is to say, relative to the modes of existence of the works. The question implicitly asked by this formula (*from text to book*) is, in fact, at the same time easy to ask and tricky to answer: *what is the difference between a text and a book?* In an article ("Transtextualités") published by *Magazine Littéraire* in February 1983 (between *Palimpsestes* and *Seuils*, but I was already involved in the preparation of the latter), I said (and I will have to quote myself at some length) that the paratext is

> the place where the essential characteristic of the literary work is put into question: its *ideality*. I understand thereby that mode of being which is proper to it among the objects of the world, and more particularly among products of art. The ontological status of a literary work is not that of a picture, nor that of a musical composition, nor that of a cathedral, nor of a film, nor of a choreography, nor of a happening or of a packed landscape [in the sense, of course, in which Christo packs monuments and, at the least, encloses landscapes]. The type of ideality, that is to say the relationship between "the work itself" and the instances of its manifestation, is no doubt in each of these cases specific and *sui generis*. The mode of being of *Remembrance of Things Past*, for example, is not that of the *View of Delft*, because, among other reasons, the *View of Delft* "finds itself" in a museum in The Hague, whereas *Remembrance* is at the same time everywhere (in every good library) and nowhere: no holder of a copy of *Remembrance* "possesses" this work as the Mauritshuis possesses the *View of Delft*. To be sure, the work of Vermeer transcends in its own way the rectangle of painted canvas in The Hague, but certainly not in the way *Remembrance* transcends the innumerable copies of its different editions [. . .], not to mention its translations. Copies, state of the text, editions, translation: we are in the midst of paratextuality, and

that is what I was thinking of in saying a moment ago that the ideality of the text questions itself in it: at the same time, it manifests and compromises itself in it. It manifests itself in it by compromising itself in it—let us say in a word that it *exposes* itself in it, and let us leave the details, which I still do not know, for the remainder of this work. But we will have understood, of course, that the ideality [. . .] of the literary text is a new form of transcendence: the one of the work in relation to its diverse materializations, or graphic, editorial, readerly "presentations": in short, the entire trip from one skull to the other.

I hope that I will be forgiven this self-quotation, not much more narcissistic on the whole than the discourse that precedes it, and that I take up again to observe that this page of 1983 contains the germ of the essential theme of a book that was not to appear until 1994: the first volume of *L'Oeuvre de l'art*, the specific title of which is, as one could expect, *Immanence et transcendance*. In this article I find that I must correct today only two things: on the one hand, the idea of an ideality proper to the literary text, having realized since that it shares this status at least with the musical and choreographic score; and, on the other hand (but I will return to this in a moment), the established confusion between the ideality of the text and the transcendence of the work. All in all, the preparation of *Seuils* had put a nasty bug in my ear that was to bear all its fruit only ten years later—if bugs can bear fruit—and not without intermediate phases. The first of these phases was the writing of *Nouveau discours du récit*, which is, as its title might suggest, a postscript, at once defensive and self-critical, to *Discours du récit*; the second was the writing of *Seuils* properly speaking; and the third the writing of a little collection of four essays, *Fiction et diction*,[36] which appears to me today as a transitional work—I mean to say: transition from poetics, or the theory of literature, to aesthetics, in the debatable, and thus provisional, sense of a general theory of art.

When I ask myself after the fact about the motives for this new enlargement (after the one that had led me from criticism to poetics), I find two that are no doubt complementary. The second is the one I have just indicated: the need to clarify the relationship between the ideality of the text and the materiality of the book,[37] or more generally of its oral or written manifestations. But the first motive (the most fundamental and without a doubt the simplest to formulate) is that—if one considers literature as an art, or the literary work as a work of art (no doubt a widely shared opinion), and if one draws from it the conclusion (somewhat less widespread but my intention from the start) actually to treat it as such—there has to come a point when one feels the need to confront, for itself and for oneself, even if it is after many others, the wider question: "What is a work of art?" if only to answer the somewhat intermediary question: "In what is the literary work a work of art?" or, in Jakobson's equivalent terms, "What makes a work of art of a verbal message?" It is this intermediary question that is the object of the first chapter, wholly transitional in this respect, of *Fiction et diction*, the chapter that gives its title to the collection. My answer, fortunately (I hope) more pertinent than original, was that the literary work is "a verbal object with aesthetic function" and thus that literature is the art of producing verbal objects with an aesthetic function. This is clearly the specified version of what will be the more general definition of *L'Oeuvre de l'art*: "A work of art is an artifact with aesthetic function."

I have just indicated two plausible motives for this new phase, but I still have to mention a third one, the triggering factor of which occurred appreciably earlier, revealing a rather long duration of intellectual incubation. In autumn 1980, when I was a disillusioned and short-lived candidate for a chair at the Collège de France, I had the pleasure of meeting, among others, some of the "scientific" (in the "hard" sense of the term) members of that beautiful institution, to whom I was supposed to expose successively, varying the tone, my program of research and teaching. Most of them listened to me absent-mindedly and with rather loose attention, their choice by the way having been already made and made well. One of them, however, whom I had never seen since our distant common years in the rue d'Ulm, the physicist Pierre-Gilles de Gennes, already future Nobel Prize winner, asked me a question that made me reflect a little at the moment and brood a lot during the following years. My program then was named "Theory of Literary Forms"—a title that I supposed to be less ambiguous for minds a little distant from this specialty, if it is one, than its (for me) synonym *Poetics*. The ambiguity became manifest where, naïvely, I did not expect it. As a good scientist, de Gennes asked me straightforwardly to explain to him, briefly if possible, "my" theory of literature. Having understood the theory of literature as a neutral discipline (the general study of literary forms) rather than as a committed explicative hypothesis, I was left more or less without voice (at the same time and definitively losing his vote), meditating with a part of myself the difference in meaning (and in force) of the word *theory* in these two fields, also accusing *in petto* my interlocutor of a thoughtless conceptual transfer, but obliged to admit to myself that I in fact did not have a theory of literature and that I did not see very well in what such a thing could consist. Thus, during several years this lacuna was to work secretly in me, up to the day when I understood that in this field "theory" could signify, in the strong sense, an attempt, if not at explication, at least at *definition*, and thus a tentative answer to the question "What is . . . ?"—be it under the form (I come back to this) "When is there . . . ?" This question once identified, "my" answer, that I already indicated earlier, imposed itself on its own during the winter of 1986–87, a little too late for communicating it to the one who had asked it and who no doubt did not care about it anymore. That is what is called, I think, "l'esprit de l'escalier."

Before leaving this specific terrain—the one of the literary work—I want to try to clear up one or two misunderstandings for which I am doubtless responsible, having failed to give a clear explanation. In the eponymous chapter of *Fiction et diction* I distinguished two regimes of literariness. The first, which I called "constitutive," concerns the texts (written or oral) that are taken as literary, so to speak a priori, because of the fact of their generic or formal affiliation: for example, fictional texts (today, typically, novels and novellas) or poetry (despite the, since at least a century, increasingly vague feature of the definitional criterion of poetry), without counting all those, like the epics or tragedies of the classical period, that present these two features at the same time; the same as, whether "good" or "bad," a picture is, by definition, always painting and an opera always music, a novel, a poem, or a drama, identified as such, is always taken to be a literary work, "bad" literature being literature, if only for a clear logical reason. The second regime, which I called "conditional," concerns the texts of which the literary character depends more strongly on an attention of a basically aesthetic order. [38] A work of history or philosophy is received as a literary work only to the degree in which the reader gives it aesthetic attention—for example, stylistic, as often happens with Tacitus or Michelet in history, with Plato or Nietzsche in philosophy— and as can happen with anyone else, depending on taste. According to this fact, the "literary" character of such works must fluctuate, depending on individual or collective conditions of "reception": what someone takes to be a page of history or philosophy subject to the criteria of validity proper to these intellectual disciplines, someone else will appreciate as a literary text, that is to say, as an aesthetic object, the relation of which to some "truth value" will be less important than its power of seduction—which will authorize him, for example, to admire it on one plane while depreciating it (even condemning it), and most often neglecting it, on the other. But this conditional character does not in the least diminish the intensity of the aesthetic relationship in play; perhaps it renders it *more* intense: when I think I am the *only one* to love something, I have a motive (not rational but the stronger) for loving it more.

Conditional literarities are thus in no sense, for me, literarities of a second rank or of a lesser degree, rather the contrary, and I would see here quite well a particular case of the difference between "aesthetic objects" in general (a tree, an animal, a landscape), which are such only in an attentional manner, and works of art, which are such in an intentional and to a large extent institutional manner: with regard to the first, the investment of the contemplator is often more intense than with regard to the second, whose power of seduction can suffer by the fact itself that it seems more willed. The involuntary seduction, or the one that seems that way, is often more effective than the other: to please (since this is the matter at hand), art must, as one says, "hide art"; nature itself has nothing of the sort to hide, since, as Kant says, it does us "no favor" on this plane and expects nothing from us in return: it is we who "receive the favor," without it having asked for anything.[39] Contrary to what has been said,[40] there is thus, in the order of the terms *fiction* and *diction* (if one takes them, simplifying a good deal, for synonyms or emblems of *constitutive* and *conditional* or of *intentional* and *attentional*), no kind of "precedence"—which would, in my view, have no meaning; and concerning the order of *preference*, if there has to be one, it would easily be the inverse for me: I have always resisted the idea that the novel was the literary genre, and, for reasons memorably expressed by Valéry (why the marquise? why at five o'clock?), fictional invention seems to me often rather pointless, and this in proportion to its more or less skillful, more or less discreet, efforts to motivate its arbitrariness.[41] This point clearly separates me from the position of Käte Hamburger,[42] for whom the domain of *Dichtung* is on the whole reduced to narrative and dramatic fiction and, already more problematically, lyric poetry, without one's knowing too well what status she accords to forms—including fiction in the first person— that do not stand out and that she seems rather inclined to exclude. As far as I can reconstruct this development, it is starting from and in reaction to this thesis I encountered in 1985—an excessive thesis but stimulating in its very excess—that I came to the distinction mentioned earlier between constitutive (roughly, those Hamburger includes) and conditional (those she excludes) literarities: a manner, as it were, of substituting a dualist theory (two regimes of literarity) for a duel of theories, the "essentialist" one (from Aristotle to

Hamburger) and the "conditionalist" one, that in its own fashion the formula of Goodman illustrates (to ask oneself not "What is art?" but "*When is art?*")—certain literarities concerning more the *what*, others more the *when*, without prevalence on principle of the first over the second.

From this rather vast misunderstanding follows one or two other, more specific ones. The first concerns the genre of autobiography, which seems to me *in principle* to belong to the conditional regime, of literarity by *diction* rather than by *fiction* (in the sense that to tell one's life or—if one wants to append this to that—to keep a journal is not first and foremost to produce a literary work, like writing a play or a novel), but in fact closer than many other genres to the constitutive regime, for reasons that one understands, at least since Rousseau and Chateaubriand. These reasons were indicated by Jean Prévost in a manner that will save me many arguments; he spoke of "spontaneous choices, insensible deformations of memory [that] give each of us his natural aesthetic; the least artistic of men would be an artist despite himself in his Memoirs."[43] According to this no doubt somewhat optimistic remark, autobiography could even represent par excellence the literary genre that pleases me most because it would consist in an as it were constitutive manner of the paradoxical—and for me precious—criterion of an *involuntary articity*: autobiography, or writer despite himself. We must no doubt not take this kind of formula to the letter because the genre has since a long time lost, at least in the field of professional literature, its (entirely relative) naïveté without always gaining aesthetically, but it is perhaps enough to show that I am diametrically opposed to believing autobiography to be an aesthetically minor genre, as one has oddly accused me of believing—I quote: "Gérard Genette, who has the merit in *Fiction et diction* of establishing the essential distinction between two modes, also distances the second from the domain of literature, or at least from its favorite domain. Here at any rate is a point common to those two theoreticians of literature [the other one being . . . Jean-Paul Sartre]: autobiography is not a legitimate form. They have held, all their lives, a certain idea of what literature is, as others have held a certain idea of what France is."[44] I hope that, "wherever he is," as one says, the author of *Les Mots* savors this inspired diagnostic as much as I do: that will give us another "common point." I am always a little surprised by the obstinacy that specialists of an object—for example, of a genre and specifically, in this case, of the autobiographical genre—have in claiming that this object, and indirectly themselves, is a victim of some generalized ostracism, as though one could not enhance one's subject, and thereby enhance oneself, without proclaiming it, and one-self, persecuted from all sides by the conspiring hydra of some inevitably dominant ideology. For autobiography, a genre that is markedly prosperous today, the skillfully ambiguous title *L'Autobiographie en procès* translates that wily form of *capitatio benevolentiae* quite well—for there is, without doubt, since Rousseau (and Chateaubriand!) as much, if not more, of rhetorical common-place as of authentic delirium, as though to plead for, even to claim public ignorance, tended today to replace the classical argument of justification by its importance, or what Montesquieu was not afraid to call "the majesty of [its] subject." [45] Philipe Lejeune illustrates this attitude a little when he de-nounces "a century of resistance [in the Freudian sense] to autobiography" since the famous article by Brunetière (1888) on "personal literature." [46] This article was in fact outrageously negative, but I am not sure that it actually set the tone for a century: a few well chosen quotes don't make up a statistic. Lejeune also picks up a formula, this time by Thibaudet ("It is the art of those who are not artists, the novel of those who are not novelists"), which he judges to be contemptuous and proper to "exclude autobiography from the domain of art"—in excluding it, of course, from the domain of literature. I, for my part, refuse such an exclusion, taking works of "diction" to be as literary as works of fiction. I suppose that the fact of giving to the former a conditional literarity, and not the constitutive one I give to fiction, places me seemingly somewhere between Lejeune and Thibaudet—which is not too bad a location, but again the conditional is not for me an aesthetically minor regime. I think I share with Lejeune the refusal of any sort of aesthetic "hierarchy," [47] and I object particularly to the underlying idea—if it is underlying—of Thibaudet's formula of a superiority of the novel; *if it is underlying*: I am not entirely certain of this, and I would be able to agree with this formula in a neutral, even laudatory axiological sense—feeling without a doubt a certain predilection for (if such a thing exists) "the art of those who are not artists." Whatever the situation, I reaffirm one last time my predilection for this genre (which in any case, even here . . .), inasmuch as one can aesthetically appreciate something besides single works; I think, despite Croce, that one can, but this point goes beyond my subject here.

I would gladly say as much about that other genre, or variation of the one I have just discussed, the one named for a few years—at least since I borrowed this term from the dust jacket of Serge Doubrovsky's *Fils*, to apply it to *Re-membrance of Things Past:* [48] *autofiction*. Expeditious and contestable as it may be, this application is perhaps sufficient to show, once again, that this is not, for me, a contemptible practice. I defined it as productive of texts that present themselves, formally or not, as autobiographical but present (more or less) notable discordances with the well-known biography of their author, like the one that separates the life of Dante from "his" descent into Hell or the one of Borges from "his" vision of the Aleph. Whence—this is said in passing—my hesitation to apply the term I borrowed from him to the work of Doubrovsky: a text that qualifies itself as autofiction clearly does not answer to my definition of the genre, any hypothesis on the fictional character of what he tells to the side; quite a few quarrels are due to this irresolvable conceptual uncertainty, from which the only way out is to specify each time to which definition one refers, and I do not pretend that mine is the only acceptable one. [49] As for *Remembrance*, one can certainly not say that it presents itself *formally* as an autobiography, but nor does it do anything (in its text) to distance itself from this qualification, and its paratext is as equivocal as one could wish. And that this type of text takes on a (more or less) contradictory status surely has, for me, nothing disparaging about it; nor does the (deliberately paradoxical) term by which one designates it; nor does the often precarious character of this status, which is itself due to its largely paratextual character: effects of the title, of the name of the author, of introductory or peripheral declarations, etc., that posterity often assumes the right to modify by modifying our knowledge of the facts or our structuration of the conceptual field. Nothing is more subject to revisions, anthumous or posthumous, than the generic definition claimed by a work: [50] one knows that Balzac denied to his own the quality of *novels*— and what destiny we gave to this denial. The status of *Remembrance*, which kept itself from claiming any in a clear way, has long hesitated between that of autobiography and that of fiction, before stabilizing itself, if one can say that and if this is the case, in the essentially mixed and ambiguous position that one admits it to have today, [51] and which one could as well attribute to the *Mémoires d'outre-tombe*, of which certain parts leave their commentators dubious at the very least. In truth every autobiography contains, almost inevitably, a part of autofiction, often unconscious or concealed, and I don't see how one could appreciate the one without appreciating the other—at least to the degree one can give a genre or a kind a feeling one should perhaps reserve for single works—but this, as I already said, is a different subject. Again, whatever the situation, if I accord an equal value of principle to literarities by fiction and by diction and if I place—to say it in the simplest way—autobiography at the halfway point of diction and fiction and autofiction at the halfway point of autobiography and "pure" (?) [52] fiction, I don't see that there is here a motive for rejecting anyone into the outer darkness.

This first chapter of Fiction et diction, and still more "Style and Signification," testify among other things—one had occasion of seeing it just now—to a meeting, a late one to be sure, with Nelson Goodman's theory of art. A late meeting, since Languages of Art was first published in 1968, but we know that one of the charms of French intellectual life consists in discovering long after the fact certain foreign contributions and drawing profit from them, the larger the more time we took to discover them: this too is called l'esprit de l'escalier, but it is perhaps worth more than no wit at all. It is thus in 1986, after finishing Seuils, that I plunged, and plunged my valiant students, into the study of this difficult but fundamental book, which brought some gratifying confirmations, and above all some decisive elucidations, to my intuitions on the status of works of art. Aesthetics called "analytical," of which I discovered other contributions in the same period, became at this point the basis, at times positive, at times negative, of my own reflection, and L'Oeuvre de l'art is importantly marked by it.

The intention of its first volume is thus to clarify the question of the modes of existence of works of art, [53] which I divide, in Goodman's terms, into two fundamental regimes: autographic, which is for me that of the works "consisting" in material objects, like those of painting, of sculpture, of artisan architecture; and allographic, which is that of works consisting of ideal objects, like those of literature, of music, and of planned architecture. I must specify that the term regime, and mainly the notions of "material object" and "ideal object," are alien to Goodman's thought and constitute for my part a connection with Husserlian analyses that does not agree with his philosophical biases. But this disagreement is not the only one. [54] The fact is that it appeared to me on my way that this ontological status does not suffice to account for the existence of works because works, in many different ways, transcend the object, material or ideal, in which they seem to consist: thus, certain works of painting, as very often those of Chardin, consist not in one but in several pictures, which give several "replicas," so that the work finds its true location—like the myth, according to Lévi-Strauss—somewhere between, or beyond, its multiple versions, and this fact of plurality can clearly be found again in all the arts, for instance in literature (see The Temptation of Saint Anthony or Le Soulier de Satin) or in music (see Boris Godounov or Petrouchka). Or, again, some works—here still whatever art they belong to—are known to us, by accident or by neglect, in a fragmentary or unfinished state, and this incompleteness does not prevent us from having a relationship to these works capable, as it were, of extending beyond the partial object that survives, like the *Venus of Milo* without her arms, or *Lucien Leuwen* without its third part; it even often happens that we have a relationship *in absentia* with a work that has completely disappeared, like Phidias's *Athena Parthenos* or the lighthouse of Alexandria, that we know only by hearsay or, more often still, with some picture that we only "see" in reproduction or some novel that we only "read" in translation: so many partial or indirect presences that do not entirely cancel our aesthetic relation to these works. Or, finally, certain works, or one would doubtless have to say all works, without even experiencing the least modification in the object that manifests them, constantly change their meaning, and thus their aesthetic function, as history changes their public: that is what gives all its impact to Borges's fable "Pierre Menard, Author of Don Quixote": the same text changes meaning according to whether one receives it as the product of a Spanish author from the beginning of the seventeenth century or of a French author from the beginning of the twentieth, which signifies, among other things, that the same text does not produce the same effect on its contemporary readers and on readers three centuries later—this fact too, of course, functioning in all the arts.

In these diverse ways works thus transcend the object in which they *reside* (rather than they *consist* in it) and which I call (to account for this restriction) their "immanent object": thus, the literary work transcends its text, as the pictorial work transcends its painting, as the musical work transcends its score and its performances. This notion is clearly altogether alien to Goodman, for whom, for instance, the literary work identifies itself absolutely and without a remnant with its text, which inevitably leads to the idea that the least modification of it, and in particular translation into another language, determines a new work, as every copy of the Chardin's *Bénédicité* constitutes a separate work and not a new version of the same work, or as a simple transposition or transcription of a musical work constitutes a new musical work. I willingly recognize that this is here a matter of simple disagreement on definitions, which are free, and that Goodman's is the only one that suits his nominalist philosophy—but it seems to me that usage imposes larger, or suppler, definitions, which take account of that "play" between the work and its object of immanence. That play accompanies, or rather it constitutes, the entire life of the works, that is to say, our relationship to them, a moving relationship ceaselessly modified by history—a history that is disregarded by the Goodmanian theory of art, in a way that is costly and difficult to sustain. Art, both as production and as reception, is to my mind from end to end a historical practice, and a theory of the work must take this into account from the start, that is to say, from the definition of its object, at the risk of missing its entire functioning; I therefore feel on this point—since "analytic philosophy" is a house with more than one dwelling—closer to Arthur Danto than to Nelson Goodman, even if I don't share the former's definition of art (I'll come back to this) nor his vision of history and the "post-history" that follows from it. It is this historical dimension that imposes, as I see it, the notion of "transcendence," a notion that is not a superfluous appendix but which opens the work to its function, that is to say, to its reception. I note in passing that it is a necessity of the same order that made me, thirty years earlier, leave behind the "closure of the text"—dear to certain adherents of the first structuralism, or, rather, to the first interpretations of the fundamental structuralist principle, which we owe (if I believe Jakobson) to Georges Braque[55]—according to which the relation between terms is more important than the terms themselves: this principle of relation cannot, without contradicting itself, be restricted to an object separated from its context, that is to say, from its field of action. As Umberto Eco perceived and expressed it as early as 1962, the work of art is a *work*, that is to say an act, only to the extent that it is open:[56] open to other works, to its own becoming, to the world where its action exerts itself. In that sense the principle of transcendence is one with the principle of relation, and it is clearly not a coincidence if the second volume of *L'Oeuvre de l'art* is called *La Relation esthétique*,[57] at the risk of a sort of pleonasm, since in my eyes the aesthetic fact can, by definition, be only relational; but a redundancy is no doubt worth more than a misunderstanding. Yet, no matter how clear one tries to be, it is decidedly not easy to avoid all misunderstandings: I have noted one or two previously, and I am now struck by the (relative) number of reviews and diverse references to this volume in which the notion of *ideality*, which applies exclusively to objects of immanence of the works belonging to the allographic regime (literary texts, musical or choreographic scores, architectural plans) is confused with the one of *transcendence*, which by definition does not concern the regimes of immanence and which applies more or less to all works, whatever their regime. These two notions are, however, evoked in two quite distinct chapters, which are, moreover, distant from each other.[58] Ideality, at least the way I define and use it, is a type of immanence (opposed to physical and material immanence) that has nothing (pertinent) to do with transcendence—even if the latter has doubtless also something ideal, in its way. I repeat myself a little here, without much hope of dispersing a confusion the roots of which are doubtless too deep to be eradicated by a simple clarification.

I had defined the work of art, in a provisional way and at the beginning of the first volume, as an "artifact, or human product, with aesthetic function," that is to say, as an object produced with the intention of arousing an aesthetic relation. This definition, though by no means original, was doubtless not as evident as I postulated implicitly because there is no lack of theories of art, today at least (for example, the one of Arthur Danto), that neglect this aesthetic criterion, which seems to them not, or no longer, essential to the function of art: it thus involved a little more of a bias than I was (or wanted to be) aware of. This bias is clearly marked in my interpretation of conceptual art, eminently illustrated by Duchamp's ready-mades. In displacing the meaning of the work, from an object voluntarily without any aesthetic interest to the "gesture" consisting in presenting it as a work of art (a gesture that can aesthetically enhance its character of provocation and deliberate transgression), this interpretation aims, as much as possible, [59] at "recuperating" from the aesthetic point of view an entire art—that is to say, the essential of a "contemporary" or "postmodern" or, according to Danto, "posthistorical" art—that, since Duchamp, never ceases to challenge this point of view and by this very fact to challenge my definition. This kind of definition is, on this point, anything but "native"—but, I said so elsewhere, I don't think that a theory must be native, rather that it must be critical, especially if it wants to account for practices that ignore or dissimulate their own significance, which is often the case of aesthetic conducts, on the side of the creators as well as on that of the receivers. In any case this definition called with all urgency for another one: that of the aesthetic relation itself; that is the specific object of this second volume, which divides itself into three parts.

The first, "Aesthetic Attention," concerns this condition prior to all aesthetic relation that is, as Kant showed by the notion of "disinterested satisfaction," to consider in an object rather the aspect than the practical function. This type of contemplative attention can concern all kinds of objects or events, natural or produced by man. It has been partially described by Nelson Goodman under the objectivizing term of *symptoms of aesthetics*, which I propose to interpret in a more subjective manner, as a set of indices of an attitude faced toward the object rather than as a set of properties of the object. For it is not some kind of object that makes the attention aesthetic but the privileged attention to its aspect that makes any kind of object aesthetic. I say "aesthetic" rather than "beautiful" because it goes without saying that a negative appreciation is as aesthetic as a positive one.

But the attention to the aspect, which can be in the service of other kinds of approaches—for example the purely cognitive search for the origin of an object, artistic or not—becomes properly aesthetic only if it orients itself toward a question of affective order, of pleasure or displeasure, and often of desire or aversion, of the type: "Considered like this in its aspect, does this object please or displease me?" This is the question dealt with in the second chapter, entitled "Aesthetic Appreciation." Kant again has well analyzed the essentially *subjective* character of what he called the "judgment of taste," but he shrank from its relativist consequence, namely that appreciation, even when shared by a large number of individuals, always stays relative to the aesthetic dispositions common to this group and that nothing authorizes one to consider a priori as universal. The famous "legitimate pretension to universality" is in fact due to nothing but the spontaneous movement, largely illusory, of *objectification*, inherent to all appreciation, and which consists in believing itself to be uniquely based on the properties of the object, whose "value" would stand out for all. I analyze this movement, discussing the objective propositions that have been supported by certain contemporary aestheticians and that, in my opinion, make up the "native theory" of that illusion.

The third chapter, "The Artistic Function," finally considers the specific traits of the relationship to artistic works alone. This relationship is fundamentally characterized by the perception, at the origin of an object, of a productive intention that some have called "pretension" or "candidature" for an aesthetic reception. This perception is, as it were, of the order of the following hypothesis: faced with an object, I can suppose, for more or less solid reasons, with more or less certitude, that it has been produced by a human being with the intention of receiving a positive aesthetic appreciation. When it is well founded, this hypothesis constitutes a recognition of the artistic character of the object, even if the appreciation is negative or neutral: what one calls "aesthetic value" is thus not at all a definition of the work of art, nor even of the artistic relationship, which is based entirely on the recognition of the intention, whether or not this intention is judged as having "succeeded." I need not appreciate a work positively to recognize it as a work: if I appreciate it negatively, I simply regard it as a failed work—let us say, more subjectively and truthfully, as a work that displeases me—which does not prevent, or rather which presumes logically, my taking it as a work. To be a "bad" work (according to Goodman most works unfortunately are) it clearly has to be a work, and what defines an artifact as such is its candidature to aesthetic appreciation,[60] not necessarily the success of this candidature. That is to say, or to say again: that I refuse any axiological definition of the concept of work, like the one proposed by Adorno[61]—and I refuse just as much the idea that an aesthetics cannot be "axiologically neutral."[62]

I will obviously say as much of the concept of *style* and thus of the status, in literature as in the other arts, of stylistic analysis: for me the general definition of *style* calls forth no consideration of value, and the description of a particular style can perfectly be axiologically neutral. If style is, as I define it, the exemplificative side, for example, of a text,[63] the description of this aspect does not necessarily *imply* any kind of judgment of value; I do not mean by this that it *must* exclude any judgment of value but only that it *can* do without it, as any description can do without appreciation, even if, for lack of rigor and objectivity, we almost always mix our descriptions with appreciative predicates. If one will forgive this simplistic example, I can describe (measure) as "long" a sentence of Proust without *having* to specify if this relative length pleases or displeases me, and it is still less necessary that this sentence please (or displease) me to undertake measuring it. To say, as I do, that "every text has style" clearly does not signify that every text has a "good" style, except to assert that style, in itself, *is* a "quality," or a value added to a text; and that *style* signifies "beautiful style," as Adorno asserts that *work* necessarily signifies "successful work," which implies that a bad work is not a work and that an ugly style is not a style, once again, seems to me logically as absurd as to say that a black cat is not a cat. One said in my youth that the adjective *military* had as its effect to cancel the noun that it qualified, as in *military music*, but, precisely, this joke worked because of its logical absurdity: military music *is* music, a *kind* of music, a bad work is a kind of work, a bad style is a kind of style, and no kind in the world escapes its genre. In pleading like this for the respect of logical categories, I do nothing but claim the freedom to appreciate freely, and sometimes passionately, objects the description—not to mention the definition—of which will not have contained in advance an appreciation: the possibility of saying "This sentence is so and so long" without giving to this objective measure an axiological connotation, setting aside my appreciation, positive or negative, about this length. And this appreciation will have for me the more meaning and force for not having been prescribed by a surreptitiously appreciative description ("This sentence is eloquent," "This sentence is repetitious"), and which, on the basis of the same "objective" description, my neighbor will be able, quite as freely, to assert a judgment opposed to my own. Contrarily to what one often seems to think, I don't at all preach an axiological neutrality *of the aesthetic relation*, even if neutral appreciations exist sometimes, even often: "I feel neither hot nor cold about this work, or this style." What I refuse is to *imply the appreciation in the definition* (of the style, the work, of literature, of art); what I wish is to liberate the former, that is to say, liberate each appreciating person (or group that has the same opinion) from the backhanded intimidation that is always contained in an implicitly valorizing or devalorizing definition or a description—and more still in the idea that a "universal" acknowledgment by "posterity" can dictate to me (us) my (our) appreciation. I want to be able to say: "This text, like every text, has its style, and this style displeases me," or "This object is clearly a work, since I know (or I suppose) it is a human product that solicits a positive aesthetic appreciation, but it so happens that my appreciation is negative."[64]

On the other hand, of course, the acknowledgment of that "candidacy for appreciation," and thus of the artistic intention that it defines, brings with it important consequences, which are due to the historical character of the act of production (and of candidacy) and a counterpart of the act of reception itself: our relation to a work of art can hardly be as "innocent" or *primary* as our aesthetic relation to a natural object, like a landscape (which is, by the way, not always as innocent as it thinks it is), it is, I repeat, historical from end to end, and even more so when it does not know it. The natural relativity of the aesthetic relation is thus not limited but, on the contrary, accentuated, as though multiplied, by the cultural relativity of the artistic relation, which establishes at once its freedom and its responsibility.

These two volumes were thus aimed at constituting a comprehensive theory of the artwork, corresponding to their main title and intended to take into account at the same time, as much as possible, the work as *object* and the work as *action*. It is clearly not for me to say if this intention has reached its goal. What is certain in my eyes is that it is the logical, if provisional, outcome of the work of progressive enlargement that I undertook some thirty years earlier, passing, to turn around a famous phrase of Barthes,[65] *from text to work*, looking in art for a reason for being of literature and at art for a reason for being in the aesthetic relationship, which transcends all that by quite a lot. The most constant trait in it seems to me, once again, this principle of method, or more simply a mental disposition that fastens itself more to the relationships than to the objects that they link—and, gradually, to the relations between these relations themselves. This disposition, were I to qualify it (not that I feel the need to do so), would be indifferently (and without too much regard for the decrees of fashion or of counter-fashion) *structuralist* or *relativist*—belonging to a structuralism that has, by definition, nothing post-structuralist and still less postmodernist and belonging to a relativism that has, in my estimate, nothing skeptical or eclectic, still less obscurantist, since it applies itself simply to conveying, as clearly as possible, the relations that it observes or that it establishes. In fact, if I must go back to my prehistory, I think I kept from Marxism as I understood it—or, rather, from what, no doubt wrongly, attracted me to it—at the end of the 1940s a desire for rationality, a wish to see clearly and a refusal to say a lot of fine words. This desire I found answered again later on, and I hope (which is not difficult) more advisedly, in structuralism and then in analytic philosophy. One has sometimes accused poetics, as I practiced it with others, to "dry out" literary studies—that is, to de-spiritualize them—and I suppose one could today address the same reproach to my conception of art. I think this reproach is largely unfounded, but, considering everything and if one has to choose, I prefer, today as yester-day, dryness to confusion or to deception.

I thus like to see not a rupture or a "conversion," as one sometimes whis-pers to me, but a relation of complementarity leading from structuralism to analytical philosophy. So, from Saussurian linguistics to analytical philoso-phy of language, and particularly the "pragmatics" issued from Austin and Searle, the passage seems to me quite natural, because necessary: Saussure had brought out the distinction between *langue* and *parole*, and he was then al-most exclusively interested in *langue*, but I do not think that he would have re-fused the clearly legitimate study of *parole*, developed by Austin and his school. The theory of "speech acts" thus seems to me an indispensable support of the formal analyses of structural linguistics, and I think it has demonstrated its pertinence for the study, among other things, of the discourse of literary fiction. As for the Goodmanian aesthetic, which presents itself explicitly as an "approach to a theory of symbols," it can be legitimately defined as an attempt at semiotic analysis of the aesthetic relation, closer than it is aware to the ones of Saussure, of Cassirer, or of Peirce. A sentence of Goodman's seems to me very revealing of this kinship, which clearly goes beyond the field of aesthetics. He says about his *Ways of Worldmaking* of 1978: "I think of this book as belonging in the mainstream of modern philosophy that be-gan when Kant exchanged the structure of the world for the structure of the mind, continued when C. I. Lewis exchanged the structure of the mind for the structure of concepts, and that now proceeds to exchange the structure of concepts for the structure of several symbol systems of the sciences, philosophy, the arts, perception, every day discourse." Between Kantian "critique," Husserlian phenomenology, structural linguistics, and analytical philosophy, it seems to me that a more or less underground, but always very intense, traffic never ceased, which the notion—Barthesian in this case—of "semiologic adventure" represents quite well. An adventure that, for me, has not ended.

All this no doubt amounts to observing that during fifty years I did not change my opinion—which is, if I believe the proverb, the happy privilege of fools. To this mixed statement I will resist adding any kind of prognosis about a possible follow-up, unless it be perhaps by variation on the unusable dialectic formula: "a little of this leads away from that; much leads back to it"— leaving vague what this and that is. I would rather note, to conclude, that this development will have consisted, in its way, in constantly putting into question what I called in the beginning its "apparent point of departure": the decision to devote myself, among the quantity of other possible objects, to the study of literary works. Because this choice, if it is one, did not, for me, go by itself: "Why literature?" To this question, which had nothing incongruous about it, my answer, as I said before, was rather quickly: "Because art"; but this answer clearly opened another question: "Why art?" I have tried to say it, but the answer without a doubt calls up a new question, and so forth; as Figaro says: "Why these things and not others?" But, as one knows, thought is not in the answers but in the questions. Let us therefore leave these open.

2

What Aesthetic Values?

The notion of "aesthetic value," in its usual meaning of objective, universal value, seems to me based on a series of ways of begging the question, of confusions, of misunderstandings that I would like to try to dispel here by looking at things from a greater distance, if not from a greater height. [1]

We can, it seems to me, state as a principle that no value of any sort is objective and absolute because nothing, by definition, can present "value," can be valuable, except in the eyes of one or several persons; to be valuable is inevitably *to be valuable for*; every value is, in this sense, relative. An object can have a high value for a subject, a much lesser value or no value at all for another. It can happen, by chance or by necessity (I will come back to this), that an object is equally valuable for all, but it cannot happen that it is valuable (whatever its nature) *in itself*, independently of one or several subjects that evaluate it—or give it value.

One can also state as a principle—but I tend to think that these two principles are identical—that the word *value* is inseparable from the word *judgment*, to which it is always explicitly or implicitly linked in the notion of "value judgment." Not that I think that all judgments are value judgments (when I "judge" it is raining, this is clearly a factual judgment, a judgment of "reality," right or wrong), but it seems to me self-evident that every value is only, can only be, the predicate of a judgment, or, if one prefers, that every value is only, can only be, judged; to be valued is to be judged. To say it in still a different way, there is value only *of* something (or someone) *for* someone. This is the reason why the usual expression "the values" (with or without a capital) follows from a reification that is absurd—absurd but doubtless highly convenient for setting up and imposing certain value judgments as absolute and universal principles. On the other hand, an expression like "the values of the Republic (or of democracy)" seems to me altogether correct (though a little overused today) if one understands by it that certain conducts and institutions have greater *value* than others in the eyes of persons or groups attached to a republican or democratic mode of government. If such a notion seems to me valid, it is not so much because I, as it happens, (more or less) *share* these values or judgments but because the modifier of the noun here clearly indicates the relative character of the invoked values: "democratic values" are the various conducts and institutions that make up the object of positive value judgments on the part of democrats. To designate these relative values as absolute *values* "in themselves" would signify that no other values than democratic ones (aristocratic ones, e.g.) can exist, which seems to me contrary to all reality, all logic, and, as must be said in passing, all democracy. It is thus legitimate to speak, in this derived or elliptical sense, of democratic, aristocratic, Christian "values," but not of Values (in themselves). Just as legitimate, though also just as derived, is the expression "our values," which evidently signifies "the value judgments I share with you"—leaving the pronoun *you* to be defined and the reality of the consensus to be established.

I have asserted on logical grounds the relative character of every value, which amounts to asserting on principle the subjective character of every value judgment. It is this feature that distinguishes value judgments from reality judgments, not in the sense that a reality judgment could not be subjective—it is necessarily subjective, since only a subject can emit a judgment and by this fact every judgment is *by definition* subjective—but in the sense that a reality judgment, though necessarily subjective at its source, can be submitted to a factual proof: if I judge that the sum of the angles of a triangle is equal to forty-five degrees, this judgment can be submitted to an empirical verification, with which I would have to agree, stubbornness and bad faith to the side. On the other hand, if I find a person agreeable or a landscape pleasant, no verification can force me to change my mind; in fact, verification is simply inconceivable here.

Thus, every judgment is subjective, but value judgments alone are irreducibly subjective because they are irrefutable—which certainly does not mean that they are true, quite the contrary, as we know at least since Popper. But before going any farther, I want to note that a judgment of *subjective reality*—of the type "I like this object," which Durkheim has shown not to be a value judgment[2]—can also be irrefutable, though for a different reason: no one can know better than I if I like or do not like an object, and thus no one can refute such an assertion. But this irrefutability is purely empirical; it depends on the weak means of investigation at our disposal concerning the subjectivity of others; it is not based on a principle: psychoanalytic adherents venture on this terrain, sometimes successfully, and lie detectors often obtain results that one can assimilate to such refutations. The irrefutability of value judgments is of a different order, properly logical and principled. In order better to determine this distinction, it is perhaps sufficient to consider for an instant a value judgment for what it is, namely a disguised subjective reality judgment: for example, "This flower is beautiful" signifies, or rather simply *takes the place of*, "I like this flower." If, having at the start produced the first statement (a value judgment), I prudently retreat to the second (a subjective reality judgment), a psychoanalyst could perhaps show me that I am wrong in *thinking that I love* this flower, but he would not be able to show me *that I am wrong to love it*—a statement as absurd as its contrary. It is in this clearly logical sense that value judgments, even those that are shared by no one, are irrefutable.

It is nonetheless necessary to distinguish, among these judgments, between those that escape every transcendent norm, which I will call *free* or *autonomous* value judgments, and those that are necessarily submitted to one or several external norms, which I will call *heteronomous*. I must first specify that this distinction does not coincide with the one between individual and collective judgments: a *subject* is not necessarily an *individual*, and a value judgment, which is necessarily subjective, can easily be one shared by a *group* of individuals, and on this ground one can consider it, still with Durkheim, as a *collective subject*, whatever the definition of this group. To chose a rather dated example, some time ago certain young people considered the Beatles to be "superior" to the Rolling Stones, whereas others believed the reverse. This disaccord concerned, generally in a rather unpredictable manner, the same age group and, we may suppose, one without other determining social distinctions, so that one was able to say that the group formed by the fans of the Beatles, or of the Rolling Stones, had no other distinctive trait than this musical preference. But let us suppose that other distinctive traits could be discerned, that one could establish, for example, that young members of the middle class preferred the Beatles, young members of the lower class preferred the Rolling Stones; this would only indicate a certain affinity between a social condition and a musical disposition, without this affinity (which would have to be explained later) being able to determine a strong norm, to produce a true obligation. A young member of the middle class could, according to this hypothesis, prefer the Rolling Stones on the basis of a purely individual deviation, defying the more or less violent disapprobation of his milieu. I could well have imagined a more mysterious disposition, duly attested by statistics, like this one: "persons whose hair is blond prefer the Beatles, those whose hair is brown prefer the Rolling Stones," a distribution that would, in this far-fetched hypothesis, have corresponded to no kind of aggregation but to a physiological determination that crossed all social divisions—at least in the population of occidental Europe, where hair color does not determine a social group, still less what one calls today a "community." Again, of course, nothing would prevent a young person with brown hair from preferring the Beatles or one with blond hair the Stones, without even in this case, as I suppose, incurring the least blame from a class without group consciousness and therefore without any capacity to formulate criteria of conformity.

I use this expression "criteria of conformity" to designate certain types of social norm that don't yet include a true *obligation*, an obligation that is recognized and internalized by the person to whom it becomes known. I am not certain that the borderline is firm between these two types, but I propose the hypothesis that the norm of social conformity (the one that, in my example, refers to the group defined as "young members of the middle class" or "young members of the lower class" and not the one between persons whose hair is blond or brown), or what we usually call conformism, is not of a nature to impose this type of internal obligation. The pressure of the milieu—when there is a "milieu," a conscious and more or less organized community— can certainly weigh in different ways on the aesthetic judgments of its members, to the point where it worries or vexes them, but it does not make for an obligation, properly speaking, because, perhaps one should say more prudently *to the extent that*, the eventual axiological deviation does not menace the cohesion or the survival of a group whose cohesion or survival are perhaps not an absolute necessity: the group "young members of the middle class" or "young member of the lower class" could easily disappear as a cultural group, or these two groups could dissolve and merge, without menacing anything vital. This merging may already have happened to some extent, owing to a relatively recent evolution that tends to endow each age category with specific cultural habits.

We must thus distinguish from these norms of conformity what I will now call "norms of obligation." Norms of obligation are those that proceed, in whatever collectivity, from a vital necessity, those whose observance determines the very existence of this collectivity. According to ethnologists, the typical example of this is evidently the prohibition of incest, whose translation in terms of value judgment is that, in its different variants, incest is a bad deed. The biblical commandment "Thou shalt not kill" is another, and I will not enlarge the list—which is well known, if not always respected by all. The judgments one calls "ethical" typically belong to this category; Kant formulated their general principle precisely under the term *categorical imperative* and under the form "Act as if the maxim of your action were to become a universal law." I do not believe that these notions of obligational norm and categorical imperative suppose the value judgments to which they refer not be subjective—which, to say it once again, would have no meaning in my eyes; they mean solely that these judgments can only determine conducts if they conform to the obligational norm in question. Kant does not say: "Judge as if the maxim of your judgment . . ."; what he says is: "Act as if the maxim of your action. . . ." Nothing on principle forbids me to *judge* that murder, rape, or incest are good actions, and nothing for that matter can hinder me from doing it. What I am forbidden by moral Law, or social norm, is to conform my actions, my discourse, and my attitude regarding the actions of others to this kind of judgment, which I can then only "keep to myself," since even its public expression in most cases is regarded as the object of an interdiction, as an "apology" or an "incitement" for a prohibited conduct. It is this prohibition that hinders, if not the internal doctrine, at least its public expression and even more so the practical application of judgments that do not conform to the norms of a society or perhaps of every society or of the human species considered as the global society that is (after a fashion) in the making. This hindrance is named "constraint" when it is endured and "obligation" when it is freely accepted in the name of some transcendent (e.g., religious) principle—or a logical one, as is in a sense the Kantian imperative, which imposes a rule of coherence to human conducts. A large number of our actions are not ruled by anything except by constraints accepted without too much internal adhesion, like the fact that we pay taxes or that we follow parking rules, and these actions do not follow what one might call "judgments of value." There is, properly speaking, a judgment of ethical value only when a rule of action dictated by the concern for group survival is accepted and assumed by an individual or collective subject. It is in this sense that a value judgment can be the object not of a constraint—which would be meaningless, since a constrained judgment is no judgment at all—but of an obligation. This is the field in which what I call "norms of obligation" apply, and this field is thus preeminently that of ethical judgments. It is well known that their universality is contested from many sides, but they seem to me to engulf all the domains of common life, including political life: the political "values" to which I alluded earlier appear to me to deserve that term only because they are assumed as moral values, for want of which they concern only entirely objective criteria of efficiency. A policy is more or less efficient in regard to its end, and this relates to criteria of fact; this end itself is more or less "just," and this criterion relates to value judgments that can only be of an ethical order. Thus, when one speaks of "political values," one is in fact thinking of moral values, the universality of which (for lack of objectivity) is based on social (and perhaps religious) norms of obligation. In this regard what is the situation of supposedly "aesthetic values"?

Kant, as is well known, qualified as "aesthetic" what he called the "judgment of taste," precisely what we today call "aesthetic judgment." This qualification was not in the least redundant for him: it in fact designated the irreducibly subjective character, that is to say, the character deprived of objective criteria, which, according to him, judgments of taste share with judgments of physical pleasure—for example, the taste of drink or food—in a system that apparently did not assume the distinction between value judgments and reality judgments. In assuming it in his place and without his agreement, one can say that every judgment is subjective but that reality judgments are based on, and thus subject to, objective criteria; value judgments, in their turn, divide up essentially into ethical judgments, which are subject to norms of obligation, and aesthetic judgments, in the large sense, which are subject neither to objective criteria nor to norms of obligation but, at most, to nonobligatory norms of conformity and often to no norm at all. It is in this sense I qualified them just now as "autonomous," since in these two cases they depend on no obligation at all. This category thus includes at the same time judgments of physical pleasure, of the type "This wine is good" and aesthetic judgments in the strict sense of the word, of the type "This flower is beautiful." The distinction between these two kinds depends, as we know, on another trait: the "disinterested" character of the aesthetic judgment, applied only to the appearance of the object, in the name of a pleasure or displeasure felt at its aspect alone, possibly illusory, without consideration of the interest we can take in its real existence. But I will now leave aside, in its turn, the judgment of pleasure, in order to consider only the aesthetic value judgment, in the current meaning of the term.

I repeat that its autonomy results from the fact that no norm of obligation weighs on it, no norm dictated by any collective or superior interest: an aesthetic judgment, extravagant as it may seem in the eyes of another, is in itself of a nature that hurts no one, neither individuals nor groups; it can distress only on account of its possible intolerance. If my enthusiasm for a certain kind of music induces me to listen to it in a manner that disturbs my neighbors (one of Kant's grievances against this art), it is clear that this nuisance is not based on my judgment but on the conduct it inspires in me, which it does not necessarily determine: it is not my taste for Wagner that disturbs my neighbor but the power of my amplifier; if I loved Wagner three times as much and turned down its volume by two-thirds, his well-being would triple, lest he be fanatical—with a fanaticism that would in turn be ethically condemnable only if he intervened in my private aesthetic conduct. The incomprehension of the contrary judgment that often accompanies aesthetic judgment, and that is even in a sense consubstantial to it, is not in itself harmful as long as it does not determine a preventive, constraining or intimidating conduct and remains in the state of judgment: my neighbor and I can, without inconvenience or prejudice, in our inner selves, take each other for philistines. Considered in itself, an aesthetic value can in no case menace the social bond or the peace of another. This innocuousness, which is the other face of its gratuitousness, in principle guarantees its liberty, except when it is constrained from without by an individual or a group—as when a totalitarian regime deprives certain individuals of the very object of their aesthetic pleasure or imposes an object of displeasure in a manifestly arbitrary manner based entirely on the use of force. Totalitarian regimes, by the way, don't have a monopoly on this type of aesthetic nuisance, since even in a democracy the taste of the majority, or sometimes simply of certain of its representatives, can impose itself on all, without possible escape, by way of public monuments or collective celebrations.

I don't want to argue—on the basis of these marginal examples, which go back to an annoying collusion between taste and power that is difficult to avoid—for an overly easy denunciation of the desire to impose on others one's own aesthetic values, especially since the desire, which Kant called "claim to universality," more or less inhabits each of us, in every one of our judgments. Nor do I want to expose here the reasons why I reject the Kantian idea according to which this claim would be legitimate, because founded on a supposed community of sensibilities, and thus of aesthetic response, between human beings. It seems to me that the historical and cultural evolution of the last two centuries has made the existence of such a universal and a priori community increasingly doubtful. I have tried to show elsewhere the simple fact that an aesthetic judgment is a value judgment taking itself for a reality judgment, a subjective reality judgment ("I like this flower") that expresses itself as an objective reality judgment ("This flower is beautiful"). This illusory movement is named "objectivization," and I believe it to be inherent in every aesthetic judgment.

It seems to me that this pretension to universality, which cannot be founded on the myth of the universal community of sensibilities, bases itself more today on a confusion between aesthetic values, by definition autonomous and relative, and ethical values, which owe their "absolute," that is to say obligatory, character to essentially social reasons (possibly sacralized by religious motives), as I indicated earlier; or, to say it differently and no doubt more precisely, it leans on a confusion between norms of conformity and norms of obligation. This is the point that I would now like to emphasize.

Like individuals, groups—to the extent that they become conscious of their identity and their community of tastes, which rests essentially on a community of culture—tend naturally to set up their taste as a "value," that is to say, to convert their empirical community into a norm of conformity and then to convert this norm of conformity into a norm of obligation capable of imposing itself on all its members and, beyond this, on all groups. The most effective notion in this regard is clearly that of "good taste," which one sometimes calls simply "taste," by an ellipsis revealing a good conscience. Of someone who shares my taste I say spontaneously that he has good taste, or, more simply, that he has taste. The first statement implies that there can in effect exist a certain diversity of tastes but that some tastes are better than others, or, more exactly, that a certain taste (my own) is better than that of others, which one declares to be "pathological" on account of some infirmity or other, as though they suffered from hepatitis and could not perceive colors: this was Hume's thesis in his emblematically entitled essay *Of the Standard of Taste*. If there is only one good taste as compared to several bad ones, as there is only one truth as compared to several errors and lies, it becomes legitimate to qualify it simply and absolutely as taste and to reject the others as absence of taste.

But this exclusive move suffers from an obvious weakness: namely, that it is reversible in every circumstance. When two groups, like our partisans for the Beatles and for the Stones, oppose each other on a set, or rather on two sets, of aesthetic values, one of them can easily try to take advantage of the other, following the depreciative posture that I describe elsewhere and which consists less in acting for its own preference ("You should like this") than in destabilizing the adverse preference ("How can you like this?"). [3] But this advantage is never entirely sheltered from a symmetric retort, and the quarrel greatly risks remaining unresolved, without winners and losers. It is here that the norms of conformity that oppose each other without success must attempt to convert themselves into norms of obligation. Explicitly or not, this conversion consists in presenting the aesthetic values as depending on ethical values, the only ones to benefit legitimately from a norm of obligation; this conversion consists in assigning certain aesthetic values (those that one favors, of course) to what I will somewhat dryly call a coefficient of ethical value, thus adding a bonus to its value.

Still, one must often take into account the aforementioned plurality of these norms themselves: thus, between the common, civic, "republican," and more or less Christian morals that preside today over the functioning of our society and those, aristocratic in their way, of certain "gangs of young people" linked by a code of "honor" and rebellion, there is clearly opposition—even if the former at times shows tolerance toward the latter. Each of these ethics can overvalue a set of aesthetic choices—one, let us say, privileging balance, the other violence. We hardly lack contemporary examples of this; the old quarrel between the fans of the Beatles and of the Stones or the one between partisans and adversaries of bebop, later of free jazz, are simply archetypes. One also knows how overinvested clashes over contemporary (plastic) art are today. [4] But there was already much of this, mutatis mutandis, in the favorable and unfavorable reception of Corneille's works (the quarrel over the *Cid*), those of Hugo (the quarrel over *Hernani*), those of Wagner, of Manet, or Picasso. In this kind of instance the aesthetic disagreement leans, consciously or not, on a conflict of ethical attitudes, where it finds no resolving path but, rather, I fear, a risk of worsening. On the other hand, at the heart of each of the opposed camps the conflictual situation no doubt only increases the confusion of norms of which I speak. It imposes "silence in the ranks," as it were, since it gives to the need of aesthetic conformity the strength of a moral obligation and to every deviance from taste the air of a sort of treason.

But without a doubt, whatever their success, these ventures of overvaluation cannot apply to natural aesthetic objects, unless one makes, as Kant wanted to, of the interest in the beauty of nature the sign "of a state of the soul favorable to the moral feeling." [5] For various historical reasons such a symbolic link has largely deserted our horizon of thought, and the privilege of morality, become since Hegel the privilege of spirituality, prefers to attach itself today to works of art, as "born of the spirit." [6] The quarrels concerning aesthetic values are thus often based on a confusion between aesthetic appreciation in general and artistic appreciation in particular, that is to say, the appreciation solely of artworks, even though it makes up only a part, perhaps the smallest part, of our aesthetic objects.

I know that this last distinction is sometimes contested in the name of the idea that aesthetic objects that are not art objects (as when I admire for its "beauty" a natural object, a flower or an animal, or when I admire an object of which I ignore the original function, an African mask or a Magdalenean fresco) are aesthetic objects only because our artistic culture has invested them with a value that they draw solely from this investment itself. The African mask would owe its aesthetic value to the echo of the proto-cubist canvases of Picasso, the landscapes of the Île de France or of Normandy would owe theirs to the destiny made for them by Corot and the impressionists, the mists on the Thames would owe all their charm, if not the fact that one sees them at all, to Turner, and so on. As this last example indicates, such a statement sends one straight to the famous paradox by Oscar Wilde, according to which it is nature that imitates art:

> Life imitates Art far more than Art imitates Life. [. . .] There may have been fogs for centuries in London. I dare say there were. But no one saw them, and so we do not know anything about them. They do not exist till Art has invented them. [. . .] That white quivering sunlight that one sees now in France, with its strong blotches of mauve, and its restless violet shadows, is her latest fancy, and, on the whole, Nature reproduces it quite admirably. Where she used to give us Corots and Daubignys, she gives us now exquisite Monets and entrancing Pissarros.

As is well known, this page by Wilde has a faithful echo in a page by Proust, a page from *The Guermantes Way*, which shows the impact of Renoir on our vision of the female body or of carriages in the street.[7]

Alain Roger, who juxtaposes these two passages in his *Court traité du paysage*, qualifies this paradox as a "Copernican revolution."[8] This expression clearly evokes the philosophy of Kant, who applied it to the manner in which he himself placed the mental activity at the center of all knowledge of the world and whose aesthetic, as I recalled earlier, places the exercise of the judgment of taste at the source of all aesthetic value, making of "beauty" no longer a real property of an object but the simple predicate of a purely subjective appreciation. But the Wildean and Proustian "revolution" clearly adds another notch to the one of the *Critique of Judgement*. Kant simply said (in substance): when I state that a flower is beautiful, I express thereby, by objectifying it, my taste for this flower, which is in itself neither beautiful nor ugly but which simply pleases or displeases me. To this first, subjectivist, reduction Wilde and Proust in effect add another, which one could qualify as *articist* and which asserts that my taste or distaste for this flower is itself not personal, even less natural, but cultural, as though it were determined, through my own artistic culture, by the evolution and the revolutions of art to which I have been exposed directly or indirectly. I like a landscape à la Corot or a woman à la Renoir because my taste concerning landscapes and female silhouettes is conditioned either by the contemplation of canvases of these painters or by my exposure to a culture that is itself soaked in the aesthetic "values" generated by these paintings. Whence the idea, defended by Alain Roger among others, according to which an aesthetic object that we think natural—a landscape or a female body—is "aesthetic" (that is to say, as I think myself, an object of aesthetic judgment) only inasmuch as it is "artialized" (to use a word that comes to us from Montaigne by way of the French aesthetician Charles Lalo), meaning that it is modified by art, either in situ (by the art of gardening, makeup, or fashion) or in visu (by the influence of painters or sculptors who have modified our vision of these objects). It is this artialization that makes us pass from natural nudity to artistic nude, from a simple land to what we qualify as landscape, only by reference to the fate of painting, of which culture has made what we naïvely call nature. Without the impact of art, nature could not be an aesthetic object and could therefore present no aesthetic value at all, either positive or negative.

This thesis seems to me at the same time just and excessive. The nuance is quite well illustrated—though undoubtedly involuntarily—by two sentences of Charles Lalo that I will quote in the order in which Alain Roger himself quotes them. The first says: "Nature, without humanity, is neither beautiful nor ugly. It is anaesthetic." The second says: "The beauty of nature appears to us spontaneously by way of an art which is strange to it."[9] There is a clear contradiction between the idea that nature is in itself neither beautiful nor ugly and the one that its beauty can appear to us in one way or another, but Lalo certainly wants to say, in his second sentence, that nature seems to us beautiful (or ugly) by way of art, which alone makes it such in our eyes. To say it quickly, I fully agree with the first sentence: nature without man is neither beautiful nor ugly because the judgment that makes it beautiful or ugly can only be the deed of a human being (this is the first "aesthetic revolution," Kant's). On the other hand, the second sentence ("the beauty of nature appears to us by way of an art"), which expresses the second revolution (the one of Oscar Wilde and thus of Lalo and a few others) seems to me excessive because it passes, and pretends to make us pass, from one extreme ("nature itself is an aesthetic object") to another: nature can become aesthetic only by "the impact of art."

I don't believe this, and I think that works of art are not more aesthetic in themselves—that is, without an aesthetic subject feeling them as such—than natural objects or nonartistic human products. According to me, the sensibility of a human being is the aestheticizing factor in all these cases, whether this sensibility be informed or not, in one way or another, by a direct and personal or indirect and socially diffuse artistic culture. In passing directly from the (pre-Kantian) idea of an aesthetic value immanent to objects (e.g., natural objects) to the Wildean idea of an aesthetic value reserved for artworks and indirectly communicated to natural objects by the sole action, in situ or in visu, of works of art on the sensitivity of human receivers, those who hold this thesis seem to me to pass from one extreme to another. And at the same time they abandon Kantian subjectivism and the relativism that (for me) follows from it in favor of art, since, according to them, works of art, and they alone, are endowed with an immanent aesthetic value, which no longer depends on any subjective appreciation: according to them, nature is not beautiful without art, but art is beautiful on its own, since it is capable of rendering nature beautiful in our eyes. In sum this thesis, subjectivist in respect to a natural aesthetics, becomes objectivist in regard to art, which seems to me altogether indefensible, since in my opinion a work of art, just like nature according to Lalo, is "neither beautiful nor ugly" without the aesthetic glance of a receiver. And this glance, surely almost always more or less informed by art, is not aesthetic in a necessary and absolute manner. To quote Proust again, in this instance more nuanced than Wilde, on the subject of Chardin's still lifes: "If you now find all this beautiful to look at, it is because Chardin found it beautiful to paint. And he found it beautiful to paint because he found it beautiful to look at" [10]—a sentence that places at the starting point of the whole thing an aesthetic appreciation seemingly free of all artistic influence. I know very well that Chardin is not the first painter of still lifes, but I also know that this genre had to be started one day by a first still life, by definition not inspired by an anterior pictorial model. In sum the "formalist" idea that art, and nature for that matter, proceeds only from art is certainly stimulating, but only if we do not take it literally for too long, do not shut ourselves away in it, are not deceived by it. If it is true, as I think it is, that aesthetic attention aestheticizes its object and if it is possible to say metaphorically, by this fact, that the object is artialized in visu, since an object rendered aesthetic is not very different from a work of art, it seems to me decidedly excessive to establish as a universal fact that this artialization inevitably passes by the artialization in actu of an anterior artistic production. I even find that such an idea abusively depreciates the aesthetic conduct's own activity: when I attribute aesthetic value, and by this fact quasi-artistic value, to a random object, for example to a landscape, it can (and often does) happen that I act in this way, consciously or not, under the influence of an anterior work; but it is, after all, also possible that my aesthetic activity in this instance is the result of a sensitivity, and thus of a quasi-creativity, that is autonomous and personal, however great the impact of artistic culture on the formation of my sensitivity. And, if my name is Corot, Pissarro, or Cézanne, it is perhaps correct to say that my aesthetic attitude then comes under the influence of an ulterior work, the one I am getting ready to produce according to the motive invoked by Proust: "beautiful to paint because beautiful to look at"—what we call look at being then already a way of painting a thing that is sometimes beautiful to look at only because it is beautiful to paint. Even if these cases are rare, are exceptional, as though they were reserved for artists and for the quasi-artists that we happen to be in our aesthetic conducts, [11] it does not seem to me a good method to move them aside a priori by an overly exclusive principle. To abuse again of Duchamp's wit, it is not always, or only, pictures that make viewers.

Concerning this rather specific aesthetic object of a natural landscape, the position of Georg Simmel, which Alain Roger compares to that of Lalo, and thus indirectly to the Wildean revolution, is in fact rather more moderate and closer to the one I hold here. What Simmel justly underlines is that a landscape is never an object given by nature but, rather, one that is more or less constructed by its "looker," at least to the extent that the latter at the same time detaches a fragment of the universe from its context and composes it into a characterizable (predictable) particularity—a fragment that would never propose itself as an isolated individual object, as would other natural objects, like a flower or an animal: "Nature, which in its profound being and meaning ignores all particularity, is modified by the human glance, which divides it up and then recomposes it into special units—into the particularities that one calls landscapes." [12] This constituent activity can, to be sure, be compared to that of the creative artist, landscapist or other. Simmel writes: "What the artist does—to remove a limited piece from the immediately given chaotic and infinite flux of the world, to seize it and to shape it into a unit which henceforth finds its proper meaning in itself and cuts off the threads linking it to the universe the better to link it to itself—is precisely what we do as well, in smaller dimensions, with fewer principles, and in a fragmentary mode unsure of its frontiers, as soon as we have the vision of a 'landscape,' instead of a meadow, a house, a brook, or a group of clouds." [13]

I spoke a moment ago of the "quasi-artistic" character of the aesthetic object, and this qualifier applies quite as validly to aesthetic attention itself, especially when it must extract and delimit its object, as is the case with a landscape. There is no doubt that this delimitation is often "unsure of its frontiers"—clearly less sure than the one the landscapist works within the limits of his picture and than the acquaintance with this type of picture works toward assuring us in this constructive activity. But it seems to me that this does not place aesthetic attention entirely in the category of art. Simmel notes with greater subtlety that the perception of a "landscape" in itself results in an artwork "in statu nascendi," and he clarifies this qualification in opposing such a perception to that of the human figure: "it is certain that the human appearance is recast in the work of art; but it starts out from the immediately given of this appearance, whereas to arrive at the picture of a landscape one has to pass through an additional intermediate step: the modeling of the natural elements into the ordinary 'landscape,' which is necessarily subjected to the contributions of earlier aesthetic categories, and which is on the way of the work of art, their pure, autonomized product."[14] It is true that this intermediate step, the one that results in "a piece of nature" turning into a landscape,[15] is of a quasi-artistic nature, but this quasi does not demand, to be such, the detour by way of properly (canonically) artistic activity; it would no doubt be more correct to say that aesthetic attention, in itself, is here already something like an art, a fact that is illustrated by the practice of photography.[16]

I may be battling rather strongly against an attractive turn-of-the-century paradox, but the fact is that the position here traced to Oscar Wilde can be taken back to Hegel himself. Recalling the famous Kantian example of the nightingale that (according to Kant) ceases to please us if we find out that it is in fact produced by a skillful imitator, Hegel reverses the statement to affirm that the song of an authentic nightingale itself pleases us only because "it gushes forth purposeless from the bird's own life, like the voice of human feeling. In general this delight in imitative skill can always be but restricted, and it befits man better to take delight in what he produces out of himself."[17] The expression of human feelings imitated by nature: we are not far from the Wildean paradox of imitation of art by nature, in an aesthetics that precisely makes of art itself such an expression. Thus, if one wants to situate it historically in this way, the second Copernican revolution in aesthetics is separated from the first only by the three decades that elapsed between the Critique of Judgement (1790) and Hegel's course on aesthetics (1818). It coincides well with the inversion worked by Hegel on the Kantian valorization of natural beauty into an antithetical valorization of artistic beauty, or, rather, with the absolute privilege accorded by Hegel to the latter as "product of the mind," to which I return now—a privilege that the confusion between aesthetic values and moral or spiritual values seeks to legitimate. Still, one often wants to pretend that not all works reflect the superiority of the spirit to the same degree, and it is here that the idea of a "hierarchy of values" figures at the very center of the specific field of works of art.

This idea becomes involved all over the place, beginning with Hegel himself, who bases his hierarchy of the arts on the supposed acknowledgment of an evolution valorized by his own attention. Today this supposed interartistic hierarchy has become much less likely; it has given way to another, this time an *intra-artistic* hierarchy, which asserts the existence within every art of an axiological range, on account of which certain works, or certain genres, would surpass other works or other genres by the fact of their greater spiritual content: thus, an oratorio by Bach would on this basis outclass a popular song or a fresco by Raphael a still life by Chardin. Assertions of this kind are not absurd, yet one feels that their axiological criterion, and thus the hierarchy that they want to establish, is *not* of an aesthetic order, that is to say, of the order of a judgment of taste. In my opinion these two strategies must be carefully distinguished so that we would eventually be able to grant to a work, or to a genre, a spiritual superiority and to its rival an aesthetic preference; to say, for example, what we think without daring to say it: "*The Passion according to Saint Matthew* is no doubt more profound, but I prefer 'Le Petit vin blanc.'" [18] I don't personally assume this last statement, but I absolutely permit its assumption, and I don't believe one can object to it. To become a little more involved: *The School of Athens* is no doubt more noble, or more sublime, etc., but I prefer *The Copper Fountain*, [19] and it is this affective preference that grounds, that even *defines*, an aesthetic judgment. Or, again, on a different plane, it seems to me perfectly legitimate to claim a work to be technically superior to another because, let us say, its structure is more complex and more accomplished, and this can pass as an objective criterion: Beethoven's *Great Fugue*, for example, is incontestably more complex than "Le Petit vin blanc." But, again, I see no necessary link between this judgment of technical merit and a proper aesthetic appreciation, which always comes back to an affective relation of pleasure or displeasure that no technical argument can prescribe or refute: I simply have no objection on this plane to those who prefer "Le Petit vin blanc" because the aesthetic superiority of the complex over the simple is nowhere established, and it is well known that classical aesthetics was not far from supposing the contrary. And, if one were to object that the (melodic) theme of "Le Petit vin blanc" is not only simpler but more *vulgar*, I would answer that this criterion, which now pretends to be based on an objective appreciation, in fact itself comprises an appreciation, that it is thus itself subjective, since I know no objective criterion concerning vulgarity or distinction. [20] Therefore, if we are to stick to these two most frequently invoked arguments, neither the reference to the nobility of the subject nor that of the complexity of structure seem to me to be able to decide between works on the properly aesthetic plane. The coexistence, and even the overlap, of these diverse data, and of many others, in the reception of works of art do not justify their confusion and still less the domination of some over others: as Pascal said in a different context, "this is impossible, and of a different order." In the same way, artistic judgment cannot legitimately apply to an art, to a genre, or to a style the possible criteria of excellence belonging to a different art, genre, or style: it is entirely permissible to prefer the novel to the gothic or the gothic to the novel, the baroque to the classic or the classic to the baroque, but it is certainly not permissible to judge one of these styles according to the values of the other. And, if, for example, we take literature to be a more profound art, one that "carries more meaning" than the others, this does not justify our judging the others according to the measure of this profundity or of this meaning, unless we want to open between them a struggle that is as sterile as it is groundless.

But to combat this confusion of aesthetic values (a notion, to say it once again, that I regard as illusory, based as it is on irreducibly subjective appreciations) and of ethical values (whose equally subjective character is legitimately objectified with respect to transcendental norms) does not authorize one to evade the question of the necessary choice between them; quite the contrary is true. Or, to ask this question more concretely: when I have to choose between a taste—an aesthetic pleasure—and a moral obligation, which course shall I adopt? The answer seems to me to follow from the difference to which I have just referred: since it is submitted to no obligatory norm, aesthetic pleasure, like all manners of pleasure, necessarily can only yield, or more exactly is *obliged* to yield, to moral obligation. The confusion of orders I criticized earlier, and which consists in judging a work of art according to its ethical value (a confusion I will call "moralism") has, as its symmetric counterpart, the inverse confusion, no doubt graver in its consequences, usually called "aestheticism," which Proust, in respect to Ruskin, qualified as "idolatry." It consists in making aesthetic values prevail over moral values (in regarding "murder as one of the fine arts"), even over the "truth values" that attach themselves to factual values or over the values of logical coherence that attach themselves to explicit or implicit reasoning. And the extremes to which this kind of overestimation of the aesthetic motive has led individuals and groups invested with absolute power in history is well known: the case, true or false, of the arsonist Nero under the alibi *Qualis artifex* provides a striking symbolic illustration. Moreover the acknowledgment of the autonomous and purely subjective character of aesthetic judgment seems to me, among other things, the surest guarantee not only of the respect for the judgment of others but also of the respect of its liberty and its integrity, on which our moral law is based. Moralism and aestheticism are thus inimical twins that I propose to dismiss together after firmly distinguishing their two different orders of values.

The objection is sometimes raised that this insistence on the subjective character of aesthetic appreciations in general and of artistic appreciations in particular is to deprive of all objective criteria, and thus of all validity, the decisions that the diverse institutions, public and private—the role of which is so important (for such a long time and by way of so many diverse procedures) in the "cultural" life of our societies—must make in buying, subsidizing, conserving, and in other ways patronizing or "helping" artistic creation. I answer this very serious objection by saying that the choices in question do not depend exclusively on aesthetic data but also sometimes on practical data (e.g., on technical and economic ones, where architecture and urbanism are concerned) for which objective criteria are not in the least lacking—which does not mean that they are always respected. And by saying that the generally (and desirably) collective character of these instances can *to a certain extent* attenuate or compensate the arbitrariness of individual preferences, *at least if we suppose* that the relations of authority, of power, of influence, or of diverse intrigues ("return of the elevator," etc.) don't come to thwart this easing effect. Many conditions, to be sure, and in any case nothing is able to hinder the action of collective habits, which can in some cases make of a commission, no matter how numerous, something of a homogeneous entity, endowed with several voices but a single taste. What results from this is that the subjectivity of such decisions in properly aesthetic matters is limited only in a manner that is itself limited and that it knows no counterweight.[21] But to recognize a fact is not to create it or even to encourage it, and I am the first to deplore this kind of consequence—at least when it offends my own subjective taste. I nonetheless think that the inverse attitude, which consists of denying evidence, is not helpful at all, or, rather, that, like every sort of ignorance (voluntary or not), it can only worsen what it conceals. If we want to avoid, insofar as possible, the most regrettable effects of what remains for me an incontestable fact (and, like all facts, more stubborn than its best-intentioned deniers), it would be better, here as elsewhere, to avoid wishful thinking and the ostrich policies it inspires or which inspire it.

By way of conclusion I will mention a recent episode that seems to me to show, though *a contrario*, the necessity to admit a plurality of criteria in matters of artistic appreciation. On the occasion of a radiophonic broadcast a music-loving and well-intentioned journalist, believing he would soften the angles by this delicate choice, made an illustrious French composer and conductor, as well known for his "impatience" as for his genius, listen to an improvisation by the pianist Bill Evans. The former, rigid as a rod and without the least nuance, answered that this music was nothing but a string of clichés and absolutely unworthy to retain his matinal attention. This appreciation was, to my mind, not absolutely "wrong" but simply, or rather doubly, inappropriate: first, the criteria of appreciation of a jazz improvisation, even the most urbane, are not those of serial music; second, it doesn't seem to me that the tenor of innovation is, any more than the complexity of structure, an absolute criterion of artistic merit or of aesthetic value. Nikolaus Harnoncourt remarks more quietly that "Mozart was not an innovator"—which does not keep him from greatly admiring a music whose depth seems to him the more mysterious: "How mysterious Mozart's music is! One has the impression of knowing all the motifs, the turns, the phrases—all that one could call his musical vocabulary. Every composer of his time spoke this same 'language.' Unlike Wagner or Monteverdi, Mozart was not an innovator in his art, he made no reforms in music. [. . .] With the exact same means as other composers, without inventing anything unheard-of, without employing a musical technique that had never existed, he knew how to give his music a depth unlike any other. This seems to us mysterious; it is impossible to explain or to understand."[22] But it also occurs to me that our illustrious French composer, whom you have certainly recognized, is supposed to have declared one day, "If what Schubert wrote is music, then what I write is not." I don't know whether this statement (and I hope, after all, that it is apocryphal) applies to Mozart as well, but, even as I grant to artists this right of mutual misunderstanding that is no doubt a condition of their creative will, I propose that the rest of us, common mortals and simple amateurs, admit at the very least—which is not always easy: after all, the amateur of jazz often professes in regard to rock the same contempt that Pierre Boulez professed in regard to jazz—that there is music and music, painting and painting, poetry and poetry, and that each of these practices holds, in common with each of its receivers, the keys to its own value.

3

Axiological Relations

I have elsewhere named "aesthetic relation" the relation that gets established between a human subject and an object, whatever it may be, to which this subject gives aesthetic attention; that is to say, to define it rapidly, an aspectual attention oriented toward an affective appreciation of the type: "This object (on account of its aspect) pleases or displeases me." One could undoubtedly just as legitimately qualify in this manner the intersubjective relationship that sometimes gets established between two or more subjects in respect to the same object (or set of objects), considered from an aesthetic vantage point—whether or not it is a work (or works) of art; when two persons consider or evoke together the same landscape and, as one says, "exchange"—that is, mutually communicate to each other—their aesthetic appreciation about it, it is certainly not improper to say that these two persons establish between them an aesthetic relation in this new, barely derivative sense of the expression. But, since it is then a matter of a confrontation (or of a meeting) of two "value judgments," it would undoubtedly be more relevant to qualify it as an *axiological relation*. This relation is clearly subsequent to the other one, which it supposes present in each of the two interlocutors or which, at the very least, it provokes in one at the initiative of the other. Two persons walk past a building; one of them experiences an aesthetic feeling in regard to this building, expresses it, and inquires about the feeling of his companion; the latter, who perhaps had not asked himself the question, can henceforth not fail to ask it in turn, and answer it, even if he does so evasively (gives an aesthetically neutral answer), since a question of an aesthetic order almost inevitably calls for an answer of the same order. The exception is when the question is explicitly refused: "Do you find this palace beautiful?—Too big (or too lavish or too expensive) for me."[1] Actually, a less than civil refusal, like all refusals of this kind, and an unnatural one to boot: if someone asks me about my feeling, I can hardly avoid asking myself about it; the correct attitude in this case—perhaps adopted later if the first speaker insists—is more likely to follow the type: "Truly superb but undoubtedly quite uncomfortable": acceptance of the question and (in this case) positive answer but together with a lateral objection; the "aesthetic point of view" is accepted at first, if only out of simple politeness, but immediately rejected as pointless, in favor of a more pertinent practical consideration.

But certainly on this plane the usual and most simple relation is the one that unites two autonomous subjects, who both spontaneously adopt an aesthetic relationship to the same object and who, on this basis, exchange their value judgments. Without giving it undue theoretical importance, the point on which I will focus, among the infinite variety of possible exchanges, is the one that plays a certain role in our daily aesthetic conduct: in case of a disagreement why is it more difficult for the one and/or more unpleasant for the other to criticize an appreciation we don't share when it is positive than when it is negative? Why is a reproach like "How can you like this?" felt—by both parties, except if the speaker is crudely insensitive—as more upsetting than a reproach like "How can you dislike this?" Such declarations of disagreement can certainly take the most diverse forms, some of which are more aggressive than others; the variations are not what matters here, but the very fact of a disaccord, even a tacit one, manifested simply by silence or by an implicitly disapproving return question: "This is beautiful.—You think so?" To say it more abstractly: between a positive and a negative aesthetic judgment on the same object (I leave aside neutral appreciations, which by definition do not lead to discussions), the axiological relation is not psychologically symmetric; the negative judgment is generally felt to be "superior" to the positive judgment. When two subjects disagree on the same object and this disaccord—to simplify—comes down to the opposition of an "I like it" and an "I dislike it," the one that "dislikes" finds himself in a situation of superiority in respect to the one who "likes"; the latter finds himself ipso facto, and without reciprocity, accused of "bad taste." "Good taste" appears more in what he rejects than in what he appreciates, and, inversely, bad taste appears more in what he appreciates than in what he rejects: it consists, in short, in liking what "must not" be liked, rather than in the reverse. When I say that it appears, I clearly mean that it appears to the eyes of another because no one accuses himself of bad taste, unless he has a large dose of bad conscience, which translates into the adoption on himself of the judgment of another (I'll come back to this); thus, when we accuse someone of bad taste, it is not ordinarily because of what he does not like but because of what he likes and which we judge unworthy of being liked. Doubtless he who liked absolutely nothing would show himself thereby to be very "difficult," at the worst very insensitive, but he would not be said, properly speaking, to have bad taste; obversely, to be difficult is often taken as a proof of good taste. Bad taste, in sum, is always positive, and everything works as though this positive nature minimized the importance of the person who displayed it in the face of his opponent. And vice versa: every negative appreciation expresses, or assumes, the superiority of the person who holds it toward the object considered and therefore toward the person who holds a positive appreciation of it. One can no doubt express this more geometrically—every positive appreciation, every admiration—goes from bottom to top: when I admire an object I place myself implicitly below that object ("I would not be able to do as much"); inversely, contempt or *condescension* (a good word!) goes from top to bottom: when I have contempt for an object, I place myself implicitly on top of it ("If I had made this, I wouldn't brag about it"). What results from this is that two admirers or two denigrators (let us suppose, to simplify, in the same degree) of the same object situate themselves on the same plane—on the same rung of the axiological ladder—but an admirer and a denigrator situate themselves (so to speak and if I dare say so) on two *vertically symmetric* planes in regard to the one of the appreciated object: the admirer places himself below the object and the denigrator above it and thus doubly above the admirer; if an object deserves his contempt, the one who admires it deserves his contempt the more. There exists however a case of disagreement in which this "the more" is unnecessary and where the disdain expressed by the negative judgment is inevitably hurtful: this happens when the negative judgment is expressed not in front of a simple admirer but in front of the author of the despised object (by definition a work of art in this case); unless of course the author (the artist) protects himself in advance against this humiliation by pretending to belittle his work himself ("It isn't finished yet," "This isn't my best work," etc.), and thus to place his own judgment above his own accomplishment, as though his self-esteem has become still more involved with the former than with the latter and to accept more willingly to fail in action than to fail in thought— which isn't that absurd, after all.

I would argue that another cause, a logical one, as it were, is responsible for this psychological dominance of negative appreciations over positive ones, but I fear that the reader will find this explication a little formal. Here it is nonetheless. By definition every negation involves the affirmation that it rejects and that it seems, by this fact, not to reject without a reason. To say, "This object is ugly"—the more so the explicitly negative form "This object is not beautiful"—is implicitly, and even explicitly, to pretend that one has considered the opposite (positive) judgment and that one has refuted it. The positive judgment itself naturally has a more "naïve" appearance: it "rejects" nothing and by this fact gives itself no "mark" on what it seems not to have even thought of examining; it is thus naïve and disarmed in respect to what Hegel, if I remember correctly, called in a different context "power"—and which I would gladly qualify as the *logical authority* of the negative. I'll come back to this.

I am not claiming that this intersubjective logic, or mechanism, doubtless as crude as it is sophisticated, applies only to aesthetic relations. It is just as applicable on the plane of ethical judgments: if I despise a conduct, I must equally, and even more, despise the person who approves it. But, paradoxically, by a peculiarity of human nature the psychological stakes are more weighty in the aesthetic field than in the moral domain: the scorn that a mode of behavior judged reprehensible inspires does not reach the self-esteem of the culprit in the same way as the one that an artistic production inspires when it is judged to be mediocre or an appreciation when it is judged to be false or naïve, perhaps because one invests more of one's ego in creations, and even more in tastes, than in actions. It is less humiliating to hear oneself say that one has acted badly than to hear oneself say that one has (if I can use this term) created badly or admired unadvisedly, a criticism that strikes head on what Freud calls His Majesty the Ego, whereas a moral criticism has a greater effect on the superego. The clearest indication of this difference is the share of ridicule: it applies far more to artistic failures than to bad actions.[2] Ridicule is simultaneously the sanction and the instrument of making one feel inferior. I can always exempt myself internally from blame ("You think that I am wrong, but I object to your judgment, because I know I am right") but not from mockery; if someone finds me ridiculous, no internal denial (nor an external one: "You are wrong to find me ridiculous" is an ineffective reply, at the limit of semantic incongruity) can do anything about it: the wound does not heal from it. One always endures contempt less easily than disapproval, vexation less easily than blame, and it seems to me that the attribution of a mistake in taste, like that of stupidity, and no doubt one or two others that would distance us a little too much from our subject,[3] results more in the first than in the second.

What I here call "axiological relation" evidently stems from this psychology of self-esteem and sensitivity, somewhat petty but omnipresent in our society and perhaps in every society. The preceding detour has made me pass by way of considerations of artistic accomplishment, but it would be wrong to think that our axiological scale functions only in regard to the appreciation of artworks. The relation that establishes itself between the two aesthetic subjects concerned is not modified by whether the object of the disaccord is a work of art, a natural object, or an artifact of uncertain status (e.g., a primitive tool): in all these instances the contemplator places himself, by the very act of his negative judgment, above the judged object and doubly above its admirer. The only pertinent difference for our subject comes from the fact that the natural object (or the artifact taken to be without any aesthetic intention) does not have a recognizable originator and that consequently its "author"—nature or the craftsman without pretension—is not targeted in the appreciative judgment that sanctions it. If I judge a postcard landscape (by which I mean a landscape that the makers of postcards prefer) banal or vulgar, my negative appreciation of this object involves no judgment about the (nonexistent) producer, but it does not fail to reach the admiring interlocutor and, by this very fact, to offend his taste—and thus his ego. And this offense, once again, involves no mutuality: if, of the two strollers, the lover of postcard landscapes is the first to express himself, his favorable judgment will not in any way offend his interlocutor, who may be surprised by it—even pained, if he estimates or likes him for other reasons—but in no case will he be affected or belittled in his own attitude, which, so to speak, comprises in itself the gratifying mark of his superiority; to despise is to be above, and one can't feel oneself disputed by what one surpasses.

This unequal relation (superiority/inferiority) between a positive and a negative appreciation is in itself, it seems to me, without solution because the debate in which it can result, judgment against judgment, cannot resolve it, for reasons that Kant explained very well: with aesthetic judgment based on no concept, on no objective criterion, each party can on principle only insist on his own, "stop [his] ears" to arguments without pertinence,[4] since the latter are incapable of affecting a feeling. The situation can only become jammed in the unilateral connection that the first exchange established, the denigrator despising the admirer,[5] without mutuality. Despisement is a vectorized feeling that functions only in one direction (from above to below); one can pretend to "answer despisement with despisement," but this pretense is illusory because the narcissistic wound puts the despised person in no condition to repay in kind the one who gave himself the advantage of the initiative. I can only reply to despisement with an impotent grudge, in other words with "resentment." What may eventually, as one says, "advance the debate"—that is to say, resolve the contradiction, generally to the advantage of one of its positions—is not further argumentation (further "demonstrative reasons," as Kant would say) about the appreciations themselves ("You are wrong to like, or to dislike, this object *in the way you perceive it*, for this or that aesthetic reason," a meaningless notion in my eyes); it is either what I will call the "action of influence," even of intimidation, or a modification, in one direction or the other, or in both, of the *attentional object*, that is to say, of the perceived object (the object *in the way it is perceived*) itself. These two possibilities appear to me quite distinct in their nature and in their appeal and also of unequal authenticity and legitimacy.

The first seems to bring a formal denial to the Kantian principle according to which one cannot establish the superiority of one aesthetic judgment over another, but this denial is only apparent because the "superiority" established in this way proceeds, in fact, from an abuse of the situation or a confusion of the orders, as when, in Pascal, the tyrant demands (and sometimes obtains) to be loved because he is strong. This is what happens when, in an aesthetic debate, one of the interlocutors is intimidated and ends up by doubting his judgment—to doubt on the subject of an example, says Kant, is to be "devoid of taste"[6]—and, on account of this doubt, to agree with his contradictor. The case mentioned by Kant is that of a positive persuasion (to persuade someone that he is wrong *not* to like "a building, a prospect, or a poem") and therefore the inverse of the one I am considering, but I think, for the aforementioned psychological reasons, that the negative persuasion is easier and therefore more frequent: intimidation can hardly function only from above to below, and the subject of the negative appreciation, as we saw, places himself right away above the one with the positive appreciation. It is clear that an act of contrite submission ends the debate only in an inauthentic fashion, repressing without modifying in depth the positive appreciation of the interlocutor. Kant comments, "A judgment of others which is unfavorable to ours may indeed rightly make us scrutinize our own carefully, but it can never convince us of its incorrectness." I would rather say that it can at the most persuade us that we are wrong in our feeling (without much legitimacy if we hold, as I do, that no feeling can be "erroneous") but that it cannot, in fact, modify this feeling. Nonetheless, the share of bad conscience and bad faith being what it is in psychic life, this movement of making one feel guilty ("I seem to be wrong in loving this object") can induce a belief in modification that is hardly different from real modification: if I come to *believe* that I no longer like an object, everything will go on internally (not to mention externally) as though I no longer liked it.

The other way toward resolution does not affect appreciation directly but what I call "aesthetic attention": this is what happens when one of the two subjects leads the other to perceive the object, as one says, "in a different manner" or "from a different angle," that is to say, to perceive in the object aspects he had not as yet perceived. This is when the object of attention, the object of appreciation itself, becomes modified, indirectly but authentically, that is to say, in an autonomous manner, not by influence or intimidation but by motivated acceptance. If I admire a flower that I believe to be natural, someone can act effectively on this appreciation by showing me that it is, in fact, an artificial flower and that I should admire it less, in a different manner, or for different reasons; we remember that Kant contrasted the song of a nightingale to that of a mischievous imitator and considered for his part that the second deserved no admiration at all.[7] If I admire the skill with which a statue that I believe to be made of marble is executed and someone proves to me later that it is in reality made out of a block of soap,[8] I will probably be able to reduce my initial appreciation, but I supposed in this case that it addressed the skill of execution, not the form itself of the sculpture, which has no reason to be affected by this revelation. The fact is that revisions of this kind refer more often to the conditions of production, easier to ignore at first sight than immediately perceptible aspects (this was already the case with the artificial flower), and that therefore they affect more specifically human artifacts and mainly works of art, but it is just as certain that the object of attention constituted by an artwork involves by definition, as soon as its artistic character is recognized, its own conditions of production, with the set of technical data, generic and historical, that situate this work in the artistic field. And, since aesthetic appreciation is always based on the attentional object, one has to admit, against Beardsley, that this appreciation concerns the entire set of data perceived and known by the appreciator and that it can therefore become modified according to those perceptions and understandings. Of course, in all these cases the appreciation changes only because it has, in fact, *changed its object*. One could say as well, or rather better, that the appreciation of a certain attentional object (e.g., a flower) has been replaced by the appreciation of another attentional object (e.g., an artificial flower). As for the positive or negative character of this indirectly worked change, it is also based on the aesthetic disposition of the subject: anybody is free to prefer artificial flowers because they are, as Hegel would roughly say, "products of the mind." Which is not wrong, after all.

But in this second hypothesis it seems to me that the abusive privilege—the psychological advantage—of the negative appreciation fortunately no longer plays a role. One might as well raise a negative appreciation by revealing to its author data that he ignored or that had at first escaped him—for example, by telling him that a work that he judged a commonplace was produced in an era when the properties attest to a certain "advance" on its time (as one says), that is, in adding to its perceptual traits the trait of innovation or originality (a nonaesthetic trait in the strict sense of the word but technical, historical, or genetic—these terms are roughly interchangeable here); or by showing him that his negative appreciation eludes the generic affiliation that he had spontaneously assigned to it; a "standard" trait in one genre can be decidedly deviant in another; the popular refrain that Stravinsky featured in *Petrouchka* ("She had a wooden leg . . .") doesn't have exactly the same meaning it has in the Moulin Rouge.

In sum both our ways of resolving the conflict are only apparent, though in very different ways. The first underhandedly brings in what at one time was called the "argument of authority"—an authority that, I insist, applies to negative propositions—with a view to sanctioning or confirming by an admission of failure an immediately proclaimed superiority. The second substitutes for the insoluble clash of appreciations a discrepancy that is perfectly resolvable, since it appeals to objective (e.g., historical) criteria—generally on the subject of artworks, [9] but this displaces the question rather than resolving it: to show me that I mistook the object does not mean that I mistook my feeling toward it (which would be meaningless); the object simply disappeared in the meantime.

To this point I have been considering this question a little artificially from a purely psychological vantage point, between two individuals that were at first separated by nothing more than a specific aesthetic disaccord, but, more or less fortunately, real confrontations often have other dimensions that come to complicate the situation. They are of an order that surpasses a simple intersubjective relation; we can qualify them as "cultural," that is to say, social. I do not necessarily designate the difference in socioeconomic classes by this adjective: the famous "gulf between generations," to which I will return, is certainly a social split; and cultural inequalities can sometimes contradict social inequalities, like when Swann, asked by the Duc de Guermantes about the authenticity of his "Velasquez" ("But you're a dilettante, a master of the subject, what would you say it was?"), after hesitating an instant "in front of this picture, which obviously he thought atrocious," laughingly answers, "A bad joke!"—provoking in his interlocutor, humiliated despite his superior rank, a typical, clearly impotent reaction of hurt vanity: "an impulse of rage."[10] When two individuals, separated by a marked difference of social rank or educational "level," oppose each other about the appreciation of an artwork (a privileged terrain for this type of disaccord), the cultural difference interferes with the psychological inequality between positive and negative appreciation, an inequality that it can sometimes accentuate, sometimes diminish, and in certain ways correct. A cultivated aesthete will easily override the "kitschy" taste of a naïve lover of garish images or garden dwarves, for whom the so-cial "inferiority complex" will often aggravate the (psycho)logical uneasiness mentioned earlier. But, conversely, the negative appreciation by the latter of a work of High Culture (e.g., of a dripping by Pollock or an installation by Beuys) will be deprived of the superiority that should on principle attach itself to it and will be quite plainly attributed to his obvious lack of competence: one will no longer say, and he himself will not say for long, that he despises this work but, rather, that he is not cultivated enough to appreciate it, that his "rejection" includes (socio)cultural resentment and goes back more to ha-tred than to contempt;[11] henceforth his "incomprehension" will be—with or without success—subject to pedagogy, perhaps imparted to his contradictor, consisting of a little lecture on the history of modern and contemporary art. If these remarks on social levels seem unappealing or this path of resolution too utopian, it may be relevant to think of the axiological relation between par-ents and children—at least as long as the age of the latter doesn't yet autho-rize them to reject the parental model, which apparently happens earlier and earlier—or, more collectively and institutionally, between teachers and their students, as long as teachers and students survive: "aesthetic education" then consists in progressively substituting for the spontaneous objects of childish taste attentional objects held to be "higher," at least according to the aesthetic criteria of the adults, whose superiority is in no way absolute but solidly based on the (sometimes justified) presumption that greater competence is acquired by age. This presumption accredits in turn the notion, in itself highly fragile, of "good taste," a privilege that the beneficiary can henceforth generously share with his less favored partner. We call this "acculturation," and I will keep from saying that it necessarily leads to "aesthetic progress," another illegitimate notion in my opinion: the triumph of one "taste" over another is simply and dictatorially qualified as progress by someone who succeeds in imposing his own taste and who no longer risks contestation from a now converted or repentant former opponent.[12] I am far from condemning actions of this kind, which give our axiological relations all their flavors. Sometimes this flavor is a bit acid; some, like Stendhal, prefer an egoist's or dilettante's tête-à-tête with the aesthetic object.[13] I merely wanted to clarify the part that games of influence and confusions of order play here. Once again, aesthetic education does not consist of exchanging judgments but information; it does not consist of forming taste but the aptitude to perceive, to distinguish, to bring together, to compare—the only legitimately "educable" basis of appreciation. Which isn't nothing, but that's a different story.[14]

4

The Two Kinds of Abstraction

It is customary to contrast two extreme types of nonfigurative painting: the geometric, typically illustrated by Mondrian, and the informal, or expressionistic, or lyrical, illustrated, for example, by Pollock. Between them would extend the entire scale of existing styles. This division is deficient, if only on account of the qualifications it uses: every picture, with the possible exception of absolutely monochromatic ones, presents the eye with a form, or an assemblage of forms (possibly most confusing), and no form is, properly speaking, more "geometric" than another: geometry clearly must be able to account for every distribution of lines and stains on a plane (the canvas). A dripping is no less geometric than a checkerboard; it is only geometrically more complex. The surface description of a nonfigurative picture goes back at every point to plane geometry. The same is true of the description of a figurative picture; simply the latter cannot be reduced to it, since the assemblage of forms that it presents refers to objects that it is considered to represent, with more, less, or no impression of depth or of perspective. What one calls "geometric abstraction" is only distinguished by apparently simpler surfaces, limited by straight lines (Mondrian) or by easily defined curves (the circles of Delaunay) and filled by pure colors, possibly primary. But the fact that one can (or cannot) identify these surfaces gives it a kind of figurative potential; I'll explain myself, taking the manifest risk of appearing altogether naïve in landing on this terrain.

Even if I don't know the title, I cannot fail to observe that the *Black Square on White Ground* by Malevich (1913) *consists* (I use for the moment the most neutral possible verb) of a black square contrasting with the white frame that surrounds it and which makes one think that the black square detaches itself from a white "ground"—whence the feeling that this picture *represents* a black square. The title represses another figurative interpretation that would be almost as good: that the picture represents a white frame on a black ground. Nothing in the notion of "ground" implies absolutely that the ground *surrounds* the figure; the contrary can be true, and I think that the relation of the (marked) black to the (neutral) white contributes strongly to giving the central square the function of figure, leaving to the white frame that of ground—whence the title; a white square surrounded by a black frame would probably inspire more easily the title Black Frame on White Ground. The white here functions a little as though this portion of the canvas had remained blank and as though the "picture" as a painted surface boiled down to an inscribed black square. As is well known, the same Malevich, some time later, escapes this hesitation by exhibiting (1918) his White Square on White Ground, in which the canvas is more visibly covered by a more painterly white, not strictly monochromatic but animated by light marblings (like the later whites of Ryman or the blacks of Reinhardt), and in which the internal square takes up a slanted position, tipped to the left, tangential at one of its angles to the left border of the picture; and this excludes, or better keeps one from introducing, as I did for the canvas of 1913, the parasitic notion of "frame."

But look: the absence of chromatic contrast and the absence of the function of frame now give more potential to the notion of ground; this time no more hesitation or rivalry is possible for the role of figure, between center and surrounding: the slanted square, which is no longer central, unquestionably appears as the figure, and the surface that surrounds it appears (almost) like the ground, a perception that the title here confirms. Despite its monochronous character, the picture of 1918 thus accents more strongly than the one of 1913 the relationship between figure and ground, which probably explains its greater fame and its emblematic role as precursor. There is something minimalist—that is, something "conceptual" before its time (and one knows the importance, in this domain, of anteriority)[1]—in the fact of basing such a relationship on an absence of contrast, the most subtle being due to the fact that the inscribed square, though above all marked by a slight effect of contour, seems in fact painted for its own sake and not merely drawn on the surface of its ground, that is to say, of the whole picture: a picture whose form, itself a square (80 x 80), has no longer the same relevance than in 1913, lest it be that the slanted effect is more noticeable than it would be in relation to a more horizontal overall format.

But in the end, to my knowledge, someone who says "figure" (and ground) says figuration, and again nothing can hinder anyone from considering this picture as figuring, or representing, a white square, in the way the Mona Lisa figures a seated young woman or the View of Delft an urban landscape. A description such as "This picture represents a slanted white square on a white background" is not irrelevant, and it is in fact this description that is stated by the title, seemingly chosen by the painter himself. One could clearly avoid this entire discussion by discharging the entire notion of "abstract" or "nonfig-urative" painting and by deleting as non-pertinent the distinction, formerly proposed by Etienne Souriau, between *representative* and *presentative* arts. But this would be a weighty move, contrary to usage and intuition, and it would at the same time suppress the thing I am trying to (re)define *inside* what one usually calls nonfigurative painting. This nuance is *almost* identical (coexten-sive) to the current opposition, recalled earlier, between geometric and ex-pressionistic abstraction: it is just about the same opposition but interpreted (in intension) no longer in terms of form but of function. It would probably be better to say that what I am after here is a functional opposition that finds an approximate but eloquent illustration in the formal opposition of the two fundamental styles of nonfigurative painting: what I would like to call—by an oxymoron that has already been used (perhaps for something else)—a *figurative abstraction* is easier to find in Mondrian, Van Doesburg, Delaunay, indeed in Malevich, perhaps in Barnett Newman, certainly in Ellsworth Kelly, without a doubt in Vasarely, than in Pollock, Kline, or Guston.

What I understand by the term *figurative abstraction* is a pictorial fact that is larger than what is currently meant by the term *geometric abstraction* (which is not ordinarily used for Delaunay or Newman, nor even for Malevich, who is protected by the official name of suprematism);[2] large enough to include, for example, a great part of Kandinsky's post-1910 work, which is on princi-ple nonfigurative: a picture—I name it almost by chance—such as *Dominant Curve*,[3] one of the most exquisite of the "Parisian" period (which is not gen-erally the most appreciated by specialists). The title, like those of Malevich already referred to, underlines a form present on the canvas, but its desig-nation is far less clearly prescribed: one could substitute another or none (*Without Title, Composition*, etc.), and the description of this canvas can easily ignore or bypass it. It presents a group of forms, curved (for the most part) or straight, of which some are based on simple geometry (isolated or conjoined circles) and of which each has its own (its very own) separate color, almost as in a collage of cut-out papers. But not entirely: certain effects of covering and transparency are no less carefully effected, and certain monochromatic surfaces are animated by traced, quasi-linear figures—the whole in a tonality that evokes more insistently a watercolor than an oil painting; one knows, by the way, that Kandinsky actively cultivated the first of these techniques, which, it seems to me, marks his practice of the second.

None of these forms evokes a real object, with the exception of a sketch of stairs in the lower right-hand corner, the perspective of which is clearly, though lightly, falsified, and which makes one see that it is here only as a figure like the others. So there is nothing that suggests the representation of a world external to this canvas, as is still the case in certain pictures (*Lyric, Impressions III "Concert"*) posterior to the 1910 *First Abstract Work* (watercolor, Musée National d'Art Moderne [MNAM]). Nonetheless, everything suggests the impression (which I do not want to verify by genetic data for the moment) that the artist has (as one can say) carefully *painted* this complex set of forms— clearly much more complex than those of Malevich and à propos of which one could hardly speak of any kind of minimalism: that he painted it in the most classical sense of the term, again as Leonardo and Vermeer painted their objects—safe for the external reference. This clause may appear flippant, presenting as secondary what is evidently a capital difference in view of the entire history of painting and the rupture that the birth of "abstract" painting produced in it.

What I nonetheless want to say is that the picture of Kandinsky gives the impression that the painter has *decided* to place in it a blue circle here, an orange one there, a sort of rectangle at the upper left, inhabited by a thread-shaped, disjointed figure, three circular, rigorously aligned black figures up at the right, etc., and that the act of painting, in the sense of "putting the paint on the canvas," has been no more than the execution of a preconceived design (in both senses of the word), as is the case for a figurative painter whose pictorial gestures are ruled by the attempt to depict his model faithfully—all differences in style to the side, but the attempt at finish and neatness (some would speak of "polish") as visible in this canvas as in all others of this period, suggesting a closer relationship with classical painting than with that of turn-of-century impressionism or postimpressionism. I would gladly say that Kandinsky here paints figures the way painters of old painted objects, subordinating his performance to the "rendered quality" of these figures as much as (sometimes more than) classical painters subordinated their performance to that of their models. The "world without object" (*Gegenstandslose Welt*)[4] of the first abstract painting is not a world without figures nor even a world without models: the canvases of Kandinsky, exactly like those of Malevich or Mondrian, adhere (conform) to models, abstract ones if you like, but nonetheless models to be imitated, no matter what their complexity and subtlety compared to those of the two others. One could qualify them as "nonobjective," to remain faithful to the formula of Malevich,[5] but I am not sure that a conceived or invented form is something different from an ideal object (an object of thought); as for universal geometric forms (a square, a triangle, a circle, a spiral, etc.) that, as one can see here, Kandinsky borrowed from the repertoire, I don't think that their "ideality," to speak like Husserl, keeps them from being objects. In this version abstract painting is indeed, if one so desires, abstract in this sense, but it is not nonobjective and still less nonfigurative: it paints (in both meanings of the verb, one of which denotes an act of representation) figures, which are abstract or ideal objects.

Before considering the other version of abstraction, I would like to mention another type of painting, equally . . . let us say clumsily "nonrealist": the one that consists of "representing" imaginary objects, that is to say, producing what Goodman calls images with zero denotation (just like the words that apply to the same objects). The emblematic case, in a very ancient tradition, is the unicorn, and other monsters or fabulous beings that are represented even though they do not exist, and which one can represent without any ontological difficulty because they "consist" of a composition of traits borrowed from several distinct beings (chimera) or displaced traits (the unicorn has nothing fabulous about it except the unique horn in the middle of its forehead). Mythological personages, including those of the Christian religion, have almost the same status, which is indicated quite well by the representation of a fictive being (Hercules, the Virgin Mary) bearing the traits of a real model that "poses" for him or her or imitating a generic image (athlete or young woman). As everyone knows, the range of these fictional beings is very extended, from the most fantastic (let us say the monsters of Hieronymus Bosch) to those that are fictional only on account of their official reference, that is to say, their titular paratext, the real model having been painted in the most faithful and realistic manner, as one can suppose for Hendrijke Stoffels posing for Rembrandt's *Bathsheba*, which without its title cannot be distinguished from a bather by Renoir or a woman at her toilette by Degas. The majority of pertinent cases is no doubt somewhere between these two extremes, but, if one considers the state most distant from common reality, one can say that the picture in question presents a nonexistent being, and that this non-existence in no way reduces its figurative, even its "objective" character, if one admits—and it is difficult not to—that an imaginary object is an object. One does not distance oneself much from the reference to Hieronymus Bosch when one evokes surrealist painting here, which itself presents one of the largest and most varied ranges, but its most typical representatives, such as Ernst and Tanguy, can be described as presenting, in their pictures, imaginary beings (sufficiently imaginary that it remains uncertain to what kingdom they belong) or, perhaps better, fantastic landscapes or worlds—which one usually calls "dreamlike," as though dream landscapes were necessarily, or typically, different from those that reality offers us.

I don't think that anyone would contest calling such works figurative (nor, with all the more reason, those of Dali or Magritte, whose relationship to reality is more obvious), even though the world they "figure" does not exist outside themselves. But we also assign, for reasons that are more or less official to the group, a painter like Miró to the surrealists—and thus, in his way, to the figurative artists, a painter whose figures are often as distant as those of Kandinsky from any kind of representation of a fantastic universe. The borderline, if there is one, and which in this case goes right across the category of "surrealist painting," no doubt results from the fact that pictures such as those of Ernst or Tanguy still give the impression of representing a set of objects; these objects, to be sure, have no counterparts in reality, but they are arranged in a three-dimensional space and often even, in Tanguy, at a great distance from the supposed observer; and in Miró, as in Kandinsky, they very often present forms that are inseparable from the plane of the picture itself. To say it somewhat naïvely, we could imagine Tanguy beginning by producing, by way of a sculpture, a set of fictional objects that he placed at a certain distance from his point of observation and then faithfully painting this bric-a-brac on his canvas; and, obversely, one could, starting from one of his canvases, compose in three dimensions a kind of scene faithful to the one presented on it. This hypothesis is perhaps not as naïve as all that, since it came to the mind of Clement Greenberg (with, to be sure, inevitable pejorative connotations): "It is possible, I believe, to construct faithful duplicates in wax, papier maché, or rubber of most of the recent paintings of Ernst, Dali, and Tanguy. Their 'content' is conceivable, and too much so, in other terms than those of paint-ing." [6] Of course, nothing like this could be said of the abstract figurations by Kandinsky or Miró—nor certainly of those by Mondrian or Malevich: they are inseparable from (the plane of) the canvas on which they figure. This test allows one to separate this form of abstraction from the representation of fictional or "impossible" objects, which distinguishes surrealist painting. A passing remark: this distinction is harder to apply to sculpture itself, in which nothing can differentiate abstraction from imaginary figuration, with both of them working in a three-dimensional space.

A different imaginary test, by contrast, would place both of them on the same side of another borderline—assuming that one can draw solid border-lines at all on a continuous scale that extends, let us say, from Poussin to

Pollock. This test consists of the possibility, or rather of the validity, of an operation similar to the one that I have just evoked but confined to the two-dimensional space that our figurative abstraction does not generally exceed. Taking a picture like Dominant Curve as a canvas, and perhaps referring to numeration by scanner, it would be a matter of producing a series not of three-dimensional objects but of surfaces and dispositions conforming to the ones the picture presents—for example, in the form of cut-out papers. This is equivalent to saying that such a canvas also represents a series of objects that can be reconstituted from it, the only difference with those represented by a surrealist being that they are objects of two dimensions; since such objects don't exist in our own world, this clearly means that their third dimension has been neglected or bracketed. As in the case of Tanguy or Max Ernst mentioned earlier, we can imagine a contrary operation: Kandinsky in fact constructs such an assembly of objects, takes it as his model, and represents it faithfully on his canvas. A similar operation, less idle certainly, has apparently steered the genesis of this canvas: a mental conception, evident in a preparatory study conserved in the Kandinsky Foundation of the Musée National d'Art Moderne (no. 609, lead engraving 13 x 21), which a catalog describes precisely as a "putting into place of the background elements" of this picture.[7] The same foundation owns other preparatory studies of the same type, in particular Milieu accompagné (1937), one of which (no. 626) is described as a "more elab-orate study put into squares, summary indication of colors in Russian."[8] It is hard to imagine a more eloquent, more probing, trace of a genesis carefully concerted by way of a preconception and faithful execution, the putting "into squares" in sum constituting a still rudimentary but rigorous form of our passage to the scanner—which itself . . .

I have said that a test of this sort (not entirely imaginary, as it turns out) would place this type of picture on the same side of a borderline as the accomplish-ments of surrealist painting. What is on the other side and for what reasons? Clearly, all abstract paintings that escape, more, if not absolutely, from the idea of figuration, in the meaning I attribute to it. Once again, it goes without saying that every picture (every watercolor, every drawing, etc.) must present to the eye a figure, simple or complex. As I said à propos of Dominant Curve, what I here call "figuration" is the fact of presenting a figure in such a way that it suggests its own representation—or, perhaps better, that it suggests being its own representation. Or, to say it still more simply, that one gets the impression not that such a form figures but that it is figured in this picture, here. Such a formulation could hardly, I think, come to mind in relation to a dripping by Pollock nor a brushstroke of de Kooning in one of his abstract canvases (nor even in one of his figurative canvases, such as the ones of the series *Women*, but I will return later to this paradox that isn't one). It is no doubt this type of abstraction Meyer Schapiro had in mind when he spoke in 1957 of the "power of the artist's hand to deliver constantly elements of so-called chance or accident," adding that "modern painting is the first complex style in history which proceeds from elements that are not pre-ordered as closed articulated shapes" and that "no art today exhibits to that degree in the final result the presence of the individual, his spontaneity and the concreteness of his procedure"; indicating, according to me, the same effect under a different angle, the historian further says, in 1959: "Abstract art today has little to do with logical abstraction or mathematics. It is fully concrete, without simulating a world of objects or concepts beyond the frame. *For the most part, what we see on the canvas belongs there and nowhere else.*" [9] These two examples (among others) from Pollock and de Kooning have historically in common that they belong to the category of what one calls "action painting," the manufacturing mark of American abstract expressionism, but also of its European version "lyric abstraction," even if the dripping belongs more specifically to Pollock— but, after all, streak effects are not absent from different forms of European painting, including again painters as figurative as Picasso himself and many others. What matters here is actually not of a historical but of a technical order (if one does not refuse to apply a term of this sort to this rudimentary, even brutal, practice—spontaneous or not) and in sum of a genetic order.

What keeps us from calling a dripping or a brushstroke a figuration (a figured figure) is that it always refers—seems to the viewer to refer—more to its cause (a *gesture*, even an accident) than to its end (the production of a figure); to the point of often excluding the idea of any sort of finality, particularly one that is figurative. Also abstract painting of this type, or rather close to this *pole* (for there certainly are intermediate cases), the one we usually qualify as expressionist or lyrical or informal was rather quickly (since the end of the 1940s) considered as abstract painting par excellence, to the point where the essential paintings of the two preceding decades were rejected to external darkness or prehistory. The exception was the work of Mondrian and Malevich, protected by the radical character of its approach, but not precisely, the final Kandinsky of the Parisian period, who concerned us a moment ago. [10] The latter was often judged too refined and too concerted for the reasons I indicated—and which are not in the least disparaging for me but which could seem that way in the climate of intolerance, of militant partiality, that accompanies each change of paradigm: one could not simultaneously militate for "informal" or action painting and appreciate the subtly *decorative* images of this series. We have certainly changed our attitudes today, when Kandinsky and Pollock, together with Matisse and Picasso, are regarded as the classics of "modern" art and when it is permissible to consider them together with the equanimity that makes us also appreciate together Ingres and Delacroix, Caravaggio and Poussin, Vermeer and Rubens, David and . . . Goya, in the ecumenism of an imaginary museum (belonging to "posterity") that does not identify difference with incompatibility. [11] But to accept a difference is not the same as to efface it: to pass from *Dominant Curve* to Pollock's *Autumn Rhythm* [12]—by going down a few blocks of Fifth Avenue—is truly to change from one universe to another.

The said abstraction immediately imposed itself as "expressionist" for evident reasons, which have to do with its ardor, its rage, but it would be entirely absurd to judge it more *expressive* than the other. In a Goodmanian sense the Parisian Kandinskys "express" as much elegant serenity (a term I use almost by chance) as the drippings of East Hampton express passion—all suppositions about the sentiments felt by the two artists at the moment of production left aside; to express is to exemplify metaphorically, and it is up to the receiver to choose the metaphorical predicates. What is less absurd is to say (still in a Goodmanian sense) that Kandinsky's picture *denotes* its figures and that Pollock's denotes nothing at all but limits itself to exhibiting its own formal and material characters (I'll come back to this), creating a perfect illustration of the type of art that Souriau qualified as "presentative."

I said that between these two extreme poles represented by the abstract canvases of the Parisian Kandinsky and those of Pollock stretched an entire range of intermediate states. No matter what was their real genesis, the Kandinskys dating to his first abstract manner of the 1910s and 1920s—such as the *Black Arch* at the MNAM or the *Improvisation XXVIII* at the Guggenheim (both from 1912)—create an impression of a liberty in their productive gesture that brings them visually close to action painting, an impression that the frequent presence of preparatory studies contradicts only in the eyes, or rather in the *knowledge*, of specialists; for the simple amateur there is no great distance from these canvases to those of Gorky or to those of Pollock before the drippings, and one knows the admiration the latter had for them. [13] The essential corpus of abstract art, European and American, between 1910 and 1960 belongs to this region, marked by the triangle Mondrian–Kandinsky (all manners)–Pollock, on which one can distribute as one pleases, and quite variably according to their diverse "periods," Klee, de Kooning, Rothko, Newman, Still, Kline, Motherwell, de Staël, Poliakoff, Soulages, Hartung, Dubuffet, Tàpies, Twombly, and many others, in whom the accent is sometimes more on representation (in the sense of denotation of the figure as figured), sometimes more on presentation, in the sense of pure exemplification and of indicial genetic trace.

It is important to understand that these two tendencies are not opposed in the way the practices are that oppose representing or not representing an object of the external world. I already mentioned the similarity of craftsmanship that exists between the abstract canvases of de Kooning and his *Women*: this similarity clearly stems from the equal significance of the vigorous brushstroke, which in both instances places the principal accent on *painterliness*, the pictorial paste taken for itself, in its thickness and in the movement it traces (but a watercolor's effects of transparency and of lightness may also capture the attention at the cost of its "subject"). We know that an accent of this kind is also present in traditional figurative painting, in which one notices it in Rubens, Hals, Fragonard, Goya, Delacroix, and many others. Its presence in impressionism and postimpressionism helps to explain the persistent appeal of this movement over a century after its birth; this includes (no matter what its detractors say) its appeal for demanding amateurs, who are quite insensitive to its boating thematics and its chromatic procedures. As Arthur Danto says: "The brushstroke became salient in impressionist painting, but that was not the intention of the movement. It counted on optical rather than physical means, and juxtaposed dabs of color to achieve chromatic intensity, but the dabs did not fuse. They were stridently visible, the way they might be in an oil sketch, when they were exhibited as finished paintings, a concept which implied the disguise of the brushstroke."[14] Simply the tension, in figurative painting, between the pictorial matter (which may be made with knife or trowel) laid out on the canvas and the object (landscape or personage) that it figures disappears or weakens in abstract painting because—or, rather, *to the degree that*—the intention of figuration disappears or weakens. The impasto and other streaks of action painting no longer compete with the figurative reference and ask to be appreciated for themselves, as a "material" pleasure, in the Bachelardian sense, which owes nothing to the art of representation. Rauschenberg and Lichtenstein seem to me to have aimed correctly in dealing, each in his own way, with this typical trait of modern painting; the first by producing in 1957, from his own gestural combine-painting

Factum, a meticulously identical "replica" that gives up—and thereby seems subtly to reject from it—any kind of physical spontaneity; [15] the second by applying several times over (1965–67) his well-known technique of pseudo-typographic enlargement to the famous expressionist brushstroke. These are two ways of "reproducing," or representing, and thus of refuting, the means by which painting had, perhaps most effectively, broken with its own function of reproduction or representation of the real. In figuring nonfiguration in this sarcastic fashion, the two iconoclastic gestures put an end—at least symbolically [16]—to a long history that had led painting, over the centuries, to its own limit. But we also see clearly that this *execution*, in all senses of the word, could open the way only to an era of ironic regression, in which irony does not efface regression.

Thus, the ambiguity that belongs to abstraction—my subject here—must not be confused with that other ambiguity, more often noted, that stems from the existence, throughout its history and across its range, if I may say, of canvases about which one does not know if they do or do not want to be figurative, in the usual sense of that term. This edge of uncertainty is present in Kandinsky, at least in canvases from the 1910s such as *The Cow* and *Naval Battle*, whose figurative impact owes a lot to their titles, without which few viewers would think of a subject; we can imagine without absurdity (and even if the generic data indicated the contrary) that these subjects were invented afterward, due to an involuntary visual effect. Moreover, it seems to me that the effect of figuration (in the sense I advocate) is weaker in *Naval Battle*—despite the forms of sails that we cannot miss once we know the title—than in the officially abstract canvases of the Parisian years; this weakening may be due to the accent placed on the pictorial matter and to the (perhaps misleading) "gestural" and formless speed, seemingly closer to the improvised "stain" than to the careful execution of a preconceived structure.

With generally more sober means, this is an effect quite close to the one we find in Nicholas de Staël, whose work—with perhaps the one of Villon, whose origin (analytic cubism), perceptible to the end, is noticeably different—seems to me the most characteristic for this capacity of a certain type of modern painting to erase, or at least to relativize, the borderline between figuration and nonfiguration. But in his case the tendency to relativization seems to me rather the inverse of the one that I indicated just now for Kandinsky (but these are merely hypothetical nuances, or, rather, pure impressions): where Kandinsky seems sometimes to discover later, and to underline with his title, a figurative capacity not at first perceived, de Staël—after a first period of purely abstract appearance (and proclamation) in what remains no doubt his most typical work—seems most often to work on his figuration, by simplification or reduction of the represented forms, by deepening of the pictorial layer, until he gives it the look of a nonfigurative "composition." By which this acclimatized Russian continues a typically French tradition that stems from Chardin, by way of Cézanne and Braque—but this time, rather, the synthetic, post-cubist Braque. Antoine Tudal attests that even de Staël's abstract canvases of the 1940s most often had a figurative origin, which he gradually submerged: "He first draws [objects] with great precision, then a succession of phases leads to an austerity that permits him to remain facing the painting and the form."[17] The difference with what follows would thus be based on the fact that, after 1951–52, the work of what I would like to call "de-figuration" is pushed less far, and the objective source, more or less recognizable, is designated, as in Kandinsky, by a title that is often helpful: see certain Football Players[18] or Figures at the Shore of the Ocean,[19] and many others. In both phases the movement goes more or less from figuration to abstraction, which is expressed quite well (voluntarily or not) by the famous pun with which de Staël thanked Bernard Dorival for having "removed [him] from the 'gang of before-hand abstraction' ";[20] in the actual genesis abstraction in de Staël is not really "before-hand" but *after* the contact with external reality and is gradually reduced to the necessary minimum: just enough de-figuration to operate on the real what, as we know, always was, in all manners, the intention of painters: its transfiguration—its transmutation into painting, what, I think, Cézanne called "to take an object and to make it absolutely painting."

From here, no doubt, stems the paradoxical feeling one cannot dismiss that even the semi-abstract canvases of de Staël are closer to a true abstraction than the Parisian canvases of Kandinsky. The fictive ("virtual") objects that figure on the latter inevitably attract and hold the attention, either by the significance of their geometric form or by their manifestly fictional, and even dreamlike, appearance: whence the evident closeness, surpassing the scholarly quarrels, between these canvases and those of surrealist painting. By contrast, the objects (still lifes, landscapes, even persons) that de Staël "makes into painting" are sufficiently current and familiar to lend themselves without resistance to their own pictorial transfiguration—that is to say, for their identification on the canvas as objects of the world not to figure as obstacles of this transfiguration in the eyes of the viewer (no more than those of the "subjects" of a Chardin or a Cézanne). There is in them, it seems to me, a sufficiently close contrast to the one that opposes, in the classical and "premodern" period, the descriptive and narrative painting of the grand genres, always spectacular on account of their subjects themselves, to those, once again, of a Chardin or of a Cézanne: one of the secrets of their attraction being precisely the banality, the domestic "mediocrity," of their objects, which Proust noted so well in connection with Chardin. No matter how great the evolution of style that separates them, the pitcher by Chardin, the one by Cézanne or by Braque, and the one by de Staël have in common that they lend themselves better, or at least more easily, to pictorial transfiguration than more "magnificent" objects—a capacity, in an entirely simple sense, for the painted material to become that other material, which painting itself is after (above) all. Referring to the work of Greenberg, Arthur Danto proposes a new formula, which finally seems to me the most correct for the opposition within so-called abstract painting that concerns me here: the opposition, he says, between *formal* abstraction, which is that of neoplasticism (but also, in my opinion, of the Parisian Kandinsky) and *material* abstraction—that of Pollock, of course, but also (among many others and still according to me) of Nicholas de Staël, "where the physical properties of the painting . . . become the inevitable essence of painting as art." [21] But no doubt we have to enlarge the consideration of the "physical properties" to those para-pictorial or quasi-pictorial materials provided by the technique of collage, from cubist paper collages to the Merz columns by Schwitters and the combines by Rauschenberg. The pictorial "material" does nor necessarily emerge from a tube or a pot: sand (see Masson or Tàpies), metro tickets, bits of tissue, and other "garbage" partake in it as well, as does, paradoxically, the medium itself when it remains visible, as in the *canvases* by Gauguin, justly celebrated by Renaud Camus:

> Nothing is as beautiful as the *canvases* of Gauguin, in the narrow sense of the word: a very rough fabric with thick meshing, the depth of which the paintbrush cannot reach. Applied to this unequal surface, color impregnates only the top. What results is the presence, in the most beautiful greens, the most brilliant yellows (those of the lemon here, in the front), in the deepest blues (those of the admirable bottle, the center of the picture, in my eyes), if I dare say so, of a void: however this void, paradoxically, is material; it is the texture of the gross tissue, the minuscule and innumerable caves, reserves of darkness from which the entire subtlety of light is drawn. Even at the heart of the most vivid shimmering, as amidst the leaves and the tawny flowers in the front of *Paysage* in the Picasso Museum, it is

always in the textile layer that the genius of the color scheme finds its true poetry. As always in the modern art that was to follow, it is matter which is the dream, the vertigo, the pleasure . . . one of the essential traits of 20th century art, its passionate interest in its own material, passed from its role as instrument to that of *artifact*.[22]

Given the snared quality of the words, it would no doubt be awkward to ask which of these two "abstractions" is the more "abstract"; but one perhaps sees which one—and in which meaning—is decidedly the most painterly. Even if "painting as art" has always been entirely able to transcend all (and even the most insistent) figurative function and to "make into painting" its objects, its materials, its "instruments," we might credit nonfiguration with having made us sensitive to it; paradoxically and outrageously, we might say: Pollock makes Poussin *more of a painter*.

Here the case of sculpture can bring a kind of confirming counter-proof. We know that classical sculpture limited its repertory to living beings, human or other, and to largely anthropomorphic, zoomorphic, or mixed divinities. The modern period can shed an ironic light on a reason for this choice, in addition to the other evident reasons, which related to the more or less strongly celebrative function of this art. Ever since the grapes of Zeuxis and the curtain of Parrhasius, a pictorial still life can attain a rigorously faithful representation that can go as far as trompe l'oeil without endangering the figurative difference—a difference between figuring and figured; this is evidently due to the bi-dimensional character of a picture. Inversely, the representation in three dimensions of an inanimate object risks at the limit to become absolutely confused with that object itself—and we know how pop art and related tendencies exploited this confusion "conceptually," from Jasper Johns's jar with paintbrushes[23] to Andy Warhol's Brillo box,[24] in fact anticipated by the ready-mades of Duchamp, who contented himself more than once with exhibiting . . . the "model" itself, taken to be its own unsurpassable representation. The expressive "deformations" that could, in the modern period, affect these figurations of objects apparently do not attract either the public or the creators. One might, at the most, take notice of a few examples of "cubist" sculptures of inanimate objects, such as Picasso's *Mandolin and Clarinet*,[25] which is more exactly a "construction" (assemblage) out of wood and whose undeniably cubist character stems from an adroit transposition into three-dimensional space of thematic and formal characteristics that belong to this pictorial style. Thus, cubist sculpture, too, most often represented human beings—or animals, with Duchamp-Villon's *Horse* as the most successful example. [26] But an expressive exclusiveness of this kind is by no means limited to this style: modern sculpture, at least since Rodin, has practiced its formal inventiveness quite generally on figurations of living beings: see, among others, Brancusi, Ernst, Richier, Moore, and Giacometti. One can thus say that sculpture in its entirety, in all cultures and periods, has had as almost its only purpose this type of figuration; it abandoned it, in the twentieth century, and quite partially, only by leaving behind figuration itself in the quite vast field of officially abstract sculpture—with another, no less vast, being occupied by intermediate productions whose figurative intention can be assumed and ensured only by their titles, such as Lipschitz's *Reclining Nude with Guitar*. [27]

To simplify without a doubt somewhat excessively, we can thus say that sculpture has until today known only two regimes in this regard: that of figuration of beings or parts of beings for which there is no doubt or illusion; [28] and that of nonfiguration. The latter, once again because of its tri-dimensional space, is characterized by a "literality," an absolute auto-referentiality of the created object, that refers rigorously to nothing but itself—think of Calder's mobiles and stabiles or, in a quite different style, of Barbara Hepworth's *Carved Form (Bryher II)*; [29] except when there is an indication, or a perceptive evidence, of the productive process, as in the compressions of César, which, without, however, figuring anything, evoke by (if I dare say) genetic metonymy the object from which they proceed, or, rather, the objects they were before this brutal transformation. [30] In this field the distinction, made earlier in the context of painting, between a pure abstraction (Pollock) and an abstraction by figuration of fictional forms (Kandinsky), cannot be made, no more than the one that Danto made between "formal" and "material" abstraction: in sculpture form and material are indiscernible, and it is impossible to imagine a "projection" into a third dimension that would be present from the outset. This is perhaps what Greenberg had in mind when he said that if "abstract sculpture meets less resistance than abstract painting, it is because it has not had to change its language so radically. Abstract or representational, its language remains three-dimensional—literal," or, further, that sculpture "stands to gain by the modernist 'reduction' as painting does not." [31] One could say just as well that sculpture *loses less* in modernizing itself, since it can renounce figuration without having to suppress a dimension: the one whose presence painting has to "reduce"—or even amputate—in order to become "literal" and thereby "absolutely modern." But it would no doubt be more valid to say that sculpture is less menaced by the unwanted return of this dimension (of depth), the "reduction" of which is, in its case, out of the question and outside the subject: it would become "illusionist" if it simulated planeness, [32] and it can stay literal, can protect itself after a fashion from all figurative function, by keeping its three dimensions.

After a fashion, certainly, since nothing escapes for good from projective interpretation: interpretation that makes someone "recognize" a personage or an animal in a simple rock "sculpted" by erosion. And up to the simple and "hard-edged" volumes by minimalists such as Carl Andre, Donald Judd, Daniel Buren, at times Barnett Newman, [33] we find at least the clear trace of a preconception that, as in the canvases of Mondrian or Albers, their more geometric character imposes. Which makes them more immediately identifiable as known forms: parallelepiped, column, inversed pyramid—these are preconceptions that one can hardly avoid referring to a figurative intention, as though one could not produce a cube without wanting to represent a cube. The instance of Robert Morris's L-forms is, in this regard, exemplary: despite their absence of titles (Untitled) and their diverse positions, no one can resist reading them as figurations in plywood painted with the twelfth letter of our alphabet heavily shaking themselves on the floor of a museum. Here again the significance of a recognizable form imposes on the abstract work, despite itself, at the very least an attentional function of representation. To say it naïvely, it is as though the form was more, or more directly, than the matter exposed to the tyrannical pressure of meaning.

5

The Stonemason's Yard

In the foreground a sort of empty lot devoted to a most prosaic of activities, that apparently of a stonecutter, whose disordered materials, crude and shaped, litter the ground. The terrain stretches between a two-story house, the angle of which occupies the entire left margin of the picture, the bank of a canal in the background, and a construction shack, with boards supported by two parallel Xs, the positions of which strongly stress the obliquity of the point of view with respect to the orientation of the terrain and to the perpendicular one on the canal. Dominating the wooden shack, a more pleasant facade, with its vaulted bays and its second-floor balcony, closes the view on the right side. At the windows of the third floor hang white linens, perhaps blinds, perhaps sheets put out to dry. On the other bank of the canal, at the vanishing point of the perspective, a church in profile, a campanile at once rustic and slender, the entire structure made of brown brick, with a rigid appearance and on the whole rather Nordic, even if one perceives the silhouette of a marble ornament that must crown the invisible facade. The base of the campanile is hidden by twin houses, neighboring but slightly shifted at their top and no doubt at their bottom, of which the light color, stressed by strong illumination, draws the attention, which is also held by the gay disposition of the windows and mainly of the facing chimneys. This double house faces the canal directly, without a quay or door at the level of the water, the entrance being doubtless on the side, the lateral square of the church, or perhaps on the left, where a sort of small garden begins. To the right of the church a series of low constructions extend, surmounted by a white belfry of a more modern and more urban style. The light blue sky, barely clouded, covers almost the entire upper half of the view. The occupations of the characters present on the shore of the canal, leaning out of the windows or dispersed on the empty lot are quite vague, some doubtless professional, others more playful, even idle or trivial: a child fallen to the ground, wriggling and presumably pissing, provokes an expressive gesture on the part of (the person I suppose to be) his mother, with (what is probably) his older sister looking on. Another woman, on her balcony, works at what must be a plant or a spindle. A third apparently cleans the interior of an enormous water font or the basin of a fountain. Nothing more routine, nothing more picturesque.

I hope the reader has recognized *The Stonemason's Yard*,[1] whose title, no doubt apocryphal, was first proposed in English. One often glosses it by this other, more conforming to titular norms of the genre, *The Campo San Vitale*—or *San Vidal*—and *the Church of Santa Maria della Carità* or *Santa Maria della Carità, du Campo San Vitale, or San Vidal*; the "court" in question, with that shed of which the weighty oblique perspective bears the principal accent of the painting, is therefore the campo San Vidal, provisionally occupied by the reconstruction site of the church of San Vidal, invisible here; the large church in profile on the other bank is the one of la Carità, today belonging, together with the buildings adjacent to the former Scuola, to the museum of the Accademia; the white belfry to the right is the one of San Trovaso. Specialists generally take this painting today as Canaletto's "masterpiece"; it has also been, quite exceptionally, admired by Ruskin (who disliked all the other works of this painter), and Whistler compared it, unexpectedly but quite gratifyingly, with Velasquez.[2] Highly regarded by specialists and also by "enlightened" amateurs but not by the general public, which favors, rather, this painter's more classical and more spectacular views of the Grand Canal, the Square of San Marco, the palaces of the Doges and of Bacino open to the vast lagoon. The slightly ingenuous notion of masterpiece clearly does not signify anything besides the objectification of a relative value judgment, or of preference; let us therefore reformulate more correctly: *The Stonemason's Yard* is, among the paintings of Canaletto, the one that specialists and enlightened amateurs— that is, persons who know at least a good part of this painter's work—prefer. Without belonging to either of these groups, I cannot—nor want to—hide the fact that I share their feeling, even if I want to qualify it by recognizing right away its eminently subjective character and by adding, without much pretension of originality, that the merits that this picture presents to me are also, at least in some details, present in others.[3]

   Such a preference (of which the exact distribution would have to be verified, quantitatively and qualitatively, by sociological means) seems to me to relate typically to what Bourdieu has described without complacency as "distinction," or again what one calls "elitism," even snobbism: its motives are of a "second" order in relation to those that in general attract "popular" (petit bourgeois) favor to a work in that they generally suppose the latter to be recognized and "surpassed." One could doubtless imagine an uninformed viewer who would admire this painting without any preceding knowledge of (the rest of) the work of Canaletto, even without knowing the name of the author, and who would right away qualify it as a masterpiece, but this improbable case would not depart much from the more current situation: that of the amateur more or less acquainted with the whole of the work of this painter who appreciates its qualities like everyone else but who finds them in some way surpassed, or rather transcended (in a quite clear sense, which I will explain), in *The Stonemason's Yard*. Indeed, spontaneously to admire *The Stonemason's Yard*, so to speak without a context, presupposes an education, or an enlightened taste (at least in painting), roughly of the same order as those that lead one to place this painting, knowing the specific corpus, above the rest of the work of its author. In both cases it is a matter of passing from a "first degree," that of the most obvious and immediate motives for admiration—for example, the primary seduction of the painted object: "beautiful" landscape, charming model—to a second degree, the one that attaches itself to an object that nothing would designate for aesthetic admiration a priori and independently of the fate that the painter makes for it by his pictorial treatment. It even seems to me that the specific "secondarity" (let us say to prefer *The Stonemason's Court* to *Return of the Bucentaurus*) is dependent on—not to say complicit with—the general secondarity that consists in preferring in every instance, to the immediately seductive objects, what Arthur Danto has in a different perspective called the "transfiguration of the banal," that is to say, here the manner in which the art of the painter exercises and manifests itself on an object that the profane viewer would perhaps have judged less worthy of his attention and of his commitment.

In this respect the purpose of *The Stonemason's Yard*—at least the one its admirers, to which I belong, attribute to it—is quite obvious: it consists of privileging an aspect of Venice as distanced as possible from the splendor usually associated with the image of the city of the Doges. Nothing, if not a topographic information external to the picture, designates as "Grand Canal" the mediocre stretch of water that separates the two banks, and everything here works toward discharging of the architectural glory that one knows— and which bursts forth in many of the same artist's other canvases. The disordered scattering of blocks of stone evokes in advance, among other things, the piling up exhibited by Corot, also in the foreground in his view of *La Cathédrale de Chartres,* [4] or again the paving stones waiting to be placed at the bottom of Manet's *La Rue Mosnier aux paveurs.* [5] In these three canvases the urban landscape opens on crude materials, the presence of which right away pushes out of the way a more glorious object: the famous cathedral, the Hausmannian bourgeois apartment buildings, and here la Carità seen in profile, its rather surly monumentality subtly eclipsed by the modest building I described. [6] I hope that the connection with these two nineteenth-century canvases sufficiently suggests the "modernity" of our painting, a feature that surely enters the motives of its positive appreciation: to know how to *disdain* (the word here has all its psychological connotations) the grand spectacles and the luxurious objects can generally—if not correctly—be taken, at least in the aesthetic order (which, of course, does not apply only to art), as a sort of late discovery, or conquest of modernity, as well as a constant trait of "good taste" in every period. In the case of Canaletto the historical theme of modernity contributes effectively to displacing this merit of the artist toward the receiver: this painter has produced, and most often answering orders (thus enduring more or less the taste, good or bad, of his diverse clients), in the two registers considered, and nothing to my knowledge testifies absolutely to his own preference in this matter. Nothing, if not, perhaps, for the painting with which we are concerned, its late public appearance (1808) and a complete absence of response, two quite notable facts that permit one to suppose, though without certitude, that he had willfully kept it for his own pleasure or that he had had more trouble than with other pictures to find a buyer in the absence of a prior order. One or the other of these two hypotheses can only flatter our attentional predilection: we gladly refuse to his contemporary clients, with a (gratuitously) supposed naïve taste, and spontaneously attribute to the artist an (intentional) system of values for which nothing proves that he shared it; the "we" thus designates a mixture of nontemporal elitism and of modernity, which it seems natural to project, or rather to retroject, on a creator that we admire for this aspect of his talent, an aspect about which we wish quite as naturally that he preferred it himself. From this spontaneous wish to the gratifying hypothesis, there is only the voluntary step of wishful thinking, and, when a contrary testimony forces us to renounce it (which might happen one day for the work with which we are concerned), there remains for us the conviction, often invoked and hardly less comfortable, that the artist was not conscious of his own modernity and of his profound genius—too profound to be conscious—and that the merit of that consciousness is entirely our own. But from this merit to the one of genius there is again only one step: in all admiration there is no doubt a part—an unconscious part, to be sure—of self-admiration.

One no doubt has understood where I wanted to get by this brief exercise in self-criticism, or, rather, in self-relativization: the relativist purpose that I defended elsewhere does not consist in denying that certain aesthetic relations, which judge themselves more enlightened than others (in a sense *every* judgment judges itself more enlightened than others, except to challenge itself), are indeed more enlightened and still less that certain aesthetic relations are to others in the relation of secondarity that I have just described; it consists (more) simply in contesting that this situation gives to one taste a real superiority over another. What is real here is the (subjective) fact that the enlightened amateur judges, rightly at times, *to know* and *to surpass* the aesthetic criteria of the naïve, if not vulgar, amateur; and the difference between the naïve point of view and the enlightened one (from here on I give to this adjective no other meaning than that of "non- naïve" and, more precisely, of "that-thinks-it-has-surpassed-the-naïve-stage") is incontestably a difference in degree, or, if one prefers, a cumulative and vectorized difference: in the movement that consists, if need be, of recognizing-and-surpassing, the enlightened one is, by definition, situated farther along, and in a sense *higher* than the naïve one, and, as long as one locates oneself in this linear perspective, he enjoys the undeniable psychological superiority (let us leave aside the sociological aspect of this relationship, certainly not lacking here) of him who knows, or understands, the other better than the other knows and understands him.

One can even without a doubt consider that in most cases that superiority will remain uncontested, for cultural reasons that I remarked on elsewhere.[7] But nothing in principle hinders one from conceiving another perspective, more dialectic (in Hegel's sense of the word), in which the naïve point of view, once informed of the reasons that sustain the enlightened point of view of the happy few, will reestablish itself at a higher level, according to this "gradation" described by Pascal in an entirely different context, where the opinion of the truly "clever ones" surpassing that of the "half-clever ones" rejoins the natural naïveté of the "people" but by a "thought from behind" and in a "wise ignorance that knows itself."[8] I must draw attention once again to the manner in which Proust, precisely à propos of Venice, illustrated this spiral gradation (one also says, "partie de main-chaude")[9] between the naïve admiration of "magnificent things," the wiser appreciation of the most humble things, and the return—that nothing guarantees as final—to the first, in the name of an even wiser capacity to surpass the consideration of the object: if the painted object has little importance, the magnificent things painted by Veronese and become, as Cézanne says, "absolute painting," deserve as much aesthetic attention as the everyday objects that are found in the still lifes of Chardin:

> the noble surfaces of marble steps continually splashed by shafts of blue-green sunlight . . . , to the valuable instruction in the art of Chardin acquired long ago, added a lesson in that of Veronese. And since, in Venice, it is works of art, things of priceless beauty, that are entrusted with the task of giving us our impressions of everyday life, it is to falsify the character of that city, on the grounds that the Venice of certain painters is coldly aesthetic in its most celebrated parts . . . , to represent only its poverty-stricken aspects, in the districts where nothing of its splendour is to be seen, and, in order to make Venice more intimate and more genuine, to give it a resemblance to Aubervilliers. It has been the mistake of some very great artists, from a quite natural reaction against the artificial Venice of bad painters, to concentrate exclusively on the Venice of the more humble *campi*, the little deserted *rii*, which they found more real. [10]

But the opinion according to which "the object matters little" is itself by no means shielded from being surpassed again, which one sees at work quite (too) well in contemporary art. In this "continuous reversal of the pro and con," which largely rules the movements of taste, each person thinks he has won over the other, and I cannot conceive a supreme and impartial judge who would remain outside the spiral and who would be able to say the "last word." The only last word seems to me to come back to the relativist acknowledgment, which is not (unless I am mistaken) a judgment of taste and which recognizes the legitimacy of each appreciation according to its own criteria. And what aesthetic relativism has a right to demand (politely) from each judgment is that it learn to expose its motives, if it has any, without ignoring or despising the contrary motives too much, and to situate the self in what Pascal, again, would call his *order*.

6

The Gaze of Olympia

The "quotation" of *Olympia* in the portrait of Zola,[1] by Manet,[2] belongs to a vast generic group generally designated by such phrases as "painting within a painting," "picture within a picture,"[3] and sometimes, incorrectly,[4] "picture *en abyme*." It occupies a very special place in this group; to situate it, we must rapidly survey the whole field, not from a historical or thematic vantage point (which has already been done at length) but from a theoretical vantage point, more precisely from one that involves a (very elementary) semiotics of pictorial representation.

By an easy but well-marked paradox a picture present in another picture can very well be invisible in it, either because its painted surface remains too blurred, as is the case with most of the canvases in *L'Enseigne de Gersaint*, or more radically because it is seen from the back or appears only in reverse; this is the case in *Las Meninas*, or in the *Self-Portrait in His Studio* by Rembrandt. The empty frame in the background of the canvas is, after all, a fairly handsome object, and we understand that a lot of painters enjoyed depicting it, professional affectation or complacency to the side.[5] But in these two cases the question of the identification of the picture, and even more of its subject, is dismissed by default; or, if one prefers, the painter represents on it a picture—allowing that the reverse of a canvas merits that name—without representing what that picture represents. A third evasion would be to represent, head on and on its easel, a still empty canvas: I lack an example for this (the canvas in Vermeer's *Art of Painting* is already partially covered); it exists, no doubt—"everything is that can be"—but an empty canvas is not (yet) a picture, at least not without a conceptual or hyper-minimalist gesture.

Visible *as a picture*, the represented work can be "real" (i.e., preexistent) or "imaginary," that is, in fact produced ad hoc on the canvas itself that is meant to represent it. I will not linger on this last case, which does not on principle relate to our *Olympia* (although I will come back to this). But a new distinction has to be introduced here: an imaginary picture-within-a-picture can implicitly refer to the author or to another clearly recognizable artist, or it can be left relatively undetermined. The medium of these implicit attributions is obviously stylistic, in the large sense of the term, which in art criticism can involve thematic traits: the second picture in Courbet's L'Atelier du peintre (The Painter's Studio) has a subject (a landscape of Franche-Comté) and a craftsmanship that are equally unmistakable.[6] When the identification is vaguer, it cannot be entirely nonexistent, since a visible picture necessarily belongs to a genre (naval in Vermeer's The Love Letter) or to a manner (style of Jacob Van Loo in Moses Saved from the Waters in his Letter). Thus, in all these cases the author follows a more or less specified pastiche; in the one illustrated by Courbet, one could say that he produces two pictures in his own "natural" manner, of which one, as it were, surrounds the other; but can a manner be quite natural, especially in this kind of situation? To "imagine" a work of one's own is always a more or less strong invitation to self-pastiche, that is to say, an accentuation of one's own traits, and Chastel is right to qualify the landscape of L'Atelier as "super-Courbet." The sensitive question is, rather, the following: can one say that a picture is "represented" when it is, in fact, produced for the circumstance?

The answer is not of an empirical order but conventional and typically semio-logical: a pictorial representation signifies, like all denotations, what it is supposed to signify, independently of what it "reproduces" iconically. Just as in chess a locket imitating the Mona Lisa can represent the king or the bishop if, in case of loss, the convention has been agreed upon, a closely resembling portrait of a naked Hendrijke Stoffels can be taken for a "Bathsheba" if the contract stipulates it. And when a second picture, because it is imaginary, is the image of no real (known) picture, and thus iconically reproduces nothing,[7] this does not hinder the first picture from representing, on this part of its surface, a picture: this is manifestly what the painter has wanted to do, and the viewer admits without wavering that he has done so. In brief, in the second degree as in the first, nothing is easier or more customary than to represent what doesn't exist, even if it "resembles" what exists.

Which leaves the case of real second pictures, a subject that, as we know in advance, will lead us to the Olympia of Zola. Based on a loan from the literary domain, this kind is quite frequently called (as I have called it) quotation. This loan is clearly not exact, for to quote, in the true sense, implies to contain: as Nelson Goodman has shown,[8] to quote is to contain what one denotes, and vice versa. The phrase "E.T. said home" denotes and contains the word home, and it can contain it because verbal objects are ideal types, whose occurrences or tokens can be literally inserted in any context whatsoever: more precisely, E.T. has uttered an occurrence of the word-type home, of which I placed another occurrence, called "quotation," into my sentence. But a picture, which can easily denote (represent) within itself another picture, cannot literally contain it, no more than any other object—except in a collage, as when, tired of reproducing titles of newspapers, brands of cocktails, or pieces of wallpaper, Braque or Picasso buy a good pair of scissors. Since it does not lead us to our object, I again leave this subject but not without noting: just as an imaginary picture generally exists within a real picture by way of a pastiche or a self-pastiche, a real (preexisting) picture can exist in it (except as a collage) only by way of a *copy* or a *self-copy*.

The copied quotation of a preexisting picture, [9] by the same artist or another, is, as we generously say, a practice as old as painting itself. I'll mention at random Rigaud's *Louis XIV* in the *Enseigne de Gersaint*, the still life (Venturi 341) in Maurice Denis's *Hommage à Cézanne* and *La Grande Jatte* in Seurat's *Les Poseuses* (*Three Models*). But the inevitable resort to the procedure of copying no less unavoidably poses innumerable questions, of which I will raise the three most pertinent to our object.

The first one is again of a semio-logic order: if the representation uses a copy, what is the difference between simply copying a picture and representing it? Physically, there is none, and nothing allows even the most careful simple visual inspection to decide between the two diagnoses in front of a "faithful" copy of the *Mona Lisa* or of the *Olympia* (if not that the second is more far-fetched); for, once again, the difference is conventional, which is to say that it depends on the meaning, or more precisely on the definition, proposed by the copyist and accepted by the viewer. It suffices that the copyist use, for example, as a title "Copy of the *Mona Lisa*, or the *Olympia*," or more simply that he indicate nothing at all, for the copy to be *received* as a simple copy (to hasten my argument, I exclude the frauds or critical blunders one may think of). If he wants his copy to have the *value of* a representation, he must indicate in one way or another that he meant not only to copy it but, in copying it, to represent it, as one represents the Mont Blanc or a bouquet of peonies. This never happens? That's too bad, nor is it certain, or, rather, it comes close to what happens. If Duchamp had taken the trouble to produce a scrupulous copy of the *Mona Lisa* and had entitled it *The Shaved LHOOQ*, instead of contenting himself for the second time with a simple photographic reproduction, this discorrected ready-made, once it had produced its small effect, could have been rebaptized—in a gesture at once conceptual and minimalist, comparable (but not identical) to that of Pierre Menard writing the *Quixote*—"the *Mona*

Lisa of Leonardo da Vinci, by Marcel Duchamp." This is, of course, valid for a self-representation by a self-copy: imagine Vermeer producing an absolutely faithful copy of his *View of Delft* and exhibiting it under a title something like "The *View of Delft* of Jan Vermeer, by Jan Vermeer."

The intentional (conceptual) difference between the two acts (to *copy* and to *represent*) consists only of a meaning that the second adds to the first, the way "voting (with raised hand) for the proposal of the president" is only a conventional meaning added, to the fact that one raises one's hand, by the moment when one raises it. But it is perhaps suitable to substitute the verb *to reproduce* for *to copy*, in order to enlarge the notion and to reserve a place for this other technique of multiplication, today far more widespread, which is the photographic print: we will need it.

We have thus reached the point where we realize that nothing perceptible distinguishes the fact of representing a picture such as it is from the fact of simply reproducing it such as it is. The phrase *such as it is* introduces (by excluding it) the consideration of two ways of reproducing (and eventually of representing) a picture *not as it is*. I set aside the latter case, which will consist of internal modifications; the first consists in reproducing a picture, as a copy or a print, by situating it, as I am obliged to say, in its *frame*. A copy of *Olympia* that would show its frame (in the literal and technical sense of the term) in addition to the picture itself would indicate, by this minimal addition, that it is not meant simply to reproduce but actually to represent this picture—no doubt because the image of the frame, in contrast to that of the picture, does not refer to an intention of "copy" but to one of representation, even if the mode of production is identical. But the addition is generally less minimal, since (to distance myself a little from fictional hypotheses) most of the representations of pictures are inserted in pictures representing a much vaster array of objects (and locations), such as living rooms, studios, galleries, and museums, which often contain by this very fact more than one picture, in fact sometimes a large number. With the almost inevitable consequence that the pictures, though clearly *represented*, are present in smaller dimensions, sometimes in oblique perspective and sometimes also only partially.

Les Poseuses strikingly illustrates these three possibilities in its representation of *La Grande Jatte*. The still life by the Master in the *Hommage à Cézanne* seems to me the most demonstrative representation: the picture is not, as is usual, represented in passing simply because it happens to be present in the depicted space: it is enthroned in the foreground, on a ceremonial easel, in a luxurious frame, surrounded by its admirers. It is *shown* to you, and you can't miss it. But it is not complete, for the two hands of Sérusier, in the position (as one says) of commentator, hide about a quarter of it. The seascape of *The Love Letter* is more complete and even more so the portrait of the artist's father in the *Self-Portrait* of Cambiaso.[10]

The second type of modification is also the second consequence of the ordinary resort to the copy: a manual copy is never perfectly faithful (nor is a photographic reproduction, but for other reasons that have to do with the technique of the photonic print, manual touch-ups aside). There would be no end to scrutinizing the internal modifications introduced in this way into pictorial representations of pictures in situ and to asking oneself about their voluntary or involuntary nature. I leave aside entirely the field of *variations*, very crowded today, illustrated by, among others, Picasso and Lichtenstein: these parodistic fantasies on the work of others don't present themselves as representations. I also leave aside the question of *modified replicas* (by self-copy), or *versions*, an ancient practice massively illustrated by the work of Chardin, among others: even if it is perfectly faithful, a replica is not (functionally) a representation but a simple duplication. Even less will I linger on what I will call, to speed things up, a *remake*, which is to say a new version produced not by a copy of a preexistent picture but by a rerun of the same motif with new expenses, the cathedral of Rouen or Montagne Sainte-Victoire[11]—though I'll observe that this case is the only one from which nonfigurative painting is on principle excluded.

The third consequence can precisely present itself only where figurative painting is concerned. When Cézanne places his easel for the twentieth time in front of the same motif of Montagne Sainte-Victoire, it is clear that this picture will (even if it "resembles" the others) represent none of the nineteen that have preceded it (which is the definition of a *remake*); when Chardin produces, by a copy of the first one, a second *Bénédicité*, identical or slightly different, we know that this picture represents in no way the preceding one but, in its own manner, their common object: a mother and (I suppose) her two children around a set table, one of the children kneeling with its hands joined for prayer. The coexistence of a process by a copy (of the picture) and of an effect of representation (of the motif) illustrates a general semiotic trait, which is the potential of certain forms of denotation for *transitivity*.

This is a complex question, and I am not certain that I see it absolutely clearly. But it seems to me that the criterion, if there is one, is based on the distinction between *usage* and *mention*. In a sentence like "*Paris* is a large city" the name *Paris* is *used*, in a transitive manner, for what it names (the city); in "*Paris* has two syllables" this name is *mentioned* (quoted) for what it is on the phonetic plane. There also exist mixed or ambiguous cases. If I casually declare in a conversation, "The heart has its reasons that reason does not know," this quotation may have, as its only function, that I take my turn, after Pascal, in expressing this opinion; but, if I say, "Pascal said: 'The heart has its reasons, etc.,' " my listeners can, depending on the context, suppose that I (only) quote the sentence of Pascal, or that I (moreover) express an opinion. In painting the picture-within-the-picture seems to me to illustrate this ambiguous case. In the first degree the large oblique surface at the left of the *Poseuses* (partially) represents the picture *La Grande Jatte*, and this degree is completely inevitable but only for someone who *recognizes* this latter picture. An ignorant or amnesiac viewer might ask himself whether there is not a window with a very special frame through which one can see the *real* landscape of the Grande Jatte. In order to avoid at least the reproach of gratuitous perversity, I remind the reader that Manet's *Portrait de Zacharie Astruc* poses a problem of this kind: to the right of the model, behind a table, a deep background opens up in the Dutch manner, and one doesn't know if it is meant to be a picture (in which case, by whom?), a mirror, or an open door. Françoise Cachin chooses the first hypothesis, but the fact that the question has been raised confirms the (general) ambiguity of this type of situation: the incontestable fragment of the *Grande Jatte* in the *Poseuses* can also function as a representation of the Grande Jatte. A viewer who ignored or had forgotten this picture could, in examining *Les Poseuses*, get some idea of this landscape, an idea that would be more fragmentary but related to the one provided by the original picture. And, in observing the "second" portrait of Cambioso senior, I can get some idea of what this personage looked like, enough of an idea, for example, to find, like Bouvard and Pécuchet, that this portrait "resembles" him. In short, the representation of a picture can function additionally, transitively, like a representation of what this picture represents,[12] just as a quotation can, transitively, express additionally the opinion of the person who quotes, even if the legitimacy of this interpretation on the part of the listener or the reader is generally undecidable.

The *Olympia* inscribed in the portrait of Zola (and I have little to add to what I have already said) clearly belongs to this kind: it is a real picture represented within another picture by the same painter and one that we might understand transitively as a representation of the subject of the second picture, in this instance of "Olympia" herself. But clearly does not always mean simply. Indeed, to recall very quickly some well-known (though not entirely certain) facts, the Portrait does not represent Olympia directly but apparently, rather, a photograph in black and white (and a partial one: the extreme right, with its black cat, is missing), not even of the picture but, rather, of an engraved copy of it made in the meantime. And, at a poorly determined point of this chain of transitive representations, one or two modifications (I'll come back to them) have been introduced. Moreover, the original picture represented the mythical Olympia with the "traits" of the model Victorine Meurent, already present in the Déjeuner sur l'herbe. But not exactly as Rembrandt represented Bathsheba with the traits of Hendrijke, for this nude became Olympia only on the occasion of the memorable exhibition in the Salon of 1865, probably baptized by Astruc, so that the picture changed its iconological and semiological status two years after its completion: first a real portrait of the nude Victorine, or of the nude Victorine "as" anonymous courtesan, it becomes the supposed portrait of an imaginary personage that is neither biblical (Bathsheba) nor mythological (Flora) and which is all in all nothing but a name. [13] The hypothesis of the photograph (the existence of which is not attested) is inspired by the fact that none of the known engravings has this dimension and that its graphism is, as it were, weakened by the intermediary reproduction. The hypothesis of the engraving (excluding a direct photograph of the picture) is based on the fact that the Olympia of the Zola picture wears a "curl" on her forehead, as on the two etchings executed in 1867, of which the second decorated the pamphlet by Zola on Manet. No one apparently knows anything about the reasons for this strange addition. The second modification, much more clearly significant, occurs only at the stage of the Portrait: it is the oblique glance of the young woman, which seems to be directed toward the writer, as though to thank him for the support that the latter had given his painter-friend, especially on the occasion of the famous scandal. For these two reasons at least the Olympia of the Portrait is a replica with variations, a new version of the original painting, and (perhaps) partially by way of a touched-up photograph. [14]

It is not unusual for a personage to be represented with an averted glance, thus evading the glance of the painter and later that of the viewer: this is the case, for example, with the young woman (Berthe Morisot) of Le Balcon—but Berthe looks straight ahead of her; it is her face that is slightly turned away. [15] The Olympia of the Zola (I dare not say the Olympia of Zola) stays with her face turned to the viewer, only her glance slides to the right, a paradoxically more expressive gesture, as everyone knows from experience. I have no reason to disagree with the classic interpretation of this expression, but I would like to underline its *metaleptic* character: the young woman of *Le Balcon* evidently looks at an object we do not see and one that is, though outside the field, inside the world of this picture, let's say the street or a facing window. The Olympia of the *Zola* looks at an object that we see but which she is not supposed to see, since the writer is not in the same picture in which she is. It is this transgression of the frontier between the first picture and the second picture that I here (like everyone else) call "metalepsis."[16] This is what gives this picture-within-the-picture its entirely special status, as though, mutatis mutandis, a Master of old, instead of introducing an anachronistic donor into the diegesis of an *Adoration of the Magi*, had inscribed this picture within the portrait of the donor and gratified the latter with an oblique wink of the Virgin. I know of no example of such an indiscreet production,[17] and, in any case, if one thinks of the supposed personality of our heroine and of the ideological role of her knight-in-waiting, the comparison is not in the best of tastes. No doubt it would be better to imagine, in this very hypothetical line and with this same function, a Mona Lisa inscribed into a portrait of Duchamp by Leonardo, who easily owes him that. According to the popular joke, one would, at long last, know why she is smiling.

7

Pissarro at L'Hermitage

Pissarro's views of Pontoise and its immediate surroundings are divided among several quite diverse sites: rare overall panoramas; private or public gardens; quays of the Oise with or without bridges, with or without barges, with or without the Chalon factory of Saint-Ouen-l'Aumône; or small street scenes, less urban than village-like, or at least middle-class, in the sense that Pontoise is then less a town than a semirural marketplace.[1] But the motif that will occupy me corresponds apparently to a dominant figure, the oldest, if I believe the catalogs, and also the most constant over a period of some fifteen years. Its most typical site is certainly the L'Hermitage quarter, where Pissarro lived several times, and in several places, from 1867 to 1880;[2] but two or three locations that are quite close to each other, like the Pâtis, in the little valley of the Viosne, Chaponval or Valhermeil, on the bank of the Oise a little uphill from L'Hermitage, present a comparable structure and are also "posed," after the fact, for a few variations on the same theme.

This structure thus appears ever since the first pictures of Pontoise, which depict the landscape called "fond de L'Hermitage"—the first dwelling of Pissarro in 1867 was in the very old street that bears that name. This hamlet administratively belonging to Pontoise in fact occupies, in the northeast of the town, following a generally dry valley, the space that extends between the southern edge of the Plateau du Vexin and the right bank of the Oise. The "fond" in question is the northern extremity of this valley, after which the plateau rises quite abruptly. The fond de L'Hermitage is thus typically a landscape below, where the village houses line up at the foot of what one might consider a hill or a slope. In order to depict it most clearly in this situation, the painter generally takes his post on an opposite slope that overhangs it slightly, undoubtedly on the other side of the valley—the later urbanization of this site has made the structure a little less readable and the reconstruction rather conjectural. The hill is thus doubly dominated, by the (small) height from which the painter perceives it, and which the spectator can only induce from the effect of the plunge, and by the somewhat steeper hillside that rises behind it. The function of this opposite slope is rather clear: if the terrain between the painter and his motif were horizontal, as it sometimes is between cliff and shore,[3] the overhang of the slope could be, at least in part, hidden by the line of houses itself and by this fact quite a bit diminished. That is what happens in L'Hermitage à Pointoise,[4] in which the painter placed himself on the same level, next to the first gardens (vegetable gardens and orchards) of the village: except for the left extremity, where a path goes up farther between field and grove, the line of the horizon hardly goes beyond that of the houses, even below the highest of them: including the color, the slope of the hill is almost the same as that of the roofs, which makes the impression of steepness almost totally disappear, the more so since the deeper perspective makes the background appear farther away: without the other views as witnesses, one could suppose that the model is a rather elevated hill but one situated at several hundreds meters in back of the village. But this is to my knowledge the only occurrence of this flattening depiction:[5] all the other canvases dramatize the site by accenting the effect of relief, stressed by the presence in the foreground of the beginning of the opposite slope (Vue de L'Hermitage, Côte du Jallais, Pontoise)[6] or of the turn of a path descending the hill, as in La Côte du Jallais, Pontoise.[7] This last one, which P. and V. take for "perhaps the masterpiece of the group,"[8] apparently gives the most ample view—shifted to the left in relation to the group of houses, including the greatest height of sky (roughly a third of the canvas) and the largest amplitude of the line of the slope—to the point of outlining, unless I am mistaken, on the left and between two couples of poplars the very characteristic Renaissance belfry of the church of Saint-Maclou, the only visible element from that point of the town itself (actually I don't know if that outline is, or was then, in fact visible from the point where the painter is supposed to be placed, but he could evidently have cheated on the perspective, like many others, to show what he did not see). A comparable spatial effect is found at the same time (1868) but at a different—though not very distant—site in Paysage aux Pâtis, Pontoise;[9] the hamlet of Pâtis is in the valley of the Viosne, in the northwest of Pontoise, and the overhanging point of view is a hill near Osny, an orientation that excludes any view of the town; in contrast to the valley of L'Hermitage, the Viosne is a true run of water, which was embellished at the time with a few mills, but the perspective adopted here hides it, which contributes to assimilating the two sites.

Paradoxically, the most constricted view, in this first Pontoisean series,[10] is the motif of the largest canvas, Les Coteaux de L'Hermitage, Pontoise,[11] in which the path in the foreground, more developed than in La Côte du Jallais, Pontoise, winds between the houses of the village, which it seems to open to the advance of the viewer; if one had to choose, without leaving this period, the most typical picture with the theme that concerns us, it would perhaps be this one, whose frankness and freshness (two features common to all these pieces) burst on one at the entrance of the hall reserved for the Tannhauser collection at the Guggenheim. This theme, whose degree of consciousness in our painter I evidently don't know, is the one I would like to call "intimate landscape." I clearly don't understand by this an inner landscape, a "chosen" metaphor of the interiority of a "soul," like the one that figured and illustrated the sequence of the Fêtes galantes; this is a wholly external landscape but one that presents—which is to say, of course, seems to present—a quality of invitation, which makes it a choice site for what Bachelard calls "intimate revery." [12] What contributes greatly to this impression is the fact that it is not a place that is wild or deserted but a built-up village: in all its versions, and especially in this one, this valley of L'Hermitage is inhabited, and the spectator can imagine he is at home, or at least received, in one of these houses, which are apparently neither isolated farmhouses nor bourgeois homes (as those constructed a little lower down, in the new rue de L'Hermitage, altogether straight, horizontal, and quite residential, where Pissarro will himself live a little later), so close together they almost touch each other, between which space tightens and arranges a familiar contiguity that is not known either by the streets of towns or by rural stretches with dispersed homes. The village down below doubles this impression of intimacy by its tightened situation, "circumvented," as Proust will say, from all sides, which in a way motivates proximity by the apparent impossibility of spreading itself farther: a home of this sort is, as it were, fortunately (for the imagination) hindered from expansion, condemned to immobility. This hollow, less of solitary "greenery" "where a river sings" (which one nonetheless thinks one hears) than of a protective and cordial habitation, is clearly a renewed image of the nest, and of the cave, [13] and thus of the maternal bosom: the intimacy that it evokes in me is not my own, the one that I contain and from which I try to flee, but (on the contrary?) the one in which I remember having been contained and which I wish to find again. To borrow again from Bachelard, this reverie of intimacy is an archetypal "reverie of rest"—but a rest outside oneself, in the refuge of a welcoming otherness: just about the opposite of what one usually calls the sublime. But enough of this village general store psychoanalysis, which I am not about to attribute to the painter himself.

I have considered to this point only the canvases of this first Pontoisean period, the one Brettell calls the period of "realist formalism." This latter expression may seem paradoxical, but it has a certain correctness in my eyes. This is due, it seems to me, to the manner in which the firmness—the robustness of the touch (which the critics of the time, starting with Zola,[14] did not fail to notice)—stresses the "grammar" (as the painter and theoretician Le Carpentier said at the beginning of the century)[15] of a landscape so opportunely constructed and so strongly structured by the readable terracing of the planes and levels and by the arrangement of the volumes: that which Théodore Duret expressed in his fashion a little later in speaking of the "absolutely seated" character of Pissarro's paintings, a quality he attributed to his "intimate and deep feeling for nature" and, like Zola, to the "power of his brush."[16] The touch certainly has a lot to do with this effect, but what has still more to do with it is the choice and the accentuation of this type of landscape: without a doubt nothing *seats* a place better than a group of houses at its base, even if they are lopsided and disposed every which way: the sensible geometry works more happily on the apparent rustic disorder than on the regular grid of industrial buildings. It is in this, without a doubt, that "realism" paradoxically contributes to the advancement of form: the analytic vision of Corot accented, as though it were made more masculine, by a touch of Courbet— I am, incidentally, not certain that the first always needs the reinforcement of the second to announce the third (in date). *Les Maisons de Cabassus à Ville d'Avray*[17] have no reason to envy, either for the motif or for the manner, the Pissarro of the first period of L'Hermitage, clearly a non–missing link between Corot and Cézanne—or, if one wants to take in more, between Poussin and Braque: the "Impressionist Poussin" that Maurice Denis will find precisely in Cézanne,[18] is, in my view, already here, thanks to the obvious agreement between a site and a vision. But we still have to consider a few echoes of this motif in the subsequent periods, which essentially span from 1872 to 1884— the (for me) decisive break between 1868 and 1872 being due to a departure, in May 1869, for Louveciennes, central site of Impressionism, then an exodus to Montfoucault in the Mayenne, then to London, on account of the war.

The period 1872–73, which Brettell qualifies as the "classic Pontoisean period", seemingly by reference to the Poussinian echoes one can find in the overall statement of the series *Quatre saisons*,[19] apparently contains few deep views of L'Hermitage, more of the plateau of Vexin or of the banks of the Oise, less irregular landscapes. The three first *Saisons* even present a height of sky, two-thirds of the canvas, quite unusual in Pissarro, which rather evokes Monet or more still Boudin, where the part of the beach, at the lower edge, would be occupied by the horizontal stretch of cultivated ground. But L'Hiver presents a village seen slightly from above, and Pontoise[20] and La Sente de justice[21] give two views of the town itself, probably painted roughly from the same spot, also from above the tower, this time of the church Notre-Dame, and Le Jardin de la ville, Pontoise[22] stresses the very marked (on this scale) slope between the inferior esplanade, where the same tower of Notre-Dame emerges, and the steep little terrace of that garden, which Julien Green rightly qualified as "mysterious."[23] Pontoise, established for centuries at the same time at the edge of a plateau, at its feet, and, as much as possible, on its sometimes a little steep slopes, surely has relief, and Pissarro, who did not misuse it, apparently preferring more rustic sites, nonetheless sometimes took advantage of it for urban views with several levels; the most remarkable is without doubt the one of the Parc aux Charrettes, Pontoise,[24] which gives to Saint-Maclou, painted in profile and from below, a very advantageous lengthening ("reality" is a little less spectacular today, but this steep slope corresponds well with my own past impressions, which are located about midway in time). A much later panoramic view, perhaps the last before the departure for Éragny, Vue de Pontoise,[25] taken from quite far to the west, by contrast shows the church halfway down below from the superior part of the village, hiding the steepness with which it actually dominates the lower part of its town and the course of the Oise.

But I have gone a little beyond my subject. It is mainly after 1875 that Pissarro comes back to our site of the fond de L'Hermitage—for example, with Coteau de L'Hermitage, Pontoise,[26] Le Sentier du village,[27] and L'Hermitage, Pontoise,[28] of which the theme (the hamlet at the foot of the hill) is identical to the one of the years 1867–68 but whose style is much more marked by the Impressionist manner that Pissarro soaked up in the meantime from his contact with Monet and Sisley: the touch is freer, the regular flats, which seemed to even out the surfaces of the soil, are replaced by lighter brush strokes. The "grammar" of the landscape fades, or at least conceals itself behind the (new) style of the painter, who now willingly resorts to effects of undergrowth, where the houses, less clear in form and at the same time more fatty and more vaporous, only make their appearance between the boles and leaves of the trees that shape a very close foreground: this is the case of the Fond de L'Hermitage,[29] in which the profile of the hill can hardly be guessed, and of the three canvases (among others?) that are characterized by a very tight point of view and a more accented relief than ever: the first Le Chemin montant, L'Hermitage, Pontoise,[30] painted, according to Brettell,[31] from "halfway up the path leading to the côte des Boeufs," where the village seems to appear in a brief vista on an almost mountainous path, is summerlike, or springlike, in tone; the two others, very close in space and apparently also in time, are markedly autumnal or wintry, where the denuded silhouettes of a few poplars and fruit trees rise up in front of roofs whose very lively color does not entirely counteract the melancholia of the whole: [32] *La Côte des Boeufs, Pontoise*, sometimes called *Côtes Saint-Denis à Pontoise*, [33] and *Toits rouges, coin de village, effet d'hiver*, sometimes called *Le Verger, Côtes Saint-Denis à Pontoise*. [34] These two last landscapes are exceptionally empty of human presences, except, in the first, two persons so thoroughly fused with the background that they seem to hide in it in order to spy on the painter, and now the viewer, with fear and distrust. This somewhat depressive tonality evidently evokes certain canvases of friend Cézanne around 1873 at Auvers—which are situated a few kilometers from L'Hermitage and in an often comparable situation—such as *La Maison du Père Lacroix*, [35] *La Maison du Dr. Gachet*, [36] and mainly, of course, *La Maison du pendu*, [37] in which the relief, more tormented than staged and even somewhat sullen, no longer inspires any sort of joy and does not suggest any kind of warm hospitality. The site seems to have exhausted its convivial capacities and perhaps gives one a premonition of its future suburban decline. The time has apparently come to pack one's bags and to go install oneself a little farther on. Yet it does not seem to me that Pissarro immediately found again elsewhere the freshness of inspiration that this privileged site of L'Hermitage had communicated to him from the start, which survives only in his work today—and in some memories that will soon be extinguished.

I would thus not say, like Lucien Pissarro and Lionello Venturi, [38] that "no one today [in 1939] would notice the poetry that emanates from the slopes of the Hermitage if Pissarro had not revealed it: through him they appear solid, reserved, not without mystery." Their mystery and their poetry have perhaps withered today, but I can attest that they were still present to us in 1939, even without reference to Pissarro, and still for a few years more, in the course of which one destroyed more than one constructed in these places. Here, as elsewhere, the magic of a representation is due to the happy meeting between the properties of an object and the sensibility of an artist, and the one of Pissarro's L'Hermitage may owe as much to L'Hermitage as to Pissarro, to the genius of the place as to the genius of the painter.

8

One of the numerous modes of relationship between literature and music is, quite clearly, the presence of a literary text in a musical work. But this presence itself can take on different modes, or degrees, which I would like to evoke briefly.

The first of these modes, which corresponds to the materially strongest degree, is that of an effective and integrated presence. This is the case of all vocal music in which the verbal text is uttered in some manner: sung (melodies, cantatas, operas), spoken (*Histoire du soldat*), or according to some mixed or intermediary state, *Sprechgesang* or other. The degrees of integration are different here, since the mode of utterance more or less espouses the melodic line or the polyphonic fabric, but the degree of presence of the text is the same, and usage is not mistaken when it still qualifies as "words" the poem of a lied or the libretto of an opera. This type is known and practiced universally, so no need to insist on it, but I want to emphasize at least one trait: by the very fact of their copresence, and, whatever the effects of the contamination that results from this (melismatization of the verbal phrase, efforts at expressivity in the score), the parts and the roles in it are essentially distinct. Except for confirming exceptions, it is the text that determines the meaning; the music wants at the most to confirm and to illustrate it. One of these exceptions would no doubt be the Wagnerian practice of the leitmotif, which may allow the score to deliver a message parallel to that of the poem: if in the course of a sentence sung by Tristan the motif of Desire appears in the orchestra, this apparition superimposes on the signified of the text another quite as determined signified, but that is because the motif has been previously invested with that meaning according to a semiotic convention that is, all things considered, closer to language than to music. There exist, in fact, kinds of dictionaries that teach us, like a language, the function of all these motifs.

The second mode, much less frequent, is of the order of reference in absentia. It consists in a musical work referring, by its title, to a definite literary text, of which it is by this very fact a paraphrase or a commentary and which it adopts, still by this very fact, as an argument, even as a "program." This is the case of certain symphonic poems by Liszt, of which the first one, *Ce qu'on entend sur la montagne* (1848), "follows" a poem by Hugo; or, further, *Tasso, Lamento e Triompho* (Byron), *Mazeppa* (Hugo), *Les Préludes* (Autran), *Idéaux* (Schiller), and *Hamlet* (Shakespeare, of course). This type can be found again at least in Franck (*Les Éolides* following Leconte de Lisle, *Les Djinns* following Hugo) and in Strauss: *Also sprach Zarathustra, Don Quixote*, and in a more diffuse manner, since there is no doubt more than one text "illustrated," *Don Juan*. The initiator of the genre (if it is one) may be Berlioz with *Harold in Italy*, "Symphony for orchestra and solo viola" following Byron's *Childe Harold* (1834). But one finds a relation of the same order in piano works such as the three "Sonnets de Pétrarque" in Liszt's *Deuxième année de pèlerinage* and, complete with a title that means without a doubt to suggest a more distant inspiration, the "Fantasia quasi sonata" *Après une lecture du Dante*, in the same volume. This repertory will seem typically "romantic," but Debussy, with his *Prélude de l'après-midi d'un faune*, or Ravel, with *Gaspard de la nuit* and *Ma mère l'Oye*, indicate the capacity of the genre to transcend the historical limits of the terrain of its origin. The evocations of *Ma mère l'Oye* are a little freer, but the three pieces of *Gaspard de la Nuit* refer in a precise manner to Aloysius Bertrand's three poems: *Ondine, Le Gibet*, and *Scarbo*.

I will not discuss the qualities of these references, in other words the "fidelity" or "infidelity" of these scores to the letter or to the spirit of the texts that are supposed to have inspired them, a relationship that each listener can interpret and appreciate as he likes. I will simply note that the degrees of imposition vary according to the knowledge or memory that the listener can have of the text in question, lest it be given to him on the score's margin, on the recording, or on the concert program. Everyone has a certain idea of Don Quixote, of Don Juan, of the *Divine Comedy*, or of Perrault's tales, but Petrarch's three sonnets and Bertrand's prose poems are not in everyone's memory, and the majority of listeners let themselves be guided—if by anything—by the meaning of the title alone (very clear for *Ondine* or for *Le Gibet*, certainly very obscure for *Scarbo*). Said differently, our second mode risks, in a good many cases, to slide in practice toward a third, the following.

The mode of presence of the text is here no longer either the effective presence or the allusive reference but, quite simply, absence, nonexistence. The musical works that I think of now, and which again are very numerous, present, except by accident, no relationship whatsoever with any existing literary text.

One can thus think that these have no role to play in this context, but I am not so sure, or, rather, I am sure of the contrary and for two reasons that are probably only one. The first is that these works include a verbal utterance, which, like all verbal utterances according to certain conditions of heat and pressure, can be qualified as "literary": it is their title, which is of the thematic type. I do not here take this adjective in its musical but precisely in its literary meaning:[1] the title of a literary work is thematic when it refers, directly (*War and Peace*) or by some detour (*The Red and the Black*) or detail (*Madame Bovary*, *Le Soulier de satin*), to the thematic content of the work it entitles; if it is not thematic, it is *rhematic*; that is to say, it designates the work itself, by some generic trait (*Odes, Sonnets, Journal*) or otherwise: *Tel Quel, Manuscript found in Saragossa*. A musical work can likewise bear a rhematic title that describes it by its genre (sonata, symphony, concerto, etc.), by its key, or by its place in the author's catalog (opus number). A rhematic title cannot, by definition, have a literary connotation; a thematic title, let us say *Rêverie* or *La Cathédrale engloutie*, inevitably has one by the mere fact that it designates a "content" (a signified)—for example, psychological or picturesque—by a verbal means that itself functions like a (brief) literary text. I would therefore say that *Rêverie* or *La Cathédrale engloutie* contains a literary text, its thematic title.

My second reason for evoking this type of work here is that the presence of a thematic title is enough to suggest the existence of a text that would be the literary equivalent of the musical work thus designated. Of this text, when all is said, we will know nothing more, and this is the whole difference between this third type and the second, for which the scrupulous listener can always go back to the "source." This text does not exist, but the title suggests to us that it could exist—and perhaps it invites the most obedient, or the most imaginative, listener to sketch a version of it. Thus, its presence here is *suggestive*, not effective or allusive. The mere imposition of a thematic title implies the possible existence of a referential text—and, if I was to learn tomorrow that Schumann's *Scènes d'enfants* or Debussy's *Préludes* illustrate as many real poems, in verse or in prose, I would have no reason to be astonished. The fact is that musical tradition has, since Mendelssohn, a term at its disposal that can designate quite well that paradoxical mode of virtual presence. This term, itself paradoxical or oxymoronic, is *Songs without Words*. I call it paradoxical because originally a romance, or a lied (the German term is *Lieder ohne Worte*) is a type of melody or of song, based on words, that goes back plainly to vocal music. The term *romance* had already served,[2] at least in Beethoven, and it will serve again with others—Schumann and Fauré, for example—to entitle purely instrumental pieces: the two *Romanzen* of Beethoven are concert pieces for violin and orchestra in which the solo instrument holds the melodic part, like a voice that would sing a melody without words. Romances without words already, but Beethoven did not feel the need to specify it. In forging the phrase *Romances without words*, Mendelssohn—if it is he—thus manifests the consciousness of a contradiction in terms: romances without words, lied without poem, as one says "dark clarity" or "glorious humbleness." But his collection does not belong in its entirety to the "genre" I am trying to describe because most of its pieces for piano do not bear any thematic title but a simple indication of tonality, as for Beethoven's *Romanzen*—and as will be the case with Fauré's whole collection of the same title. They have from the romance, or from the lied, merely the perceptible presence of a melodic line that could belong to a chant or perhaps of the standard lied form (I did not verify this). Others, by contrast, accentuate their relation to the vocal genre by the use of a title that indicates the thematic content of the absent poem: *The Harp of the Poet* (*La Harpe du poète*), *The Flight* (*La Fuite*), *The Spinner* (*La Fileuse*), *The Shepherd's Complaint* (*La Complainte du berger*), etc. The reference to vocal music thus uses two means here: for one thing the structure in an accompanied melodic line, for another the choice of a thematic title. But this second means can also act by itself, in conferring by its own semantic function a significant value to a piece that imitates in nothing at all the appearance of an accompanied melody, such as "The Prophet Bird" from *Scenes from the Woods*.

It is, in fact, Schumann who, during the romantic period, best illustrates this genre, which tends to organize itself according to the model of a cycle of lieder that bear a common thematic title, *Scenes from the Woods* or *Scenes from Childhood*, aimed at unifying a group of pieces individually characterized by their respective thematic title (*Of Foreign Lands and People*, *A Curious Story*, etc.). Despite the (unequal) disappearance of the form of accompanied melody, such collections deserve, it seems to me, the cavalier denomination of "songs without words," in the sense I understand it here.

Thus defined as a piece, most often for piano, provided with a thematic title ensuring by itself its affective or descriptive meaning, songs without words are by no means the monopoly or the invention of the romantic period. Most of Couperin's harpsichord pieces thus bear picturesque, often quite precise or quite refined titles (*Les Matelotes provençales*, *Les Petites crémières de Bagnolet*, *Les Barricades mystérieuses*, *Les Vieux galans et les Trésorières surannées sous des Dominos pourpres et feuilles mortes*)—and I doubt that such a practice was completely isolated in his period. And, closer to us, it is well known that Debussy's *Préludes*, his *Images pour piano*, his *Estampes*, his *Children's Corner*, Ravel's *Miroirs* and Albeniz's *Iberia*, among others, prolong the Schumannian type of unified cycle with thematic intention, without including such isolated pieces as *Jeux d'eau* or *Pavane pour une infante défunte*. One also knows that for *Préludes* some sort of bad conscience about these effects of the title led Debussy to place them at the end of the piece and between parentheses, as though he wanted to avoid too great an influence on the interpreter or the listener. A vain precaution: they are as a rule unmistakably understood as titles, and *Danseuses de Delphes* or *Des pas sur le neige* wield their suggestive power with as much intensity as *The Poet Speaks* or *The Prophet Bird*.

Another sign of reserve with respect to the title, and one that was perhaps not alien to the somewhat playful choice of Couperin, is the systematic recourse, in the work of Satie, to a sarcastic or provocative title: *Aperçus désagréables*, *Embryons desséchés*, *Sonatine bureaucratique*, *Morceaux en forme de poire*, *Véritables préludes flasques pour un chien*, etc. In these two cases (the second may be seen as a caricature of first) the indiscretion and above all the impertinence (the refined absence of pertinence) of the title clearly express and produce a derision of the thematic title and of its way of imposing a meaning on a score, in other words of the arbitrariness of thematic entitulation in music, and in this regard Satie clearly plays the role of gravedigger of the genre, which he terminates by pushing it to absurdity. But the process is not without risk because such a marked use of the title ends up by making us forget the score, which will perhaps be the first victim of it: one does not make fun of the paratext with impunity.

But the influence of the thematic title is not limited to these piano pieces, whether or not they are grouped into cycles. It rules another genre as well, also very characteristic of the romantic and post-romantic period, the symphonic poem. We must observe in this term a paradoxical effect comparable to the one in *song without words*, for *symphonic poem* signifies also something like "poem without words."[3] The symphonic poem, such as it is eminently illustrated in works by Liszt or by Strauss—with the exception of those, already mentioned, that refer to a specific literary work—has of a "poem," that is to say of a text, only the title, and sometimes that sort of development of the title into a narrative argument that one calls the "program," which imposes on it its significance from the outside: see, among Liszt's works, *From the Cradle to the Grave* or, among Strauss's, *Tod und Verklärung* and *Heldenleben*.[4] But here, again, the genre extends far beyond its romantic origin, since one finds it again, more or less well disguised, for example, in Debussy or Ravel, with a sort of synthesis between the type symphonic poem and the cyclical type as a bonus, in the form of thematic orchestral suites: see Ravel's *Rhapsodie espagnole* (four pieces: "Prélude à la nuit," "Malaguena," "Habanera," and "Feria") and, in Debussy, those "symphonic tryptics"—the *Nocturnes* ("Nuages," "Fêtes," and "Sirènes"), *La Mer* (three "symphonic sketches": "De l'aube à midi sur la mer," "Jeux de vagues," and "Dialogues du vent et de la mer") and *Images* ("Gigues," "Iberia," and "Rondes de printemps"). The same structure, as we know, is found again in de Falla's *Nights in the Gardens of Spain*: "At the Generalife," "Far-away Dance," and "In the Gardens of the Sierra de Cordoue." These groupings clearly have a semantic effect: the two-floored titular device in a manner confronts itself in confirming the overall title with the title of its parts, and reciprocally. We can thus say that the cycles of songs without words or thematized symphonic sequences exert a priori by this semantic convergence a greater force of suggestion than isolated works such as *Jeux d'eau* and *Tod und Verklärung*: the listener becomes established immediately in the evoked climate by the main title and finds in each part a particular specification of this climate, just about the way he does in a collection of thematically homogenized poems such as *Les Fleurs du mal* and, more clearly still, *Fêtes galantes*.[5] The search for effects of this kind no doubt affects decisions to group after the fact, like the one that rules *Années de pèlerinage* and even perhaps the symphonic poems of Liszt (in which the overall title, no doubt for lack of a better one, remains rhematic).

The literary—and, more particularly, poetic—fact thus has here a paradoxically stronger function than in vocal music, in which its effective presence assigns it a place that is limited by this presence itself: in these poems without words the poetic, without effective presence or determined reference, plays the most elusive but perhaps the most pressing possible role: that of a *model*. Music here no longer tries to sustain and surround the present text nor even to illustrate an absent text; it tries, one might say, to *make itself into a text*, as though it wanted to honor its title (even if, in many cases, it came only after the fact), to *make itself* language and poem, as though the literary model had entirely taken hold of its imagination. Vocal music was music *with* words, musical paraphrases of the *Mazeppa* type were music à propos of words; in instrumental music with a thematic title the absence of text joined with the suggestion of a text by the title, the contradictory situation of a *with words without words*, in a certain way forces the score to take the place and to play the role of the text it suggests and which it is lacking. The relationship is thus no longer one of copresence nor of evocation but one of substitution and imitation: ut poesis musica. This is decidedly the formula suggested, among others, by the 1841 preface to Années de pèlerinage:

> As instrumental music progresses, it tends to imprint itself with that ideality which has marked the perfection of plastic arts, to become not a simple combination of sounds, but a poetic language better suited perhaps than poetry itself to express all that, in us, goes beyond the usual horizons, all that is beyond analysis, all that attaches itself to inaccessible depth, eternal desires, infinite feelings.

There would no doubt be something a little ridiculous in such a statement if one did not know it to be in a way compensated (or aggravated) at the end of the century (and no doubt before) by the reciprocal temptation, as Mallarmé said, to "retake its own from music." An ut musica poesis, which has during the nineteenth century taken the place of the classical ut pictura . . . , corresponds to the romantic and post-romantic ut poesis musica. There is, incidentally, a little of ut pictura in the descriptive pruritus of music in the nineteenth century, for which not only Granados's Goyescas, the Pictures at an Exhibition, the Debussyan resort to the term esquisses, and the musical term impressionism testify. It would no doubt not be very difficult to find symmetrical features of some ut poesis . . . (Delacroix) or of some ut musica pictura (Klee), as though all the arts more or less felt this nostalgia or trans-artistic utopia that sometimes induces them to borrow from or reciprocally imitate each other, forgetting (or in order to forget) their respective specificity, to deny the heterogeneity of their means in the, perhaps illusory, name of a convergence of their ends.

To his daughter, who asks him what are the words of a theme that he dedicated to her for her birthday, Dale Turner answers, with an infinitely tired air: "One is not obliged to put words to everything." [6] One puts them, in truth, more than one should and often more than one would want to, as though one could not accept that music was, according to the scornful phrase of Liszt prefiguring Stravinsky, nothing more than a "simple combination of sounds." This inherently religious incapacity to the Es ist so has resulted in innumerable apocryphal titles, imposed by a public wanting meaning for works that did not want it, recently including the thirty-three Diabelli Variations. This often childish indiscretion is clearly a result of semiotic hypertension, a chronic condition of the human mind. It would no doubt be vain to complain about it and unjust to deny that the thematic titles of certain songs without words add to their charm. One can only wish that this addition may remain marginal, detached, floating, as it were, and that its ad lib presence may serve not to weight them with an authoritarian meaning but, rather, to lighten them, to air them, like a silence, a question without an answer: that the problematical relation between the combination of sounds and the proposition of meaning may resound not as a perfect chord but as an unresolved dissonance. I am sure that this is what a Couperin, a Schumann, a Debussy, asks of us, and this would be the good (and difficult) usage of the thematic title, so that the song without words does not turn into *words without song* (to repeat Adorno's cruel phrase—and title).

For music and literature are neither parallel nor symmetrical: they are simply two different practices—but nothing is more difficult to think than a simple difference—which fortunately meet only because of their difference. Like all uts of this kind, the *ut poesis* is a mirage or a goad. *Aliter poesis, aliter musica.* The one sings; the other speaks. To exchange roles is not always the best thing they can do and to confuse them is certainly not the best way of loving them both together.

9

The Other of the Same

Who is the one who said: "At the beginning was repetition?"[1]

I would like to elucidate the nature of, or the reasons for, the variable and re-current fascination that the fact—and at the same time the idea—of repetition and variation exert on me, as undoubtedly on everyone else. I doubt that I will succeed, here or anywhere; I'll at least try to measure its force and to identify a few of its occasions.

Without much risk of appearing absurd, one can state as a principle that every repetition is already a variation: a variation at degree zero, if you like—a degree that, as we know, is never nothing, since, in any system, an absence contrasts with one presence as effectively as with another.

Saussure, asking himself the delicate question of synchronic identities, noted that during a lecture each occurrence of the address *Gentlemen!* (in those days it appears that only men attended conferences) seems to us a unique "word," identical to itself despite the "variations in speed and intonation" it presents "in different passages with very appreciable phonetic differences." In the same way (I here follow the sequence of the *Course in General Linguistics*)[2] the "express train Geneva-Paris of 8:45 p.m." retains its identity despite the daily changes of locomotive, of railroad cars, of staff. Roland Barthes, on his side, often evoked the vessel *Argo*, which remained the same *Argo* after changing its sails, its hull, its crew; others refer to the knife of Jeannot, with its new blade and its new handle. The key to the mystery—and it is one—rests for Saussure in the ideality (he does not use this word) of an entity "rooted in certain conditions for which its occasional material is foreign." What makes up the express train of 8:45 is not its material composition nor even its hu-man cargo but "the hour of its departure, its itinerary, and in general all the circumstances that distinguish it from other express trains." What makes up the knife of Jeannot is that it belongs to Jeannot; what makes up the vessel

Argo is no doubt the simple fact that it is called "Argo." In the same way (I here arrive at the end of the repertory of Saussurean metaphors), if in a chess game "I replace the wooden pieces by ivory pieces, the change is indifferent to the system" and, therefore, to the pertinent identity of the pieces. As we know, I can even replace a lost knight or bishop by a pants button, which will do the trick by convention.

This relationship between the opposition identity / difference (repetition/ variation) and the opposition ideality / materiality being established in passing; it is no doubt not foreign to the theoretical stake of the first. But let us not try to study this matter in greater depth.

And let us return to our *Gentlemen!* Saussure specifies that the identity of this "expression" does not stem from an identity of its meaning: "A word can express quite different ideas [I can *adopt* a mode or a child; a *flower* can be from an apple tree or from the aristocracy] without its identification being seriously compromised"; it stems from the conventional identification of a unique word across all the nonpertinent variations of its pronunciation. And "this feeling of identity persists, even though from a semantic viewpoint there is no absolute identity from one *Gentlemen!* to the other."

In fact (I here embroider freely on a well-known theme), at least the context is different in each case, if only because of the place each *Gentlemen!* holds in the inevitable duration of an hour-long lecture. And, even if I said in sequence, without taking a breath (easy) and without any change in voice (impossible) three *Gentlemen!* in a row, these three expressions would be stylistically different *because of the very fact of their repetition*, which makes of one the first, of the following the second, and of the third the last. In short they are different by *the very fact of their identity*. Didn't I speak of mystery?

In sum at first we state that three necessarily different emissions make up one single and same word, then that the three successive emissions of the same word do not have the same value. Which is actually to pass from difference to identity then from identity to difference. From variation to repetition, from repetition to variation—one and the same thing. We cannot vary without repeating nor repeat without varying.

Music is clearly the supreme art of repetition-variation, the art that has this as its absolute principle. As soon as a theme has been (ex)posed, the entire device of development gets going, grounded in the different procedures of imitation-transformation: transposition, augmentation, diminution, inversion, retrograde, retrograde inversion, counterpoint in canon, in fugue, etc., without prejudice against literal reprises (repetitions) or instrumental migrations, as in Ravel's *Boléro*.

There is nonetheless something more immediately seductive in the form (more) correctly said to be a *variation*, as it is used, let us say, from Bach to Webern, no doubt because it is more perceptible to the uninitiated: inversions to the side, the initial theme serves as framework and guide here, and the game consists in trying to identify its recurrence by way of its metamorphoses— and reciprocally: the pleasure of research, *ricercare*, as (it seems) one said earlier regarding these themes hidden in the polyphonic fabric and which the auditor was meant to flush out from under their counterpoint, like a needle in a haystack or a hunter in an ambiguous design. When a certain threshold is passed—that is to say, when one has entered the phase where it is unrecognizable (as happens rather quickly in the *Diabelli*)—this pleasure fades away in favor of another, even as the hope subsists that a renewed audition will allow it to be prolonged by a stage—whence the inexhaustible pleasure of listening. I rather dislike anyone telling me (as sometimes happens) that the last *Diabellis* no longer have any relationship whatever with the theme of the waltz; even as it discourages a good intention in advance, it at the same time also, I think, depreciates the composer's work: to produce an entirely autonomous piece is less commendable than to produce a variation whose relation to the theme is sufficiently wily to remain enigmatic for a long while.

Inversely, some variation sets that are too transparent, like those of the *Eroica*, or the first movement of Mozart's twelfth sonata, perhaps don't offer sufficient resistance to the desire of identification. But the contrary holds for the final reprise, as in the *aria da capo* of the *Goldberg Variations*, which disturbs a quite paradoxical epitome: the one, of course, of the disquieting familiarity. I can well imagine that this disturbance influences interpretation in one way or another: Gould 1981, for example. But even if the interpreter contented himself, on a record, with the reproduction of his initial delivery in a magnetically identical fashion, I would still swear that something has changed. Not without reason: at least the auditor has changed. So that here again to repeat is to vary.

I perhaps find the happiest balance between transformation and repetition in the variations of jazz, in which the principle (free jazz to the side) is to improvise each *chorus*, meaning each series of thirty-two measures (twelve in the blues), leaning on the sequence of chords given by the theme: a sequence whose incessant reiteration, *basso ostinato* as in the baroque *chaconne* and *passacaglia*, [3] authorizes an indefinite number of melodic illustrations. We know that during the lovely nights of jam sessions in Kansas City or at Minton's in Harlem groups could improvise, chorus after chorus, for more than an hour on the same theme; we also know that the freedom of interpretation of themes did nothing but progress, [4] from the timid New Orleans–style paraphrases to the polytonal explorations of bebop, without thereby, save exceptionally, renouncing the harmonic thread. The principle of this pleasure is thus simple for the auditor, though sometimes demanding in its application: to perceive at the same time, in each measure and in their relation, the unforeseeable melodic invention and the *obligato* progression of chords, formulated by the rhythmic section or suggested by the soloist. This coexistence, or rather this reciprocal manifestation, of an unchanging bass and of an aleatoric melody makes listening to jazz one of the most active and, contrary to prejudices, one of the most intellectual activities that exist.

For the lover of variation, whose portrait I have perhaps sketched indirectly just now, one would imagine that plastic arts and literature are places of frustration, since their principle, if they have one, is elsewhere. This is not exactly the case, thanks to our patron saint Proteus. A few words on this.

It is evident that architecture—the "music of space," according to the irrefutable cliché—often proceeds by varied repetition, from Ictinos to Bramante and from Bramante to Mies Van der Rohe. For figurative arts, sculpture, painting, design, I would say that the relation repetition-variation lies in the very fact of representation, or, as Pascal said, of "resemblance." It is true that we don't always have the means to call on the "original" for comparison, but at least we sometimes have the occasion to confront two or more resemblances, that is to say, two or more versions, or *replicas*, of the "same" work, even if they are present in museums that are far apart. Certain exhibitions have no other merit, but this one is sufficient to us. In nonfigurative painting (or sculpture) the obsessional character of an autonomous theme accentuates this fact: this is made clear if we move around a retrospective exhibit of Pollock or Rothko, true labyrinths of more or less distorting mirrors.

But what about literature? I don't dare to pretend that its mimetic function gives it, more than painting, the possibility of comparing the resemblance of the text to the originals of the world. But the powerful fascination of works such as the *Human Comedy* and *Remembrance of Things Past* is perhaps due more than one believes today to what Balzac called his "competition with the civil status" and Proust his "translator's task" and thus to a certain *relation* (of similarity or dissimilarity) if not with the real at least with the idea the reader has of it and which takes its place. Whether it is competition or translation, the realist simulation is still, or already, a variation on an obligatory, which is to say an agreed-upon, theme that we call history, society, truth, happiness, lost time, whatever, and that the most "faithful" representation invites us, not without detours, to *ricercare*.

Jakobson taught us some time ago the poetic significance of the "principle of equivalence," and, if I sometimes grumbled, it was in fact against an overly reductive interpretation of this principle, an interpretation that did not read in it the simultaneous presence of similarity *and of dissimilarity*, which is clear from the simple work of meter, of rhyme, of strophe, and in which Wordsworth already saw the main source of poetic pleasure. Narrative texts, to be sure, too rarely exploit this type of resource, except for the regular parallelisms of tales and the recurrent formulas of epics. Novelistic discourse ordinarily follows its course without turning back on its traces, often pursuing a linear suspense; only the New Novel has introduced into it, by the play of unstable descriptions, imperceptibly metamorphic, a dimension we have to call "musical."

But the comparative study of manuscripts and of successive editions comes to the rescue here: from one state to another, a "same" page by Flaubert, by Proust, by Joyce, unfolds its fan of repetitions and repentances, of deletions and substitutions, in restorations that are increasingly rigorous and increasingly disconcerting: indefinite tremblings and stutterings of a creation that proceeds always and everywhere from a vigilant and constantly adjusted improvisation, like the dance on a tightrope. The radiographic study of pictures and live films, like the irreplaceable *Mystère Picasso*, offers a similar spectacle. In the absence (?) of analogous effects in music, we at least have at our disposal, like in the theater, the infinite variety of interpretations or, as one says, of *executions*.

At the limit, and contrary to the surface evidence, all the arts are, in their productive gesture, performing arts; no performance is identical to any other, and, as a Valéry or a Borges felt correctly, there is no definitive state, except for reasons of fatigue or superstition. Completion—the repose of identity—is no more the aim of art than of life; it is its end, the fall into entropy, whose other name is death. Let Apollo and Dionysus grant us some time yet, some leisure time to repeat and to contradict ourselves.

Who is the one who said, "At the beginning was variation"?

10

A Logic of Literature

Here we have, at long last, the French translation of one of the most celebrated monuments of modern poetics.[1] It is also, no doubt, since its initial publication in 1957, the most massively glossed and most fiercely debated. This turbulent reception is due to its radical and (intentionally or not) rather provocative presentation. The controversy, however, has largely addressed points of detail, logical consequences of a fundamental choice that, for some strange reason, has not received as much attention on its own.[2] These points of detail concern, among other things, the exclusion of first-person novels from the fictional domain; the characterization of lyric poetry as reality statement— not, to be sure, on the same basis but to the same degree as ordinary statements of daily life; the absence of the narrator from fictional narrative; the atemporal value of the "epic preterite" and, more generally, of grammatical tense in the language of fiction.

This brief preface is hardly a suitable place for further debate of these controversial issues. I believe, moreover, at the risk of offering a purely personal interpretation, that it will be more useful to stress the grounds of the work's overall argumentation.

An attempt to anchor its boldly innovative thesis in the secular tradition of Western poetics would locate its ideal starting points in a Hegelian remark and an Aristotelian gesture, both in fact invoked at the book's inception. The remark by Hegel is that "poetry" (in the broad meaning that the author of the *Aesthetics* gives to the word *Dichtung*, coextensive with our concept of literature) is an art "where art begins to dissolve and to verge, from a philosophical viewpoint, on its point of transition . . . to the prose of scientific thinking." Freely interpreted: literature, unlike painting or music, is not an art that can be defined in itself and immediately identified with the employment of specific material; its medium, language, is the most trivial in the world; and nothing is more difficult to trace a priori than a clear borderline between literary usages of language and its everyday usages once the existence of prose literature has come to invalidate versification as a differentiating criterion. This criterion itself had already appeared irrelevant, or insufficiently rigorous, to Aristotle: his *Poetics* excludes from the field of *poiesis* all discourse in verse (lyric or didactic) that does not apply to the mimesis of human actions, which is to say to dramatic and narrative *fiction* (as Käte Hamburger incisively insists on translating the Aristotelian term). Non-"mimetic" verse does not pertain to *poiesis*: it simply uses verse (and some related formal and semantic devices) to ornate a discourse that remains simply a discourse (or, as Hamburger would say, a reality statement) aimed at communicating knowledge, opinions, feelings, without in any sense calling on the power of *creation* that defines *poiesis* and gives it artistic status.

In its way the Aristotelian partition thus anticipates an answer to Hegel's question—a question that, despite its banality, cannot be dismissed: "What is literature?" Elaborating somewhat on the Stagirite's thinking, one might articulate the relationship as follows: "In the loosely defined field of what one commonly and confusedly calls literature, the only acreage to which one can assign the status of art (in the sense of creation) with any degree of certainty is fiction, both in its dramatic and its narrative modes. All the rest, whether or not it is adorned by verse, is only discourse. The aesthetic feeling that may or may not arise from its fluctuating reception will not, at any rate, be subject to indisputable and objective criteria."

It thus appears that this partition results from the refusal of a purely aesthetic criterion, one that would follow a judgment of the type: "this text is literary because it is beautiful," which in actuality always means: "this text is literary *for me* because I *find it* beautiful." In the wake of Aristotle, with the field of fiction widened to include prose, this approach has inevitably become strengthened and justified: the aesthetic criterion was further "dissolved," that is, subjectified, by the removal of the doubtful but formally decisive mark the employment of verse imprinted on it. Since the advent of the novel and prose drama, and even more clearly since the invention of "free verse" and "prose poetry," since the "dissolution," in sum, of the partition between verse and prose, the choice Aristotle had refused ("I call literature all and nothing but writing verse") has quite simply become untenable—proving, if nothing else, that Aristotle had flair. By the same token it has become increasingly hazardous to rely on an aesthetic criterion, since it allows all texts, and even entire "genres," to enter and exit the literary field in response to individual and collective judgments: according to readers, eras, cultures, a certain text (say the *Essay on Customs* or the Gettysburg Address), a certain genre (autobiography, oratory), will figure as literature or as informative or rhetorical prose. This attitude may well be justifiable, perhaps even reasonable, and it has clearly ruled, though more often than not implicitly, our entire critical discourse since the nineteenth century; but one should at least perceive and assume, as does Roland Barthes among others, its subjective foundation, resistant to all manners of generalization and, accordingly, all manners of rationalization.

To this attitude, which is precisely the one she qualifies as "literary aesthetics," Käte Hamburger opposes another, which she calls the "logic of literature." It consists in taking the principle of the Aristotelian partition, if not this partition itself, seriously, with a view of drawing up a list of genres (or types of verbal production) whose assignation to literature as art is incontestable and *independent of any kind of evaluation*. It should be noted that this principle leads not only to obligatory exclusion (of texts promoted to literary "dignity" on account of judgmental taste or pleasurable feeling) but also to prescribed non-exclusion, that is, obligatory inclusion. The fact is that arts such as painting and music have a great theoretical advantage: "bad" paintings or "bad" scores are nonetheless incontrovertibly painting and music and thus ontologically protected from all fluctuations in taste, all aesthetic value judgments; as a famous saying has it, "there are three sorts of music—good, bad, and Ambroise Thomas's." Some literary genres, to be sure, cannot be ontologically dislodged by aesthetic evaluation: a bad tragedy, a bad epic poem, a bad novel or sonnet, are nonetheless tragedy, epic poem, novel, and sonnet; their evaluation cannot affect this status, which is a matter of fact, not of value. And Käte Hamburger would no doubt agree that literature, in the strong sense of the word, consists of a group of genres to which this factual status applies. Which is why her logic of literature is a logic of literary *genres*.

Logic: the term may seem surprising, implying as it does a choice that authorizes a different (in this case larger) partition from the one Aristotle had proposed. The latter had opposed a priori to an aesthetics of literature a poetics in the strong sense of the word: "I call poetry everything that imitates [*mimeitai*] human actions by way of dialogue or narration." Hamburger's choice of a "logic" is prompted by criteria based on the differentiation of language types according to their usage or function. Normal (nonliterary) usage consists of the production of "reality statements," characterized by a polarity between the statement-object and the statement-subject. Hamburger discerns three types, according to the implied type of statement-subject: a statement is "historical" (in the peculiar sense she attributes to this term) when the statement-subject is personally involved, as in the sentence "I am a professor" or "How difficult life is!" (these examples, synonymous or not, are Hamburger's own); a statement is "theoretical" ("Parallel lines meet in infinity" but also "Napoléon won the Battle of Jena in 1806") when the statement-subject is not personally involved, when he states a fact unrelated to his own existence; a statement, finally, is "pragmatic" when it is oriented toward action, as in a question, an order, or a wish.

In its literary usage, by contrast, language is defined by the fact that it produces no reality statements aimed at intervening in the world. Here language has one of two functions: either to constitute fictional realities in their entirety, and more specifically characters functioning not as statement-objects but as autonomous objects: the case of narrative and dramatic fiction; or to produce reality statements whose function is not to communicate but to constitute a lived experience inseparable from its statement, its origin remaining essentially undecidable, impossible to assign to a subject conceived as real (the poet) or as fictional (an imaginary speaker): the case of lyric poetry. This is how the major, properly literary "genres" of fiction and lyric poetry (in verse or prose) are determined. Clearly, the term *genre* (*Gattung*) is here given a far more extended sense than usual, since the first alone engulfs all narrative and dramatic genres customarily distinguished by literary theory.

Designed in this manner, the field of literature could be said to consist, first, of the Aristotelian field of fiction; and, second, of the adjoined field of lyric poetry. This latter addition is clearly bolder, even as it fully displays the change in criteria: for it does not represent a facile annexation that would correspond, as is sometimes proposed, to making the lyric statement-subject into a purely fictional subject (a "character," more or less specific, involved in a kind of monologue). Käte Hamburger quite decisively refuses this kind of annexation, except of course in the case of poems attributed to fictional characters, as in *Wilhelm Meister*. Lyric statements have an entirely specific status for her, even if their distinction from the communication statements of ordinary language (and of nonliterary writing) is far more subtle than the one that applies to fictional language.

I said earlier that I would not take up the discussion raised by various details in this system, but I do have to insist on one of them—rather weighty in itself—to give a more complete, if inevitably summary, idea of the whole: namely, the aforementioned exclusion of the first-person novel from the field of fiction, though not of course from literature itself. For Hamburger first-person novels, regardless of whether they take the form of continuous (autobiographical) retrospection or of intermittent narration, single (as in a diary novel) or multiple (as in an epistolary novel), always result from a series of reality statements that can in no way be distinguished from the series of statements that constitute an authentic autobiography, diary, or correspondence. To wit, this *Life of Sinouhe* stemming from the second millennium BC, whose status—authentic memoir or fictional text?—Egyptologists have as yet been unable to decide. To wit also, I would add, the foundational text of the picaresque genre, *Lazarillo de Tormes*: were it not for the generic assumptions, it could easily be read as the actual autobiography of an authentic picaro. The fact is that a fictional autobiography—*Gil Blas* or *Felix Krull* (to cite only examples clearly above suspicion of authenticity)—preclude on principle all recourse to the typically fictional devices of the third-person novel, such as interior monologue, free indirect discourse, or psycho-narration, that would permit it to present as subjects any characters besides the protagonist or witness-narrator himself. In practice this abstention turns out to fluctuate unevenly: see the numerous infractions of this norm in *Remembrance of Things Past*, in which the novelist on occasion forgets the homodiegetic cast of his narrative and thereby unwittingly slides into the properly fictional regime. Käte Hamburger, far from ignoring these exceptions, nonetheless maintains (and to my mind correctly) that a strictly homodiegetic novel can be distinguished from real autobiography only by way of external criteria. First-person narrative accordingly does not derive from fiction but from *feint*, from the apocryphal simulation, as it were, of authentic autobiography. By way of this simulation it functions as an *intruder* within the field of fiction, whereas its natural habitat is much rather the field of lyrical statement.

Disconcerting as it may appear at first sight, this proposal nonetheless seems to me ultimately irrefutable on its own terms. It follows quite naturally from a highly rigorous definition of *fiction*, a definition that, aggressively but no doubt beneficially, perturbs our habits. Inversely, Hamburger sees in the ballad (understood in the Romantic sense) and in monodramatic poetry a kind of symmetric intrusion into the field of lyric poetry, with these crisscrossings constituting the order of what she calls "mixed" or "special" forms.

One might well decide that this final rubric reveals a kind of repentance, a correction after the fact applied to an overly rigid totalizing system: a system that—not unlike the Ptolemaic cosmology—can function properly only with accommodations that turn out to be costlier than a complete redesign. At the very least, however, the forcefulness of Hamburger's detailed argument prompts one to suspend such a verdict. What to my mind speaks most forcefully in favor of this argument is its quite evident and entirely explicit promotion of narrative fiction to the rank of what naturalistic classifications call a *type*, as opposed to a *species*, which is to say a category more essentially characteristic than others. On account of its more pronounced break with the ordinary functions of language, narrative fiction is manifestly for Käte Hamburger—rather in the way tragedy is for Aristotle, though for quite different reasons—literature par excellence. Dramatic fiction is a somewhat derivative form by virtue of its "diminution," which is to say its eviction of narrative segments and its reduction to pure dialogue; it is accordingly deprived of the potential to evoke the inner life of another person directly, a privilege granted solely to narrative fiction and the supreme achievement of literary creation. Cinematic fiction—whose presence in such a restrictive system might at first seem surprising but which is amply and strongly justified—turns out, by virtue of its animated image, to be in many regards closer to narrative fiction. Lyric poetry cannot be reduced to fiction, but its status as *Dichtung*, though wholly based on textual (internal) traits, is clearly more tenuous; the first-person novel, as already mentioned, glides into fiction surreptitiously, and all the rest is *not* literature.

This privileged attention accorded to narrative fiction has resulted in various misunderstandings, stemming from its apparently inevitable collusion with the discipline—"narratology" by name—that studies the devices of narrative in general and of fictional narrative in particular. Franz Stanzel has recently shown that Hamburger's thesis concerning (among other things) the absence of a narrator in fictional narrative can be seen to be compatible with narratological categories (which are almost always based on different positions envisaged for this narrator and correspondingly diverse types of "mediation"),[3] provided only that one situates each of these analyses on its own proper level: those of narratology on the level of surface narrative structures ("narrative discourse"), those of Hamburger on the level of deep structures productive of fictional worlds. More generally, it seems to me that the work of fictional narratology, always more or less focused on the comparison of discourse and story, assumes (by virtue of a provisional methodological decision) that the nonserious pretense of fiction—to tell a story that has actually happened—is taken seriously. Hamburger's methodological decision, by contrast, is to take fiction at face value and to examine it for its manner of creating a purely fictional diegesis by way of characters or imaginary actions (without granting the least attention to the notion of mediation). These attitudes, each legitimate at its own level, are compatible, but, since *one cannot simultaneously study fictional narrative as narrative and as fiction*, they remain disconnected: the "as narrative" of narratology implies by definition that one pretends to accept (the fiction of) the existence, *prior* to the telling, of a story to be told; by contrast, the "as fiction" of Käte Hamburger implies the refusal of the methodological hypothesis (or fiction), and by the same token the notion of narrative itself, since there can be no narrative without a story—for which reason a fictional narrative is nothing more than a narrative fiction.

To repeat: there is no connection between these two attitudes, but each is entirely legitimate on its own ground, anchored as it is to one of the sides of the paradox of fiction that demands of its reader, at one and the same time, faith ("I'll tell you a story . . .") and lucidity (" . . . which never happened"). The same dichotomy, it seems to me, would hold for dramatic fiction, which likewise, by its own means, "represents" an action that never took place. All told, three attitudes can be conceived in the face of these fictional arts: the first, clearly naive (and groundless), is the one taken by infantile realism: "to believe that it happened." The second, methodologically legitimate, is the one of narratology and "dramatology": to proceed as though it had happened in order to study the relationship between what is supposed to be happening and the manner in which it is "represented." The third is Käte Hamburger's: nothing whatever happened; we have before us neither story nor narrator but only a "narrative [or dramatic] function" that progressively *constitutes* what it pretends to represent. This radically formalist position is ontologically legitimate, for, if the fiction of fiction is that it is not fiction, its truth is that it is fiction. It is this truth that Hamburger obstinately states and restates and that she displays by examining not narrative techniques but *devices of fictionalization* (interior monologue, free indirect discourse, epic preterite, etc.).

It now becomes clear that this "logic" is closely affiliated with an enlarged linguistics: a statement linguistics, to which pragmatics has long since introduced us but which Hamburger—drawing at once on Wittgenstein and the philosophy of language—has had the merit of anticipating. It also becomes clear that the criterion she adopts excludes from the field of literature anything that does not derive either from fiction or from the lyric in strictly defined meanings, that is, everything that, in one way or another, derives from communicative reality statement: oratory, for example, or history, the essay, autobiography, all of which Hamburger, true to the rigor of her proposal, excludes without mention, in conspicuous silence. But it is clear that the potential conditions that would allow these genres—or, rather, their textual incarnations—to accede to literarity can in her view only emerge from an aesthetics, which is clearly not her purpose. For her literarity—for this is clearly what is at stake—entails a certain employment of language, or, rather (and this reminds one of what Sartre, in an entirely different perspective, said about poetry), from a certain *refusal to employ* language; it entails, in sum, the decision to constitute a fictional world made of language, an imaginary experience inseparable from its own resources. No matter how great the aesthetic achievement of a historian's work or an orator's or an essayist's, its essential purpose is to use language to communicate knowledge or opinions, and this excludes it from the realm of *Dichtung*.

The radicalism of such a proposal may be shocking (no doubt not intentionally: Hamburger merely wants to remain faithful to the evidence of a principle); indeed, it would be rather a pity if it were received without resistance, without scandal, for this is the price it demands for the "furious" (and perhaps infuriated) thinking it provokes. But, since my presentation has been limited to a summary statement of its thesis without reproducing its argument, I must warn the reader: this book is not merely paradoxical in the etymological sense and thus banally disturbing; it is also, in the details and steps of its analyses, terribly *convincing*. One can no doubt push it aside, either by refusing to read it or by pretending to have read it. But one cannot read it seriously—that is, listen to its arguments and understand its motivations—and emerge unscathed. I said a moment ago that the current (aesthetic) definition of *literature*, which stems more or less from Romanticism, is perhaps more "reasonable," by which I, of course, meant more prudent, more convenient. This one is at its antipode: it imposes the discomfort of an intrepid but in no sense delirious rationality, confronting the sincere reader with the irritating question: what if she were, quite simply, *right*?

In other words: what if we were unable to propose rational grounds for attributing literary status to such works as *De Natura Rerum* or the *Essays* or the *Confessions* or the *Neveu de Rameau* or the *Vie de Rancé* or *La Sorcière* or *L'Amour fou*? The acceptance of Käte Hamburger's theses demands this price, and I doubt anyone will pay it willingly. But who speaks of acceptance? It is much rather, in my view, a matter of disquieting our evidence and relativizing it; by realizing, for instance, that our implicit definition of *literature* is lame, that it is incoherent to include at one and the same time certain genres (tragedy, the novel) in which literarity is independent of all evaluation and others (the essay, history, autobiography) in which it is almost wholly dependent on evaluation. By refusing, or at any rate revealing, this incoherence, Käte Hamburger is certainly, as one says nowadays, "somewhat" right. Go see for yourself; you won't be sorry you took the trip.

11

The Diary, the Anti-Diary

One of the last texts published by Roland Barthes is that "Deliberation" on the diary[1] that was published in the November 1979 issue of *Tel Quel*.[2] It does not want to be a reflection on the genre ("There are books on this subject") but only "a personal deliberation, aimed at allowing a practical decision: should I keep a diary *in view of publishing it*? Can I make a "work" out of a diary?

Even more than his last book, *Camera Lucida*—but not without at least a thematic relation to it—this text remains for me inseparable from his imminent disappearance and from what, very personally, I feel about it. The most immediate reason is that we talked about this article when we last met, in the beginning of December 1979. It would no doubt be more accurate to say I muttered a few phrases that he listened to with patience and that he answered with a few evasive words, having on his part exhausted the subject with the text itself and having turned the page. I will not try to reconstitute this "conversation" here but to articulate my feeling a little better than I did on that day—it was a rather gloomy afternoon, in the backroom without warmth of a café on the Place Saint Sulpice.

The first sentence of that *deliberation* coils around a slight and almost unnoticeable anomaly of discourse: "I have never kept a diary, or, rather, I never knew if I should keep one." The anomaly is clearly in the corrective *or, rather*, which links two propositions the relationship of which is not one of correction: one would "rather" expect an explicative *for* or a reinforcing *and even* or else a corrective of enunciation of the *que dis-je?* type—it is the figure of the rhetorical *correction* itself, which always introduces a semantic reinforcement—or, finally (but in this case the second proposition would have to be formulated not negatively but positively, even as it designates the same situation of thought), an adversative link like *and nonetheless*: "I have never kept a diary, and nonetheless I often asked myself if I should keep one." Compared to all these hypothetical formulations, the one of Roland Barthes presents the particularity that the *or, rather* there retracts the first proposition not as insufficient but as inexact.

This kind of statement has nothing that is abnormal in itself ("I have never seen Peter, or, rather, I have seen him only once and from a distance"), but this one is clearly abnormal because the implicit retraction introduced by the conjunctive locution contradicts the second proposition: according to "good logic," or popular wisdom ("When in doubt, abstain"), when one does not know if one should do something, one does not do it; there is thus an apparent lack of logic in saying or in suggesting: "I have never kept a diary, or, more exactly, I never knew whether I should keep one." One remarks, however, that this last sentence becomes more "acceptable" if one develops its implication in the form: "I have never kept a diary, or, more exactly, I did keep a diary, but I have never known whether I *should* keep one." More acceptable, without a doubt, thanks to the *but*, which admits, and thus assumes, the lack of logic or the paradox, like all explicitly concessive sentences: "Even though I never knew whether I should keep a diary, I did keep one," or "I never knew whether I should keep a diary, but I did keep one" (understood: "Yes, I know that it's not logical, but it's a fact, I am like that, these are things that happen, etc.").

But these normalizing rewritings are clearly not faithful to the Barthesian statement, the characteristic of which is precisely not to evacuate the contradiction by stating it but, on the contrary, to maintain it by veiling it—the (very light) veil being the use of the equivocal *or, rather*. For, finally, Barthes does write, and not without reason, that he never kept a diary, and until now our only reason to doubt it is the *more exactly* that we think we must read under his *rather*. The question is thus asked whether he has, or has not, kept a diary, and, for lack of being able to draw other indications from this first sentence itself, we are forced to refer to its context, that is to say, to its sequence.

The following sentence, in fact, is enough to enlighten us and perhaps, in a certain way, to eliminate the contradiction: "Sometimes, I begin, and then very quickly I let go—and yet, later on, I begin again." Roland Barthes has thus several times embarked on keeping a diary and (but) has each time very quickly stopped. This can or cannot be called "to keep a diary," depending on the definition. For Barthes the answer is negative, but, more or less silently, he feels that for others it could be positive. Whence the compromise that one knows, and that I will now gloss heavily but, I think, faithfully, thus: "I have never kept a diary, at least in the sense I give to this locution, for, each time I begin, I stop very quickly because I don't know if I should continue."

One could compare this intermittent practice (the third sentence begins: "It is a slight, intermittent desire . . .") to, among other things, one of these systems automatically regulated by means of a thermostat: the diarist's "desire" triggers diarist writing, which, very quickly, discourages and de-motivates him, whence the halt of writing, whence the renewal of the desire, etc. In the absolute (that is to say, in the absence of all internal erosion or external intervention) such a system could function indefinitely on the mode of an assumed, even a demanded, intermittence: "I keep my diary when it pleases me, namely, to be precise, from time to time." Is this called "keeping a diary"?

In the strict sense, or at least in the etymological sense, clearly not, unless the rhythm of intermittence is precisely daily—which is manifestly not the case here: to keep a diary means to note each day what one has lived and thought. But a lot of diarists exempt themselves from this daily discipline, which would perhaps often lead them to a laughable "nothing to report," to the "existentialist" degree zero of Roquentin: "Tuesday: Nothing. Existed," or the auto-referential minimum: "Today, wrote this sentence." One can thus quite well keep one's diary in a less than daily rhythm (or, inversely, a more than daily rhythm), weekly or monthly, or, as in the CNRS,[3] in a yearly report (that would not be so bad), or, of course, without a predetermined frequency or periodicity. This hypothesis does not respect the strong meaning of the verb to keep, which definitely does not imply that one "lets go," but this meaning cannot be maintained except in a Sternean or Borgesian sense of a writing that is rigorously constant and uninterrupted; even if one disregards the physical difficulties, the logical impossibility of such a practice is immediately obvious: a diarist who would rigorously spend all the time he does not need for sleep or subsistence (without even letting go of it during these interludes) in front, or in back, of his diary would not have much to record, except to detail his dreams, his meals, etc., and would quickly escape toward some form of fiction or of meditation outside the thematic norms of the genre.

Let us therefore say that the diarist practice is by definition intermittent and that no one can without pedantry determine its optimal, or even its minimal, frequency. What is it, then, that excludes from the field of this practice the Barthesian type, which consists, from time to time, of beginning and then "letting go" of a diary? Externally, probably nothing, and, supposing that Roland Barthes conserved and left in order the totality of the written signs of his successive attempts, nothing would forbid one on principle from publishing them under the title of Diary, or better, and according to an attested custom, Pages from a Diary. The exclusion is clearly altogether internal, and it does not relate to a practical decision such as destroying a copybook or forbidding its publication: it relates to the fact that the intermittent diarist (let us understand by this phrase not the one who keeps his diary intermittently—

the case of all diarists—but the one who only intermittently takes on the diarist *project*), each time he "lets go" of his diary, thinks he does so definitively and because he (again) persuaded himself by a (new) diarist attempt of the vanity—in what concerns him—of this practice. Putting down his pen after a few pages (a few days) he is not a diarist who (provisionally) interrupts himself but a diarist who (definitively) renounces, and by this not only stops but denies, perhaps legitimately, having ever been a diarist: "I have never kept a diary." What defines a diarist is less the constancy of his practice than the constancy of his project.

I have written "*perhaps* legitimately" because a doubt exists here and a difficulty: would a person who kept his diary for ten or twenty years and who abandoned it one day with the intention never to return to it (I suppose there are many such cases) thereby exclude himself from the class of diarists? To be a diarist, does one in sum not only have to keep a diary without intermittence but without final interruption except death? This would doubtless be a condition as absurd as the preceding one or at least as exorbitant: one does not stop having been a diarist if one stops being one, and one is not a diarist by a nontemporal essence, even if some people—this is, I think, the case of Amiel—have written almost nothing else during their lives than their diary. And many writers have been at the same time diarists and, for example, novelists (Gide, of course), and others have alternated the practice of a diary and that of other genres, or types of writing: sometimes, therefore, *occasional* diarists. The borderline between the diarist and the non-diarist is thus not easy to draw, and the first proposition—immediately withdrawn but nonetheless stated by Roland Barthes—"I have never kept a diary," is thus not entirely justified.

It becomes perfectly justified, it seems to me, if one takes account, again, of the second proposition, which places the borderline elsewhere than on purely factual criteria of frequency or duration and which one has to read now as an annotation of the first proposition: "I have never kept a diary *in the sense that* I never knew whether I should keep one." This second proposition, or this second stage of the first, is by no means retracted by what follows— and not even by the words "it is a slight, intermittent desire." Desire is not a feeling of duty or of justification: I can desire and then—especially after having satisfied my desire—think it is wrong or simply state that this desire was not a reason. It was not nothing, but I'll come back to this. The truly distinctive trait of the diarist would then be that he does not generally put into doubt the legitimacy of the practice of the diarist but only his own in particular. He can provisionally, even definitively, stop keeping a diary, but he does not stop thinking retrospectively that this past practice was justified. In short the diarist is less the one who keeps a diary than the one who believes in the virtue of the diary. One could, going farther—too far, no doubt—define *diarism* not as an activity but as an opinion (a certitude): the one that consists in not doubting of the virtue of the diary. One would be a diarist the way one is a Baptist or a Taoist—without necessarily practicing and perhaps without ever practicing.

The fact is that Roland Barthes never stopped *doubting* the diary, or at least *his* diary. *Doubting*, to be sure, does not denote here a negative certitude (a positive disbelief) but a simple uncertainty: as he well states, it is a matter of an "insoluble doubt." But this uncertainty does not relate to what I have purposefully called, to defer the necessary distinctions, *the virtue* of the diary but only to one of its possible virtues: "the value of what one writes in it"; and the sequence specifies without ambiguity (we have already seen this) the order of value that matters here: it is the *literary* value, the value of the diary as "work." The quotation marks are Barthes's; they connote the modesty, or more exactly (*or, rather*) something like a mixture of tact and irony in respect to his own ambition, or nostalgia and the perhaps reprehensible, or ridiculous, system of values that it implies; but the nature of this ambition, *or, rather* of this demand, is clear: it is an aesthetic demand. What Barthes doubted was the literary value of his possible journal as a work, and, if I dare say so, what periodically reinforced his doubt was the reading (the "rereading") of the few pages resulting from these aborted attempts at a diary.

I said that literary (aesthetic) value is only one of the possible "virtues" of the diary, and I suppose that many diarists did not think of it; perhaps the very ones on whose example he is meditating, or brooding: Tolstoy, Gide, Kafka. The diary (close to memoirs) can fulfill a documentary function for another person, for a posterity not of admirers but of curious people: "don't I have a vivid pleasure reading in the diary of Tolstoy about the life of a Russian lord of the nineteenth century?" or in the one of Pepys about the life of a middle-class Englishman of the seventeenth?—but Barthes certainly did not consider himself as a representative personage, nor even as an especially interesting one, of his era or milieu. Or cathartic, for himself: "for example, Kafka kept a diary to 'uproot his anxiety' or, if one prefers, 'to find his salvation.' This motive would not be natural to me, at least not constantly. The same is true for the purposes one traditionally attributes to the diary: they no longer seem pertinent to me. One related them all to the benefits and to the prestiges of 'sincerity' (to tell oneself, to enlighten oneself, to judge oneself); but psychoanalysis, the Sartrean criticism of bad faith, the Marxist criticism of ideologies, have made confession futile: sincerity is only an imaginary to the second degree." This makes the round, for Roland Barthes, of the practical functions of the diary, which he thus objects to successively, in general (the myth of "sincerity" and the examination of conscience) and in particular: I am not sufficiently anguished; my life is not sufficiently interesting. And he concludes: "No, the justification of a Diary (as a work) could only be *literary*, in the absolute, even if nostalgic, sense of the word."

One notes here the very surprising omission of one of the most obvious and most well-known functions of the diary, its role as memory help. The more surprising since Barthes, without actually complaining about it, often qualified his own memory as weak and "hazy." This, I must specify here for my own sake, is an infirmity that we shared. Two or three things that mattered, and that still matter, happened to me some time ago, but I can hardly designate them with a vague, or at least abstract, formula. From an intense effort at willful reconstruction I can only draw a destitute and suspect scenario, laboriously illustrated by a few erratic, hazardous, and contingent images. As for "involuntary" memory, not everyone has the miraculous gifts of the Proustian narrator. When I happen to evoke these things, I feel very intensely, and painfully, the bareness of my archives (discarded letters, photographs lost or never taken), and the absolute lack of what a diary, even of a half-page per day (what a multiplication!), would provide by way of details, which would fortunately interest only myself—that is to say, testimonies, perhaps one should say *proofs* of existence. Incidentally, but strongly, Barthes evokes this "flaw of the subject," which is neither more nor less than a "flaw of existence": "what the diary asks is not the question of the Madman, 'Who am I?' but the question of the Dumbfounded: 'Am I?'" The person without memory is this comical dumbfounded. The amnesiac, like the deaf or the shortsighted, is a comic role (whereas the blind is, as Sophocles understood, a tragic role), and the amnesiac without archives is, like Professor Tournesol, without hearing aid, like Mr. Magoo without glasses. The diary is a prosthesis, but it is a preventive prosthesis, the necessity of which reveals itself only after the fact, that is to say, too late for him who did not take the care (or have the taste) in time. It is possible, however, that the care of a diary, by one of these ironies that occur often in real life, is more urgent for those who need it least (the non-amnesiacs), like money always goes to the rich and water to the river—unless the diarist exercise is itself at the same time a substitute and an auxiliary: a *supplement* to memory, the fact of noting each evening the event of the day, fixing it not only on paper but in memory. In short one should train every young child to keep a diary and take care as much as possible that he never loses the habit. *Nulla dies sine linea*: this precept of the poet should be a universal maxim. For the diary does not limit itself to posing the question *Suis-je?* It answers it, and in the affirmative.

As far as I remember (!), it was on this point that I had tried, that dusky afternoon, to shake the uncertainty of Roland Barthes on this theme, preaching the diarist cause as nonpracticing believer: the literary value is of little importance; keeping a diary is a beneficial exercise and a necessity, perhaps a *condition* for existence. Vaguely taken by the voluntarist topos (there was in him a sort of semi-nostalgic fascination with any sort of asceticism—it is not for nothing that he had written his *Spiritual Exercises*—and he liked from time to time to sketch out some moral reform, *vita nova*, new regime, new timetable for work, etc.), he played with this suggestion for a moment, until he "realized" that first of all it came a little late (none of us, I hope, suspected *how* late), since it in no way answered *his* question: "Should I (now) keep a diary with a view of publishing it? Can I make a *work* out of a journal?"

For this was, I thought so and I still think so, a real question, I mean a question he asked in this text of his readers, not only of himself. To wit the dialogic tone in this sentence, placing onto the scene the inner image of another: "The question I ask myself: *Should I keep a diary?* is immediately provided, in my head, with an unpleasant answer: *Who gives a damn*, or, more psychoanalytically: *That's your problem.*" And as *uncalled-for* (next to the question) as my answer was, I believe—I hope—that it will have indicated to him that someone, among others, could have answered him something else.

But, finally, "his problem" was not the one that I ingeniously tried to foist on him—and it remained whole. The diary really attracted him, for his part, neither as a document (Tolstoy) nor as an instrument (Kafka) but as a work, that is to say, as a *monument*, and he felt this monumentalization of the diary was forbidden him by three principal defects: the subjective contingency ("I cannot invest in a diary like in a unique and monumental work that would be dictated to me by a crazy desire"); the objective lack of necessity (no page of a diary is indispensable to its entirety, the diary is thus a text that is "infinitely deletable"); and, finally, perhaps principally, the inauthenticity: diarist writing (nominal sentences, abbreviations, etc.) is not doubtless the most coded but the most *contradictorily* coded: "to report a mood in the coded language of the Statement of Moods." An unbearable practice that constantly sends back to you, like an indiscreet mirror, the pale and vaguely obscene image of a *naked* writing—it is not by chance that I use a Sartrean vocabulary here: the retrospective uneasiness of Barthes before his own diary is a reduced version of *Nausea*, and this disgust with contingency is based, in him as in Roquentin, on a valorization of Art as a domain of necessity and thus of justification (his *Some of These Days* was, certainly, the work of Schumann).

The aesthetically negative aspect of the diary (its literary anti-value) was so dissuasive for Roland Barthes and its practical value so negligible that one can ask oneself why its fascination, or rather its temptation, remained so vivid for him—perhaps constantly since his first published text, "Notes sur André Gide et son journal," which appeared in 1942 in Existences,[4] and apparently growing in the last years, marked as one knows by works very close to the diarist model (*Roland Barthes par lui-même*, *Fragments d'un discours amoureux*, and already in a certain way *Le Plaisir du texte*, without taking account of the chronicles in the *Nouvel observateur*, which he interrupted, in an impulse manifestly similar to the one retraced in "Deliberation"), formally (by the fragmentary writing) and thematically: by the declared egotism—though he notes precisely here, "of egotism I am fed up."

One immediate reason for it is indicated here, of which one must not ignore the weight for a writer constantly tormented by the rhetorical question of the *inventio*: "In a first period, while I write the (daily) note, I feel a certain pleasure: it is simple, easy. There is no need to suffer in order to find *what to say*: the material is there, right away; it is like a mine under the open sky; all I have to do is bend down." But the ransom of this "easiness" is seemingly the weak pleasure of the reading: there would be here something like an iron rule of textual (libidinal) economy. Nonetheless, it was not only a matter of the easiness of writing or of the substitute for a failing "inspiration"; it was, rather, a matter of a way (the only one perhaps) of discharging the famous (and problematical) "intransitivity" of literary writing, the diary being here the closest to the *book on nothing*.

I think nevertheless that I perceive a different, more obscure, more emblematic reason, across the very fact, paradoxical at first sight, to *publish* here, framed by the deliberation, a few pages, typical performances of a writing practice whose publishability is the very object of this deliberation—of this uncertainty. To the question publicly asked: "Can I publish this?" an irritated answer, and perhaps still more unpleasant than the foreseen (and defensive) "no one gives a damn," might have been something like: "A tardy and definitely hypocritical question, since you have just done so." This answer would itself have been sophistic, pretending to take "Can I publish this?" literally, when it clearly signified "Can I *continue* to publish this *kind* of text?" To which the cruelly salutary answer that Roland Barthes perhaps expected could have been, for example: "Okay for this once, but don't come back to it." This is no doubt the one he gave to himself, contemplating in the end as the only resolution (from above) to this deadlock a new type of work (a new literary genre?) that I don't want to describe in terms other than his own: "One would doubtless have to conclude that I can save the Diary only under the condition of working it *to death*, beyond extreme fatigue, like an *almost* impossible Text at the end of which it is possible that the Diary kept in this fashion would not resemble a Diary at all." If one defines the diary, among other things, by the facility of the daily happening, this almost impossible and *worked-to-death* Text (let us respect the uppercase) is in truth no longer exactly a diary (though it no doubt keeps its material, or its absence of material) but a kind of inversion of the generic model perhaps comparable to what Malraux aimed at in naming his Memoirs *Antimemoirs*. This almost impossible and mortally difficult diary would have been like an anti-diary. Is the *almost* too much? Let us not give in to the easy temptation of setting up the accident as a symbol, and let us dream in our turn this interrupted dream. Let us interpret in its light (for dreams, and even death, also have their light) the paradoxical design of this ultimate deliberation. Let us go back to the enigmatic first sentence from which we started, and let us reread it a little inversely: "I keep a diary to know if I should keep a diary—that is to say, if I can make an anti-diary out of it." A singular modulation of that question characteristic of a certain modern literature (Flaubert, Proust, Kafka) that he never ceased, anxiously, to interrogate: "I write to know if I can, if I am supposed to write."

12

Fantasy Landscape

My purpose here is to try to define the specificity, as a collection, of Verlaine's *Fêtes galantes*. This specificity can clearly be defined only in relation to the general appearance of collections of poems, which demands a detour by way of a question that is less textual than paratextual, often largely editorial, a little too much neglected by the critical tradition: what is a poetic collection? This question may seem too easy (perhaps the reason for its disregard): a poetic collection is a more or less thick volume—from the thin booklet that will occupy us to the imposing folio of Ronsard's *Oeuvres complètes* (1584)—made up of more or less short poems that,[1] separately, would lend themselves badly to the commercial practices of bookstores in the years before and, more so, after the invention of Gutenberg. This answer can in fact serve as a minimal definition, that is to say, one with maximal applicability: every collection of poems surely answers it. But it is just about as clear that most collections call for a more comprehensive definition, at least capable of indicating some common denominator for the collected poems: for example, the fact of having been produced by the same author; a more than commonplace, if not obligatory trait today, but we have to remember, without even having to go back to the disparate manuscripts of the Middle Ages, that the classical period (or at least the baroque)[2] consumed more or less periodic collections of the type *Parnasse satyrique* in large quantities, a practice still attested in the nineteenth century by the *Parnasse contemporain* (1866, 1871, and 1876): two of the poems of *Fêtes galantes* were first published in a *Gazette rimée* that seems to belong to this tradition. These modes of publication occupy with different nuances the entire space that today separates the mono-authorial (if one will forgive me this term) collection and the literary review. I will now leave them aside to restrict the field to the question of mono-authorial collections—with the exception, however, of collections that are less collective in the current sense (where the neighborhood of authors goes back to an essentially editorial choice) than pluri-authorial (where the said plurality proceeds from a voluntary and intentionally significant cooperation): the case, clearly, of the

Lyrical Ballads of Coleridge and Wordsworth,[3] in which the plural is reduced to two, but I suppose that one could find, by looking thoroughly, more numerous, if perhaps less famous, teams.

I will thus henceforth call "poetic collection" a collection of poems, in verse or in prose, published or at least created by one, or exceptionally more than one, poet, in principle before his death; a collection published posthumously but created anthumously, such as Vigny's *Destinées*, strictly corresponds to this definition; but posthumous compositions with a more strongly editorial initiative or organization, such as Chénier's *Oeuvres poétiques* and Hugo's *Toute la lyre*, could also reveal themselves (though quite differently) pertinent to our inquest: the grouping principle more or less freely adopted by an editor can be as revealing (of usage) as the one by the author himself. But this principle, whatever its source, can be of different orders: thematic, structural, formal, generic, purely chronological, even less than that if the collection coincides, explicitly or not, with the entire (poetic) work of the author, whether it bears (Whitman's *Leaves of Grass*) or not (Théophile de Viau's *Oeuvres poétiques*) a thematic title. Each of us can, according to his own criteria, consider one principle more significant than another: for example, the one that inspires the thematic title *Spleen de Paris* as more significant that the one indicated by the formal title (competing for the same collection) *Petits poèmes en prose*—but one has, in this last case, at least to recognize that the change of title is sufficient for modifying the "character" of the collection in the eyes of the reader, which should invite a certain prudence in appreciations of this kind. The character that is involved here, and elsewhere, is doubtless the degree of "unity" of the collection, and we know the nuance of value that is generally tied to this notion: a collection judged heterogeneous or disparate is by this very fact a little depreciated, and the critic who favors it nonetheless, making it for a time the object of his study, will try to efface this stain by discovering some principle of unity. The effort fortunately never exceeds his (our) strength, at least as long as it is a matter of deciding on a thematic unity, for this is a domain in which the criteria are highly elastic and the interpretive resources just about unlimited; the demands for formal unity escape speculation a little more because the hermeneutic is of no help to someone who would want to present *Les Fleurs du mal* as a collection of ballads.

For reasons that relate not at all to the relative merit of the vanquished difficulty but to the implicit and spontaneous axiology of the "world of literary art," thematic unity is generally taken to be a positive value—the most positive of them all—which one is honored to ensure, beginning most often with the

author (and/or the editor), by way of the title and/or the preface or other paratextual means. Those who insist on the "diversity" of the assembled elements
are actually rare; Borges often does, and Baudelaire, who, in the preface-
dedication (to Arsène Houssaye) of the *Petits poèmes en prose*—without critics,
more royalist than the king, assenting—recognized the uncertain character
of a structure without head or tail, in which everything is "at the same time
head and tail" and of which the dispersed sections could be joined *ad libitum*,
in whatever order they needed. I will evidently not say as much of the *Fleurs
du mal*, of which the overall theme and the subordinated motifs are carefully
(if not, for me, always convincingly) indicated by titles and subtitles and for
which Baudelaire "solicited" this unique praise "that one recognize that [this
book] is not a simple album and that it has a beginning and an end."[4] I point
out in passing that this collection in fact belongs to the aforementioned category of complete poetic works, even if certain poems escape it, without this
mattering much. Let us note that the notion of thematic unity can be interpreted in at least two senses: the rather simple one of homogeneity, or what
Proust qualified (laudatorily) as "monotony" (if all the poems of a collection
treat the same theme or—to speak in a more distinguished fashion—go back
to the same thematic), and the one, more subtle in my eyes (and impossible to
define in general terms), of complementarity in diversity: it is perhaps the one
that Mérimée (or his editor) suggests in entitling his first collection of 1833
Mosaïque. It is true that this one played equally with several formal or generic
modes (novellas, *Lettres d'Espagne*, popular poems, little plays), but the said
complementarity can clearly also act on this plane, and nothing prevents one,
for example, from perceiving its action in a collection of poems of systematically diversified forms and of which the very contrasts make the structure and
the meaning; we will precisely find this trait in the one we will be concerned
with. The Flaubertian title *Trois contes* withholds even all suggestions other
than generic (and numerical)—which evidently never discouraged passionate
hermeneutes from attributing unity to it.[5]

I therefore do not think that it would be suitable to arrange the diverse
grouping principles enumerated here according to some gradation of importance: nothing obliges us to consider the supposedly thematic unity of Ronsard's *Amours* more pertinent than the one, supposedly formal, of his *Odes* or
of his *Hymnes*. I will thus consider these few types without basically attaching
too much significance to the order of their mention.

I just qualified as "formal" the unity of two of Ronsard's collections, but
it was by trusting their titles and supposing that their choice indicates, on

the contrary, that their author did not wish to suggest another common trait between their elements—which each reader, once again, can discover at will and perhaps advisedly. Nothing forbids one from finding a common theme to the poems of a collection with a formal title, such as Shakespeare's or Michelangelo's *Sonnets*, and it goes without saying that Du Bellay's *canzoniere*, *L'Olive*, *Les Antiquités de Rome*, and *Les Regrets*, are at the same time formally homogeneous,[6] collections of sonnets, and collections containing the thematic unity that their titles indicate, which signifies at least that these two principles (and perhaps others) are by no means exclusive and can rule together over one same grouping. But especially in the classical regime—in the large sense of the word that goes back to Greek antiquity and extends to the beginnings of romanticism and which Ronsard belongs to—a concept such as the one of *ode* or of *hymn* (or even that of *sonnet*) is not of a purely formal order (whatever one understands by this) but, rather, of a *generic* order, an order that most often includes thematic traits as well: the ode, the lyric genre par excellence (the term *lyric verse* is for a long time, as precisely in Du Bellay in 1549, a synonym of it, just like *La Lyre* of Tristan l'Hermite in 1641) contains, for example, in addition to the strophic complexity, that of exaltation in celebration, which is associated with it at least since Pindar, and that of "beautiful disorder," which Boileau will still assign to it; and everyone still knows today the thematic traits that (more or less) mark genres such as the elegy, the iamb, the fable, the satire, the epistle, the eclogue (or bucolic), and the ballad (of medieval origin and diverse functions, at least according to national traditions). This grouping principle thus clearly dominates the classical period, up to the *Odes et ballades* of the young Hugo, and it generally orders either the composition of collections with generic titles (Pindar's *Odes*, Virgil's *Bucolics*, Boileau's *Épîtres*, etc.) or the subdivision of collections of more or less complete (or *diverse*) poetic works, and often, at least in the sixteenth and seventeenth centuries, increased from edition to edition: thus, Théophile de Viau's *Oeuvres poétiques*, Saint-Amant's *Oeuvres*, and Boileau's *Oeuvres diverses*; typically in this regard the posthumous edition of André Chénier's *Oeuvres complètes* (after 1819), in which the poems are arranged under *Bucoliques*, *Élégies*, *Épigrammes*, *Amours*, *L'Invention* ("*poème*"), *Épîtres*, *Hymnes*, *Odes*, and *Iambes*. The romantic dislike, if not for genres (and for forms: we know Hugo's spectacular—given the immensity of the context—abstention from the sonnet), at least for their official denominations, will result, from Lamartine's *Méditations poétiques*[7] and Hugo's *Orientales* onward, in a generalization of thematic titles; these had almost been reserved up until then for narrative (more or less epic) "poems" of a certain size, such as Ronsard's *La Franciade*, Saint-Amant's *Moyse sauvé* ("Idylle héroique"), La Fontaine's *Adonis* or Voltaire's *La Henriade*, or didactic "poems" like Boileau's *Art poétique*, and Chénier's *L'Invention*. I say "almost," because fables and tales (see La Fontaine) always bear individual titles, and we know at least the short poems with thematic titles of Saint-Amant and of Tristan l'Hermite (but not those of Théophile de Viau), but these are not collections, and the collections to which they belong bear generic titles. And these two poets, though they certainly belong to the classical period, belong to its "baroque" side; the most typical title (of a collection) in this respect is without a doubt Gongora's *Solitudes*.

But the adoption of a thematic title in no way guarantees the real thematic unity of a collection, or, more exactly (since the elasticity of this notion allows one to assign a unity to every grouping, even the most fortuitous one), it in no way guarantees that a collection has been effectively composed—and still less produced—as a function of the theme that its title suggests. [8] The romantic period inaugurates a usage that exists until our own day and which consists in collecting the poems produced during a certain period, dressing up this grouping with a more or less evocative title. The most glorious illustration of this practice is found in Hugo, with the four volumes of the 1830s having titles that are more or less arbitrary and interchangeable: *Les Feuilles d'automne* (1831), *Les Chants du crépuscule* (1835), *Les Voix intérieurs* (1837), and *Les Rayons et les ombres* (1841). What follows will conform more to the displayed significance, since Hugo foresaw as early as 1848 a thematic division of his future production into "Contemplations," "Petites épopées," and "Poésie de la rue"; [9] the coup d'état will come to jostle this program by prescribing the satirico-polemical collection of the *Châtiments* (1853–70), but *Les Contemplations* will be published in 1856, waiting for *La Legende des siècles* (first installment in 1859) and *Les Chansons des rues et des bois* (1865). One can thus consider that Hugo, after *Les Rayons et les ombres*, renounces periodic groupings to impose on his poetic works a kind of a priori thematic classification, for which his exile production will have provided the principle, each poem written during this long period having more or less its marked destination or at least one determined by its character; the last anthumous collections, *L'Année terrible* in 1871, *L'Art d'être grand-père* in 1877, and *Les Quartre vents de l'esprit* in 1881, seemingly adhere to this same principle, which is further accented by the practice of subdivisions, thematic as well, inaugurated for *Les Châtiments*, thanks to the Bonapartist slogans ironically quoted as intertitles—and for *Les Contemplations*, despite the trompe l'oeil chronology of the "Autrefois"/"Aujourd'hui." [10]

Baudelaire will in his turn adopt this usage of thematic subdivision for the *Fleurs du mal* ("Spleen et idéal," "Tableaux parisiens," etc.).

The classical principle (more or less strictly used in its own time) of generic grouping is thus, not without exception, [11] abandoned, the modern practice making its choice between the model I will call "Hugo of the 1930s," more or less thematically entitled chronological collections, [12] and the model "Contemplations/Châtiments," collections authentically ordered by a thematic unity. I will not search through a century-and-a-half history of worldwide poetic production to provide two series of contrastive illustrations. It seems to me more useful to recognize that the difference between these two types is more gradual than categorical and, as I have already noted, strongly subject to interpretations and controversies and also that nothing, of course, prevents a chronological period from coinciding with a thematic preference, or perhaps a formal one, as in Baudelaire passing after 1857 from the verses of *Fleurs du mal* to the prose of *Petits poèmes*. It suffices for this that an author, after the publication of a collection, takes up the composition of another collection, whose principle of unity is strong enough to orient, all at once or gradually, the essential of his production during the following period—a little the way a novelist or a composer of operas stays a few months or a few years with a work and then devotes himself completely to the following one—even if it often happens that Balzac writes several novels at the same time (that is to say, alternately writes pages for each) and that Wagner abandons *Siegfried* in his forest (and thus the whole of the Ring) for more than ten years—the time, among other things, to write and arrange for the performances of *Tristan* and *Meistersinger*.

Be it said in passing: this comparison cannot get rid of—or, rather, it stresses—the difference in status between these works with a manifest and constitutive unity such as novels and plays and those composite works with an uncertain and largely artificial unity (or at the least an "ulterior" and "retrospective" unity, as Proust said of *La Comédie humaine* or, less justly, of the Tetralogy), [13] which collections of poems (or of novellas or of essays) represent; it stresses at the same time the difficulty of what I will call the quantitative concept of *work*: if *La Chartreuse de Parme* or *Tristan* can without hesitation be qualified as works, the same is not true of a collection of poetry, even if it is (relatively) as homogeneous as *Les Fleurs du mal*, since one can also give this quality to each of its constituents; to say the truth, *Les Fleurs du mal* is a work and *La Mort des amants* is at the same time a part of this work and a work in its own right—and this would be more difficult to say of a chapter of the *Chartreuse*;

the same ambiguity is clearly found in music: each piece of *Kinderszenen* or of the *Winterreise* is at the same time a work and part of a work, and it would be more difficult to say this of an act of *Tristan*. But there is no point stopping too long at this (onto)logical obstacle, which is perhaps nothing but a difficulty of language—even though the Latin word *opus*, which one uses in music, presents analogous difficulties: we understand that a movement of a quartet (or of a sonata or of a symphony) is not the entire work (despite the exception of the *Great Fugue* of the Thirteenth Quartet of Beethoven, separated after the fact into opus 133), but without a doubt only editorial considerations explain that there had to be six quartets to form opus 18, or three for opus 59.

Fêtes galantes,[14] as we know, is the second poetic collection of Verlaine, published in July 1869. The first, *Poèmes saturniens* (November 1866), illustrated quite well the practice I spoke of earlier of chronological collections with a retroactive thematic unity: the essential of the anterior production (going back, if one believes the late project of a preface, "Critique des Poèmes saturniens," to the lycée years),[15] placed after the fact[16]—in a rather artificial and not very convincing manner, by way of title and introductory poem—under the invocation of Saturn and with internal subdivision à la Baudelaire: "Prologue." "Melancholia," "Eaux fortes," "Paysages tristes," "Caprices," "Épilogue." The passage of the first to the second collection illustrates a thematic conversion of which I have not yet given an example. For lack of authorial testimony and of genetic traces in the manuscript,[17] we ignore at what moment Verlaine conceived the purpose of the whole, but one can infer it with some verisimilitude from the chronology of prepublication: two pieces, then named "Fêtes galantes" and "Trumeau" (the future "Clair de lune" and "Mandoline"), appear in *La Gazette Rimée* in February 1867. Four further pieces (and again those from the *Gazette*, now with their definitive titles) will appear in January 1868 in *L'Artiste* under the title "Fêtes galantes,"[18] six more under the title "Nouvelles fêtes galantes" in the July issue of the same revue,[19] and two finally in the issue of March 1, 1869.[20] The transfer of the title *Fêtes galantes* from the piece first so entitled, and which will remain the first in the final grouping, to the whole of 1868 suggests that Verlaine only perceived, after the fact,[21] not certainly the kinship of the two pieces from 1867, which was obvious right away, but the fertility of their common theme, which this transferred title designates with perfect accuracy. The two rebaptized pieces thus become six, then twelve, then finally twenty-two—if one omits those of March 1869, which cannot have been written before the rest of the collection (the printing of which was finished on February 20) and which thus do not have a locatable place in the process of amplification. A certainly modest amplification (*Fêtes galantes* remains—with the subsequent *La Bonne chanson* and *Romances sans paroles*—one of the thinnest collections published as a volume or, better, as a booklet), but it testifies to a real constancy of purpose, even if it is certain, as Bornecque remarks, that the years 1867–68 were not devoted exclusively to the writing of this collection: "In total, in 1867–1868, there appear, independently of the Fêtes galantes, twenty-one pieces, of which fourteen are in verse, seven in prose, without counting a music-hall revue written in collaboration with François Coppée."[22] These other "pieces" will be taken up later in other collections, in particular *Jadis et naguère* (1884). The "thematic conversion" of which I spoke is thus not without division, but it is altogether clear and proceeds precisely from a very distinct division (like the type *Contemplations/Châtiments*), in those few months, between those poems that correspond to the theme of the *Fêtes galantes* and those that Verlaine, whether or not they were published in journals, leaves aside because they are irrelevant to this purpose, including a "Pierrot" that a less strict choice would have included, given its titular personage. This poem, which is not second-rate, will remain unpublished in a revue until 1882 and will then be included, dated 1868, in *Jadis et naguère*; it no doubt owes its exclusion to its gloomy climate, which would not have agreed with the at most melancholy ("quasi triste") climate of the *Fêtes galantes*, and this decision (if one trusts the chronology given here) testifies to the precision of feeling of the author in respect to this work—the exact contrary of a ragbag and one that no doubt merits a different term from that of collection. I propose one that I borrow from musical vocabulary and that I will now try to justify by clarifying it: *Fêtes galantes* is a poetic *suite*.

Critics agree, without difficulty, on the thematic unity of the work: one qualifies it, since the article by Edmond Lepelletier (solicited for a long time by the author), as "homogeneous."[23] The motif is clearly indicated by the title, which relates to the favorite subject of Watteau, Lancret, Pater, and other painters of the Regency, recently made fashionable again by different historical studies, including the one of the Goncourts, and by many poetic variations, or "transpositions of art," among others in Gautier (to whom we owe this last quasi-generic designation), Glatigny, Banville—and Hugo, of course, whose "La Fête chez Thérèse" Verlaine knew by heart, according to the same Lepelletier.[24] I will not go back to the question of sources, well elucidated today, except to observe that the kinship is complex: a kinship that is many-barreled, since the pictorial reference itself borrows certain of its traits from an older "literary" genre, if one wants the one of the commedia dell'arte, with its Pierrots, its Harlequins, its Cassandras, its Scaramouches, and its Colombines; and that the baroque or precious pseudo-pastoral of the Théophiles or the Tristan l'Hermites is not without its echoes in the scenery, the climate, the onomastic repertory (Dorante, Clymène, Églé . . .) and the refined diction of certain of these pieces;[25] the hypertextual game is thus of an evidently deliberate double or triple mechanism here. I do not believe, moreover, that homogeneity is the most characteristic mode of unity in these poems. The most active trait seems to me, rather, to be the complementarity and mutual resonance of pieces with a very different accent and form that compose together a more inseparable sequence than would a more constant and monotonous series (which suggests, in this case wrongly, the quality homogeneous).

What makes these pieces most obviously diverse is their formal variation: unless I am mistaken, these twenty-two pieces do not share any metric schema.[26]

I do not pretend that this kind of diversity is entirely exceptional in a period particularly leaning toward formal virtuosity. I am not even certain that the two following collections, La Bonne chanson and Romances sans paroles, are much less diversified. But it seems to me that the undoubtedly willful contrast between these incessant ruptures of rhythm and of accent and the displayed unity of purpose is glaringly obvious; to measure it, it is enough to compare this disposition to a thematic series as homogeneous as Du Bellay's Regrets or Sponde's Sonnets de la mort, whose homogeneity is also in the adopted form, systematically reproduced from one piece to the other. I said before that this diversity contributes to the unity of the collection, which is, according to the already quoted title of Mérimée, that of a mosaic. It may be necessary to justify this apparent paradox further: I want to say that each piece, by its very difference, seems to bring a specific, and on this account irreplaceable, element to a whole that draws its coherence from it—or perhaps, rather, its cohesion—as in those complex chemical molecules in which each physical element contributes, in its way and in its place, to the stability of the whole. To draw on a less far-fetched analogy, let us say that each piece of Fêtes galantes behaves a little like the rhythmically and melodically "heterogeneous" pieces of a baroque suite (of dances), the succession of which produces, by its very diversity, an effect of necessity;[27] an undoubtedly largely illusory effect but one that the formal variation sustains more than would the simple, identical repetition, always marred by a suspicion of gratuity: after three identical forms, why not a fourth, and so on? The succession of the same is deprived of points of reference and thus seems deprived of reason; the diversified succession, as capricious as it may in fact be, seems, on the contrary, to proceed from a formal reason: after the overture an allemande, after the allemande a gigue, etc., each contrast suggesting a structured whole, and a regulated order, more significant than it is no doubt in reality: I suppose one can without damage mix up the cards of this game; one would certainly get different effects, which would seem no less necessary, given the irrepressible desire of the mind to motivate what is. The fact is, at any rate, that Verlaine wanted this order. If one could give to each metrical and/or strophic form used by Verlaine in *Fêtes galantes* (others evidently exist, even an infinite number of others) a generic name—rondel, sonnet, ballad, etc.—one would see this collection order itself in a manner quite comparable to the one that seems to rule suites of dances: after a piece of three quatrains of decasyllables, a piece of two sextets of octosyllables, etc. Without spelling out the twenty-two missing generic terms, one can imagine the motivational effect that would result from such a nomenclature, parallel, even analogous (a strophe being a sort of verbal dance), to the ones that music utilized for quite a long time.

Much as in a musical suite each piece distinguishes itself from the others at the same time by its rhythmic pace and by its specific musical motif—even, at least in Bach's *Suites for Orchestra* by its instrumental size[28]—each of the twenty-two poems of *Fêtes galantes* presents a climate all its own, or at least contrasts with that of the pieces that precede and follow it, and is in agreement with its rhythmic particularity, if it is not to a large extent induced by it. I do not want to detail these effects of thematic declension, which have been sufficiently pointed out by Verlaine's critics. One could define these twenty-two pieces as so many facets of the overall situation, which contains its aspects of furtive pleasures, of melancholy dreaminess, of libertine allusions, of hyperbolic oaths, of cajoling serenades, of ironic dialogues, of silent ecstasies, of poignant regrets, with the contrastive emotions circulating from mask to mask, from grove to tree-covered path, from grotto to meadow, from treetops to waterfalls, without ever fixing on a stable tonality—except perhaps on that of a disillusioned organ—point, the (again saturnian) blackness of which seems to me a little artificial, as though to end on a serious note a whole that is not serious.[29]

This leaves for me to indicate what I believe to be the most specific unifying motif of this poetic suite. It again relates to a fact of disposition: the role played by the first piece, "Clair de lune," which, as I remind the reader, initially bore what became the name of the whole, a transfer that assigns it emblematically after the fact a sort of seminal function, as though the entire series emerged from this first poem.[30] But the most important, and also the most certain, is not this unverifiable genetic hypothesis but the relationship that this "overture" has to the pieces that follow it. This relationship, it seems to me, depends essentially on the initial sentence: "Votre âme est un paysage choisi . . . ." Bornecque sees the similarity with the Baudelairean formulas in which we get "that enlightenment of the internal universe by reference to an aspect of the external world" and for which he quotes several examples: "Mon âme est un tombeau . . ."; "Notre âme est un trois-mâts . . ."; "Vous êtes un beau ciel . . ."; "Je suis un cimetière . . ."; and "Tu ressembles parfois à ces beaux horizons . . . ," to which one must certainly add the "pays qui te ressemble" of the Invitation au voyage. We see that the "internal universe" evoked by metaphor is, in Baudelaire, sometimes claimed by the poet himself, sometimes attributed to some listener, sometimes generalized to a community that can be humankind as a whole: the procedure can apply to every personality with whom the poet enters into the privileged communication that this metaphorical description of psychic intimacy supposes. Robichez is probably right in supposing that the addressee of the first verse—and thus of the entire poem—is imaginary.[31] He perhaps forces the interpretation a little when he adds that this instance is apt to be "the poet himself"; at any rate this narcissistic hypothesis effaces precisely the "communication" (in the rhetorical sense of the term) that assigns this interior "landscape" to a virtual addressee and which seems in fact to be composed of two instances: the first, which the reader can only identify as feminine—poetic usage being what it is: the poet addresses a more or less imaginary woman, to (the soul of) whom he attributes the "paysage choisi" that the first poem describes; the second instance is clearly the reader himself, who will share this symbolic attribution as it develops in the sequence of the collection.

As a matter of fact, the nocturnal landscape here "chosen" and evoked (and at its origin specifically related to the world of Watteau) is not only a place, rather a park than a natural landscape, with its waterfalls and its marble statues—close to what Baudelaire called "fantasy landscape":[32] it is a scenery, in the theatrical meaning of the term: a stage, where immediately no less fictitious characters, "masques et bergamasques," come to evolve ("que vont charmant"), whose own psychology, clearly conventional, soon occupies the foreground. The seven verses that follow the first are devoted to them, which gives the whole of the poem a purpose that does not conform to the Baudelairean topos, quite simple when all is said, of the landscape as metaphor of the psyche: here "the soul" of the addressee resembles a landscape that is itself not at all deserted but peopled by characters, and these characters live their own interior lives, which one knows ("quasi tristes") or which one supposes ("Ils n'ont pas l'air de croire à leur bonheur"), and of which the relationship to the one of the addressee, which they are supposed to inhabit and "charm," becomes quite problematic. Everything happens as though the soul first invoked opened up like the curtain of a scene that it was supposed to present and which in its turn would have the function to present, as a prologue, the actors of a comedy (Italian, Marivaudian, or, as one has sometimes claimed, Shakespearean—dream of a night of the four seasons) of which the rest of the collection will trace the successive episodes (in a sequence, here again, interpretable *ad libitum*) of picturesque evocation, of gallant comedy, of melancholy ecstasy, of precious eroticism, of playful buffoonery, and other mixed feelings. This multi-barreled presentation thus places the whole on a plane of fictionality quite rare in collections of "lyric" poetry, usually devoted to the more direct expression of feelings more or less sincerely "experienced" by the speaker. What happens, is felt, is declared, and is played in *Fêtes galantes* happens, is felt, is declared, is played, between these fictitious characters that have first been presented to us in the overture called "Clair de lune," as in an opera in which the overture announces and sums up in advance, by the succession and the interlacing of its themes, the plot that is to follow. The anonymous "masques et bergamasques" of "Clair de lune" will later identify—unmask—themselves more and become animate, under their fantasy names, in diverse scenes, dialogues, processions, more or less discreet frolickings, pantomimes, shared and finally challenged feelings. And in this largely (though subtly) fictional context, the *je* and the *nous* that appear here and there do not refer anymore quite or simply to the "author": we have to take these diverse "first persons," plural and singular, as characters among others, as though the poet had little by little (since "A la Promenade," unless I am mistaken) himself entered the scene and had become one of his creatures; after which, the speaker of "Dans la grotte," of "Coquillages," of "En patinant" and the mock–letter writer of "Lettre" can *ad libitum*, and without obligation—without penalty—identify or not with the famous (and as we know always ambiguous) "lyrical I" and his (their) addressee(s) with the unknown addressee of the prologue to the moonlight. It is sufficient to compare this enunciatory situation to the one, of course more classical, of *Poèmes saturniens*, of *La Bonne chanson* or of *Romances sans paroles*, to perceive, by contrast, the generic originality of our "collection." *Fêtes galantes* is decidedly less a collection than a *lyric suite* but of a lyricism in which the feeling expresses itself in dramatic fiction—or, to say it better, dramatic *fantasy*—in the scenery, surely dreamed, of what we will later call "a love lesson in a park." I will not swear that this is a unique case, only that I know no other that is as perfectly accomplished.

13

Egotism and Aesthetic Disposition

"I feel through every pore that this land is the home of the arts. I believe they hold the place in the hearts of this people that vanity holds in those of the French." Those two sentences, from the *Diaries* of 1811, [1] present to my knowledge one of the first formulations of the antithesis in which is rooted the Stendhalian theory of what I will call "aesthetic disposition," this sociopsychological condition seemingly necessary, if not sufficient, of aesthetic experience. The antithesis is double, if one may say so, since it opposes at the same time two feelings, vanity and love of the arts, and two countries, France and Italy, each being the "homeland" of one of these two feelings, which it cultivates and symbolizes in a privileged, even an exclusive, manner. [2] The statement seems at first to concern more the *practice* of the arts (Italy as the homeland of artists rather than amateurs of art), but one immediately sees that it is here a matter of the "place they hold in the heart" and thus, if the words have meaning, of the feeling that one brings to them, the artistic vocation of the creators apparently depending on the aesthetic disposition of their compatriots.

The opposition of France and Italy, a recurrent and so to speak obsessive motif with this author, here only doubles—by illustrating it—the thematic opposition between vanity and love of art. Its largely mythical character is glaringly obvious, Beyle having decided very early—if one believes the *Life of Henry Brulard* and for almost too obvious "oedipal" reasons—to attribute, or rather to *affect*, to Italy everything he loves and, contrarily, to France everything he is disgusted by. I will thus neglect here (without being able to avoid its omnipresent manifestations in my references) this conceptually redundant allocation, in order to adhere to what it supposedly illustrates. The division is, in fact, more complex, even more unstable, than it wants to be because each of its terms is apt to reproduce it, *en abyme* as it were, within itself: France is divided between north and south, or between Paris (the realm par excellence of vanity) and the provinces, and Italy, eminently diverse, presents at least a significant opposition between Roman energy and Milanese tenderness and even an exception to the affective vocation that Stendhal assigns to it: namely, Florentine intellectuality, which "whithers the heart."[3] As for the Venetians, so likable and so "tremendously cheerful," they are quite simply (but doubtless in the best, or least bad, sense of the word) "the Frenchmen of Italy."[4] One can thus be a Frenchman of Italy and, conversely, as Beyle certainly wants himself to be, the most Italian of Frenchmen. Each city, by the way, can still diversify itself morally from one district to the other: thus, Roman violence is strongest in the Trastevere, or in the Monti: "These are terrible people," his neighbor says to the author of *Promenades dans Rome*, concerning some bloody incident; and the latter comments: "Note that this district is two steps from us, on the side of Santa Maria Maggiore; in Rome, the width of a square changes customs"[5]—and thus, without a doubt, at least the *color* of aesthetic disposition.

As one can observe, our initial statement still presents the antithesis in a weak version, and it barely indicates the motif, as though vanity and love of the arts were simply alternatives due to a lack of mental "space," whose narrowness cannot contain two feelings at once, like a garret that cannot hold more than one inhabitant. This crisis of psychic habitation does not yet imply a basic opposition between them but a simple, quasi–material impossibility of cohabitation: nothing tells us if, and still less why, vanity would be in some way contrary, and even hostile, to the love of the arts, and/or reciprocally. This weak version, if it were to be definitive, would certainly result from a strange conception of interior life; one suspects it to be provisional, and we will soon see what makes up the inherent incompatibility that motivates it. One also notes that the reason for this division of fact (exclusive predominance of vanity in France, of love of the arts in Italy) is not indicated; the explication (by climate, by history, by all sorts of other mysterious causes) that Stendhal will give throughout his work is rather complex, if not confused, but we will fortunately not have to worry about it here, since we bracket its geocultural investment in terms of *Volksgeist*. I observe incidentally that the excellent chapter that Michel Crouzet devotes to this point does not answer the question that entitles it:[6] "Why the Italian has no vanity." The answer, if it were there, would clearly be Stendhal's (I don't imagine that the critic would want to imagine another or propose his own), but it is not there, so that the correct title of this chapter would be more simply: "*That* the Italian has no vanity." The reason for this absence of (clear) reason is perhaps simply the imaginary character of the fact, a character that Crouzet does not stress but which the subtitle of his book pertinently suggests: "Essay in Romantic Mythology." *Moral Italy* is for the essential, it seems to me, a Beylist myth.

One last remark before proceeding: the opposition is established here between vanity and love of *the arts*: what follows will show, but we might as well state it now, that this feeling is only a particular case of what Stendhal hesitates less than we do to name "love of the Beautiful" and which I named earlier—in as banal a manner but less objectively (and thereby, as we will see, more faithfully to the Beylist position)—"aesthetic experience": what (French or not) "vanity" opposes (what it *prevents*) is not only the taste for the music of Cimarosa, the painting of Correggio, or the dome of Saint-Peter but also for the bay of Naples, the banks of Lake Como, or that famous (feminine) Lombardian beauty that sends us back to the very phantasmatic *Herodiades* of Leonardo (in reality of Bernardino Luini). The word that opens our sentence—at the same time atypical (in this usage) in common language and typical of the Stendhalian idiolect—will become the keyword of the aesthetics concerned (since it is one): "I *feel* through every pore that this land is the home of the arts." Such a fact (if it is one) is not ordinarily among those that we can "feel" but, rather, one that we can conclude, quite metaphorically and not without risks, from a complex set of diverse observations. The verb *feel* seems to me unconsciously suggested by the context and to proceed from an implied sliding of the object to its perception: the particular disposition of aesthetic experience relates to the presence in the individual or collective subject of a certain *ability to feel*. This point, which we will meet again, of course, perhaps gives the beginning of a justification to the initial antithesis: "vanity" would hinder, specifically (and reciprocally?), the ability to feel. What is actually at stake here?

What Stendhal constantly names *vanity* is not exactly what this word designates in current usage: "[excessive] self-satisfaction and display of this satisfaction,"[7] even if these two attitudes are related and if the second is as contrary as the first to the aesthetic disposition: the vanity (in the usual sense) of the duc de Guermantes, which he reveals in saying of the *View of Delft*: "If it is to be seen, I have seen it," hinders him no doubt from truly appreciating this work, and perhaps simply from "seeing it," for a contemplation of this sort demands a minimum of self-forgetfulness, which this Proustian personage (who has a few relatives in Stendhal) is manifestly incapable of. But in the end the Stendhalian use of the term does not designate so much an excess of self-worry as a worry about other people, or, as our author prefers to say, *about others.* It is understood that this worry does not address the existence of one's fellow man; it consists not in an interest, still less in a disinterested sympathy, toward other people; it consists (and this is what motivates here the use, even indirect, of the word *vanity*) in worrying about the *opinion* of other people about myself and, among other things, about my taste—which contributes so largely to defining and manifesting me—and thus necessarily about the objects of my taste. The proofs of this meaning abound; here is one among hundreds of others, in which the keyword is opportunely equipped with italics: "This is the excess of our *vanity*: we want to know, before laughing about a pleasant trait, if the people of good taste find it so."[8] The clearest synonym of *vanity*, according to Beyle, which shows up frequently in his text,[9] is thus in fact the worry about *what one will say*. Another, less expected equivalent is *bégueulisme*, defined thus in *Racine and Shakespeare:*[10] "In common life, *bégueulisme* is the art of taking offense on account of the virtues one does not have; in literature, it is the art of enjoying the tastes one does not feel in oneself"—the case of literature being clearly extendable to all the arts, to all aesthetic situations. *Enjoying the tastes one does not feel in oneself:* what this severe oxymoron, in which the verb *feel* is again used, designates is clearly aesthetic pseudo-enjoyment, which consists in adopting "good taste" and in regulating one's taste according to that of others. But I am no doubt wrong in saying "aesthetic pseudo-enjoyment": enjoyment here is no doubt real, though entirely mental, and what it lacks is being *aesthetic*, for it is precisely an enjoyment of "vanity," the joy of affecting (*affectation*, or the worry about "appearing," is still another synonym of *vanity*)[11] good taste and no doubt of persuading oneself that one truly shares it; it is thus in fact a *pseudo-aesthetic* enjoyment, an enjoyment that pretends, wants itself and at the limit believes itself aesthetic but which is only *social*, in the superficial and futile sense of the term, that is to say *worldly*, and which flourishes in the place carefully denounced by Beyle (who knew and no doubt regretted that he was not very brilliant in them): the salons.

Vanity, according to Stendhal, thus does not consist in overestimating oneself but in an almost contrary trend: subserviently looking for models outside oneself. Crouzet has it right: "The Italian is without vanity only because he has avoided interiorizing the existence of others; the other is real outside, not inside the self, as an image or a model."[12] All we have to do is to reestablish the antithesis in order to find here the reverse portrait of the typical Frenchman (let's say the Parisian), that is to say of the anti-aesthetic subject, who interiorizes the other as guide (as arbiter and as master) and, inseparably though reciprocally, as "image"—I interpret freely: as a mirror assigned to send back a flattering or reassuring image; a certain worry about the other is nothing more than an oblique, worried, [13] variant (but are there others?) of narcissism—"it is a terrible thing in France to be alone in one's opinion." [14] We still don't know why such an attitude is anti-aesthetic, but it seems to me useful, before asking that question and better understanding the answer, to consider the other term of the antithesis.

The contrary of supposedly French vanity rightly bears an Italian name: *disinvoltura*. I don't know whether the meaning that Stendhal gives to it conforms entirely to the usage (in his period) of this language—it clearly does not correspond to the rather pejorative usage of its French replica. But it is at least altogether clear: it is the indifference to the judgment of others on myself, on my actions, and still more, for what interests us here, on (the object of) my taste: "There is carelessness [i.e., insouciance] in this country only toward the what-will-one-say; that is *disinvoltura*." [15] Its other name, French this time (but the thing is not), is *naturel*: the Italian (since it is still he who is charged with illustrating the Beylean ideal) [16] "is the most natural being in Europe, who thinks the least of his neighbor"; [17] the music lover of San Carlo or of the Scala, "fully involved in the emotion he feels, not concerned with judging and still less with making a nice phrase about what he hears, does not worry at all about his neighbor, and does not think about having an effect on him; he doesn't even know if he has a neighbor"; [18] and one of his fellows, in Brescia, "whenever he sat at a concert, there would come a point when, in sheer delight at the music, he would proceed quite unconsciously to remove his shoes. Then he would sit quietly, shoeless, until the coming of some really *superb* passage, at which, unfailingly, he would fling both shoes over his shoulder into the crowd of spectators grouped behind him" [19]—apparently not to solicit their opinion. Stendhal presented him as "the true music lover, a ridiculous person quite rare in France, whereas you meet him at every step in Italy." But "there is no such thing as ridicule in Italy," [20] whereas in France the "lack of originality" is related (among other things) to "the despotism of ridicule": [21] "The only danger for a Frenchman is ridicule, which no one dares to defy North of the Loire," [22] because the Beyliste Italy, as one knows, often begins at this climactic borderline: "The South of France, especially Toulouse, has striking relationships to Italy; for example, religion and music. Young people are less terrified by the fear *not to be in the right*, and much happier than North of the Loire. I have seen much real contentment among the youth of Avignon. One would be inclined to think that happiness disappears with the accent." [23]

The essence of the "unselfconscious" or "natural" subject is thus to think by himself, [24] trust only his personal taste, and judge "all alone like a big boy." [25] In the realm of facts and ideas such a self-sufficiency of judgment can be a default or a weakness, since it hinders one from taking account of the most solid arguments. [26] But the aesthetic relationship precisely does not belong to this realm because it is nothing but an affective relationship, a feeling of pleasure or displeasure. A feeling does not judge itself, and, no more than I must let another judge my pleasure, I must not, and cannot, judge my own pleasure: "Here people do not spend their life *judging* their happiness. *Mi piace* or *non mi piace* is the great way of deciding everything." [27] The aesthetic appreciation is "so to speak an instinctive pleasure, or at least not a reasoned one, of the first moment [without which] there is no painting or music. Nonetheless I have seen the people of Königsberg arrive at pleasure in the arts by reasoning. The North judges according to its anterior feelings, the South according to what currently pleases its senses." [28] The mention of Königsberg (where Beyle in fact stayed twice and where he started, without apparent displeasure, to write *Mina de Vanghel* and *The Pink and the Green*) alludes spitefully, and perhaps wrongly, to Kant, whom Stendhal likes to take as the Germanic emblem of an abstract and nebulous metaphysics (without having read much of him) [29] and a fortiori without suspecting how much his own aesthetic subjectivism resembles the one of the *Critique of Judgement*— which he only pushes to extremes; it even happens to him to lend to Rossini a kind of rage "against some poor pedant from Berlin, who had the effrontery to stand there, armed with a few thin quotations from Kant, and to oppose the *instinctive feelings* of a man of genius": [30] difficult to do worse, but let us leave that typical moment of the history of misunderstandings. The fact is that for Stendhal, exactly as for Kant, pleasure can't *reason* with itself nor communicate by demonstrative reasons. "There are things one does not prove . . . how can one prove to someone that a thing that inspires a feeling of insurmountable repugnance can and must give one pleasure [and reciprocally]?" [31] Such a pretension is as absurd as would be a question like "Pray, Sir . . . am I amused?"; [32] for pleasure (or displeasure) does not obey orders any more than reasons, and to consult another (or to accept his advice) on a *duty* of pleasure is as inept as to consult him on the *fact* of one's pleasure—or of one's desire: "*To make it a duty* [to listen to the continuation of a concert]! what an English sentence, what an anti-musical idea! It is like making a duty out of being thirsty." [33]

This last comparison seems to illustrate an obvious trait of Beylean aesthetics, which one could easily qualify as *hedonism* and which would consist—this time, contrary to Kant—in often assimilating aesthetic pleasure to physical pleasure. [34] A manifestation of this tendency can be read in his musical tastes: his predilection for pure melody, the little interest he has in harmony, according to him too frequent in German music, Mozart, and sometimes even Rossini included, show it clearly; as does his pictorial preference for Correggio, the fact that he is devoted to the aesthetic emotions that are the "easiest" and the most favorable to what he constantly names *voluptuousness* ("*voluptuousness*, first aim of art"). [35] But this trait must not be exaggerated: Beylean voluptuousness is not basically of the order of "flesh"; the modest place he reserves for "physical love" is well known, as is his preference for Werther over Don Juan, in the very name of the "quantity of pleasure" provided by passionate love. As for eating: I don't know much about Beyle's alimentary tastes besides his passion for spinach, but his references to food in the whole of his travel "tales" are remarkably rare, and the fact of qualifying as "admirable" a coffee with milk and even as "sublime" (oh Kant!) "a coffee with cream, as one finds it in Milan," [36] does not seem to me to show a very demanding gastronomy. It seems to me, and I suppose that a lexical statistic would confirm it, that he calls "voluptuousness" (or enjoyment) not necessarily a bodily pleasure but an intense pleasure and that the most physical pleasures are not for him the most intense. The most revealing expression to designate the aesthetic relation is the use of the verb *feel*, as we have already seen. The "beautiful," in art and elsewhere, must be "felt," and he opposes all other approaches: "The more a Frenchman has a spirit like Montaigne, like Voltaire, the less he feels the arts." [37] In reverse, of course, the Italian is in all things the man of *feeling* (the noun *feeling* is seemingly a little rarer, perhaps because it is weaker or duller: the true *feel* is of the order of passion, possibly insane or violent): [38] "The true *feeling was made for them* [39] . . . the most sensible people in the universe," [40] and "the manner of *feeling* of Italy is absurd for the inhabitants of the North. I cannot even conceive, after having dreamt of it for a quarter of an hour, by what explanation, by what words one could make them understand it." [41] The relation to the beautiful is of the order of feeling and privileges beings "endowed by heaven with a rarer gift of sensibility. . . . In respect to painting, music, architecture, etc., the distinction between one nation and another rests upon the intensity of pure and spontaneous *sensation* which the average representative of the race—even among uneducated classes—derives from these arts." [42] The most refined description is found in this page of *Promenades in Rome*: Stendhal has just assailed the French spirit once again, "a sure preventive against artistic feeling," and for once he explains himself about this matter at some length:

> The French spirit cannot exist without the habit of attention to the *impressions of others*. The feeling for the arts cannot form itself without the habit of a somewhat melancholy reverie. The arrival of a stranger which comes to trouble it is always a disagreeable event for a melancholy and dreamy character. Without being egoistic, or even *egotistic*, the great events for those people are the profound impressions that come to upset their soul. They look at these impressions attentively, because from the least circumstances of these impressions they gradually draw a nuance of happiness or of misfortune. A creature absorbed in this examination does not think of coating his thought with a spicy turn, he does not think at all *of others*.
>
> The fact is that the feeling for the arts can only be born in souls whose reverie we have described. [43]

But this state of "somewhat melancholy reverie," which he also often calls "tender reverie" and which is clearly not the mark of an amateur of purely physical "sensations"—once again, the aesthetic subject is closer to Werther than to Don Juan (or to Falstaff)—is not only a condition for the aesthetic relation; it is also its effect. Rossini's duet from *Aureliano in Palmira*, is an example: "by plunging the listener into the remotest, most mysterious depth of reverie, it performs the miracle which is the surest hall-mark of truly great music." [44] One could ironize the profitability of this strange device, which produces nothing but what it has received, but it seems to me once again that the condition is of the order of the setup: the Beylean aesthetic subject is *carried* to reverie, and he finds in painting or in music the occasion to feel, or at least to maintain, it. This state of *absorption in the examination of one's own impressions*, which defines aesthetic voluptuousness at its climax, not only disdains the worry about the opinion of "others"; it cannot even bear their presence ("My stand is taken, I will always see the celebrated monuments *absolutely alone*," and again, "One must be alone in the Coliseum . . . in Rome, every cicerone kills pleasure"); [45] or at least it bears that presence only when it is silent and mainly capable of accepting your own silence: in Florence, in front of Santa Maria del Fiore, Beyle feels "happy to know no one, not to be afraid of being obliged to speak," and he adds: "I am ashamed of my story, which will make me appear as an *egotist*" [46]—with the occurrence of the word in this passage enlightening the meaning of Beylean egotism, which has nothing of a satisfied egocentrism but which is closer to a form of solipsism or at least of unsociability; [47] here he is on the Appian Way: "in order not to be obliged to speak, I pretended to sleep. I would have enjoyed it much more if I had been alone." [48] The point is that the "sensations" that such spectacles provide "can be indicated, but not communicated. . . . What a deception to speak of what one loves! What can one gain? The pleasure of being moved an instant by the reflection of the others' emotion. But a fool, irritated to see you speak to yourself, can invent a pleasant word which dirties your memories. From this follows, perhaps, that modesty of true passion which common souls forget to imitate when they pretend to have passion." [49] Solely solitude permits the growth of imagination, which itself alone allows one to respond to aesthetic "sensation": "The triumphs of vanity are rooted in a process of contrast, in a series of comparisons, deft-fingered and drawn with lightning rapidity between oneself and *other people*." [50] Already in the *History of Painting in Italy*, Stendhal evoked "those great rare men [of the Renaissance] that are today suffocated by the great principle of the century, *to be like another*." [51] This principle today seemingly suffocates great men in Italy as well as in France, which confirms the entirely relative character of the Beylean myth: Italy of the Renaissance is to modern Italy as the latter is to France—an ideal *elsewhere* (in time and/or space) and rather utopian.

We have seen how the enthusiast of San Carlo and of the Scala ignores his neighbor, the existence of whom he disregards, unless the latter menaces his ecstasy, doubtless by some inopportune commentary: "Plunged in a contemplative ecstasy, he has only anger and impatience to give to *others* who would keep him from soulful enjoyment. . . . There is soul only in his eyes, and, if one warns him of this fact, he hides his eyes with his hand." Some lines earlier, there is a furious assault: "Why *do* we start talking? Why do we feel impelled to appeal for sympathy to this vast *extinguisher* of enthusiasm and sensibility? *Because of our obsessions with other people!*" [52] And one must not think that this manifestly amused picture contains the least bit of criticism toward such excessive behavior: the question "Why do we start talking?" addresses itself seriously to the "poor sensible enthusiast" who "has in him still a little of the French character"—enough to want to "communicate" his feeling— and whom one strongly invites to get rid of it, following the example of the Neapolitan or Milanese music lover.

These tones of elitism or intolerance must not suggest, however, that Beyle assumes the monopoly of "good taste" and of aesthetic truth. His assured judgment—or rather *feeling*, of course—does not keep him from acknowledging the right of others to "feel" differently, providing they do not challenge him. In truth a relativism of principle is the best protection against every debate: I feel as I feel, my neighbor feels as he feels, and these two feelings are as "incommunicable" as they are legitimate and as legitimate as they are incommunicable: "Everyone has reason in his taste, however weird it is, for one is called upon to vote by counting heads. The error happens in the moment when one says: 'My taste is that of the majority, is the general taste, is the *good taste*.' "[53] And he affirms in *Life of Rossini*: "It will be only too evident that an expression of admiration can never prove anything save the degree of emotional excitement present in the admirer, and can have no possible bearing upon the degree of merit implicit in the object admired."[54] At the end of this same work Stendhal reproduces, under the clearly approving title *Apology for what my friends call my exaggerations, my enthusiasms, my contradictions, my similars, my etc. etc. etc.*, a letter by Julie de Lespinasse in which she declared: "I judge nothing, but I feel everything; and that is why you never hear me say: *this is good, this is bad*; but I say hundreds of times a day: I love."[55] This is how, in truth, we should always express our aesthetic appreciations.

In the absence of a Kant, whom he misjudges absolutely (and who would not have followed him as far as he went), and of a Hume, who ended up by denying his own "All sentiment is right," the guarantor of this profession of subjectivist belief is the Voltaire of the article on the "Beautiful" in the *Philosophical Dictionary*, whom he paraphrases in these terms: "Voltaire said it in a style that I would not dare to allow myself, so much has scrupulousness progressed since his time! Nothing is as beautiful in the eyes of a toad than his female toad, with her eyes sticking out of her head. Does one truly believe that a courageous black general, from the isle of Santo Domingo, admires the fresh color of the Madeleine of the Guide? Men have diverse tempers."[56] But in the *Promenades in Rome* he offers us his own relativist fable, which he places in the mouth of the economist Nestorre Gioia addressing the illustrious Canova: it is about the nightingale and the mole, each of which prefers his mode of living and feeling and both of which are wrong to want mutually to impose it on each other. And here is the aesthetic application: "Someone prefers the *Flood* of Girodet to the *Saint Jerome* of Correggio. If this person recites a lesson that he has just learned in some poetics, one has to smile at him agreeably and think of something else. But if he is friendly and presses us in good faith to respond to him, continued Melchior Gioia, I would say to him: 'Sir, you are the nightingale and I am the mole; I am unable to understand you.

I can only discuss the arts with beings who feel roughly like myself. But if you want to talk about the square of the hypotenuse, I am your man, and a quarter of an hour from now you will think as I do"[57] (from which one sees that aesthetic relativism does not necessarily entail epistemological, moral, or political relativism). The "philosophical" version of this relativist belief is the rejection of the notion, inherited according to him from Plato, of an *absolute ideal beauty*, a notion that leads one to uphold that, "if Raphael and Titian had been able to perfect themselves more at each instant, they would have arrived one day at producing *identical* canvasses [. . .] I dare not lead the reader to the amphitheater of the Jardin des Plantes; and it would perhaps be indiscreet to propose to him thereafter a little journey to Saxony, followed by a stay of two months in Calabria. If nonetheless he was willing to study literature in this fashion, instead of reading every second year, in *Le Philosophe à la mode*, a new explication of the *beautiful*, he would soon conclude, from hundreds of observed facts, that there are different tempers and that nothing differs more than the phlegmatic inhabitant of Dresden and the irritable scamp of Cosenza. I would tell him then, or rather he would tell himself (which is better), that the *ideal beautiful* of these people differs; and, six months later, he would finally arrive at this enormous proposition, which seems to him so bizarre today. Each man would have, if he really thought about it, a different *ideal beautiful*. There would be as many *ideal beautifuls* [sic] as there are different forms of noses or different characters." As it is true that "taste is local and instantaneous, so it is true that what one admires on one side of the Rhine is often despised on the other side, and that the masterpieces of one century are a lie in the following century."[58]

The first occurrence in Stendhal of what I call the relativist fable presented itself, in a quite typically elliptic form, in chapter 68 of the *History of Painting in Italy*:

> A blade of grass said to its sister: "Alas, my dear, I see a devouring monster approaching, a horrible beast that tramples on me with its large feet; its mouth is armed with a row of sharp teeth, with which it cuts, tears, gobbles me up. Human beings call this monster a lamb." What Plato, Socrates, and Aristotle missed was to hear this conversation.[59]

This historio-geographic, cultural relativism, in which an entire tradition inherited from the Age of Enlightenment—from the theory of climates of Montesquieu to the ideology of Cabanis and Destutt de Tracy—brings an important nuance to what I characterized earlier, and no doubt a little strongly, as "a form of solipsism." The diversity of individual tastes is at the very least framed by the diversity of collective tastes, in a set in which each one is determined from the outside more strongly than he thinks or wishes: I may not know "if I have a neighbor," like the music lover of the Scala, but the fact is that I have a few of them and that several factors can lead us to "feel" more or less in the same manner, possibly without knowing it and with each one thinking himself more autonomous than he actually is; as the Chinese proverb says, "one thinks oneself original, and one is a statistic." And one knows that the "Romanticism" of *Racine and Shakespeare* is defined (and recommended) in typically historical terms as "the art of presenting to the people [and not to individuals] literary works that, in the actual state of their habits and beliefs, are likely to give them the greatest possible pleasure," whereas classicism "presents them with literature that gave the greatest possible pleasure to their great-grandparents." [60] This enlargement of the field, from idiosyncrasy to what one could call *sociosyncrasy*, by periods or by generations, is certainly not reserved for literature nor dictated by the specific context of a militant pamphlet. The "Italian" works of Stendhal abound in indications of this sort on the comparative tastes of peoples or of centuries in music or painting, "according to races, climates, periods, government institutions";[61] and, after all, the very opposition between France and Italy, which permanently illustrates his thesis, relates to a doctrine of collective psychology: there is a French taste and an (or some) Italian taste(s), even if the Beylean bias most often prefers to see in it the radical conflict between a basic aptitude and inaptitude for the aesthetic feeling.

Another nuance concerns more specifically (but not exclusively) the realm of artistic relation. It pretends to proceed from a late observation, although it appears rather early in the Stendhalian text. Its first mention, if I am not mistaken, is found in 1815 in the *Lives of Haydn, Mozart and Metastasio*: "A thing I would not have believed is that in studying the arts one can learn to feel them." [62] Another occurs in 1817 in the *History of Painting in Italy*. It concerns here the ideal reader of that book, "some tender soul . . . unique reader, and that I would want unique in all senses. . . . Gradually the number of pictures that please him will increase. . . . His knowledge increases; he has new pleasures. He would never have believed that thinking makes feeling; nor would I have thought so; I was surprised when, studying painting only out of boredom, I found that it brought comfort to cruel sorrows." [63] I know that these two works are in part a tissue of plagiarisms, but the repetition, based on quite different hypotexts, seems to me a guarantee of authenticity, and here is a third occurrence, which comes from the less suspicious *Life of Rossini* (1824): "If only we took the trouble to study their scores with the care and attention that they deserve, we should suddenly be startled one fine day to find ourselves perceiving and feeling qualities in their music, whose existence we had never suspected! In all art, the road to appreciation lies through reflection."[64] The convergence is obvious; it relates (I synthesize without great effort) to that discovery—surprising in all three cases, without doubt because it seemingly contradicts the spontaneous certainties of affectivism: that in the matter of art to study and to reflect "makes one feel," that *feeling is learned*. Here is another testimony, more negative in its tonality but teaching the same thing, from the *Promenades in Rome* (1829): "It is a sad truth: one has much pleasure in Rome only when the education of the eye has ended." What follows confirms a theme we have already seen: "Voltaire would have left the halls of Raphael shrugging his shoulders and making epigrams, because wit is not an advantage for enjoying the kind of pleasure that these paintings can give. I have seen timid, dreamy souls, that often lack assurance and presence of mind in a salon, appreciate more quickly than others Luini's frescoes in Saronno near Milan, and those of Raphael in the Vatican";[65] which at least indicates, in passing, that the *wit* of the salon—specifically the "French," that is the Parisian, salon ("Paris, thanks to the superiority of its conversation and of its literature, is and will always be the salon of Europe) and,[66] as such impossible south of the Alps ("There is no room for *French wit* in an Italian salon" and "the Apennine mountains will become a lowland before it can be introduced into Italy")[67]—is one thing that masks badly, or betrays well, the absence of sensation (and no doubt hinders the necessary education of the eye and the ear) and that *thought*, or reflection, or education, is another. That is what we must stress before we end.

To think makes one feel: this statement is paradoxical only if one summarily opposes the affective (or emotive) to the cognitive and if one forgets that the voluptuousness of (positive) aesthetic appreciation comes inevitably from a "contemplation" of the object that itself involves a virtually infinite number of stages and levels. In fact, the "aesthetic object" is nothing else than an object considered in an aesthetic manner—that is, in an inexhaustible diversity of its aspects (inexhaustible, at least compared to the limited number of its functions). To this, as it were, primary diversity of aspects of every object, the work of art adds a secondary diversity that relates to its technical and historical character as a human product, which can be perceived only at the price of what Stendhal calls an "education," capable of bringing out what he calls its "style," that is to say, its specific meaning in the field of its production and reception. This meaning thus depends on historical and technical considerations relative at the same time to its own genesis and to the situation of the person who constructs them. This work, which each person must do on his own, "all alone like a big boy," is clearly of the order of knowledge and of reflection, and it *informs*, in both senses of that verb, the manner in which the subject perceives and appreciates a work. *To feel* designates at the same time the (infinite) cognitive activity of perception and the (unstable) affective act that results from it, which explains an observation like this one: "Today Mozart is more or less understood, but his music is still very far from being *felt*."[68] This purely intellectual understanding lacks the affective response that would make of it a truly aesthetic relationship and which is hindered according to Stendhal by a disaccord of sensibility between German music and the Latin temperament. A more personal experience attests elsewhere to a hindrance of the same kind, though due to a quite different cause: "The view of the islands that the Rhone forms in the neighborhood [of Avignon] is not bad. To tell the truth, I *have judged* that all these views were agreeable, but I have not enjoyed them; I was in a state where I could not enjoy anything. A furious *mistral* has started again this morning; that's the great *drawback* [Translator's note: the English word is used] of all the pleasures that one can encounter in Provence."[69] It seems to me that *drawback*, which Stendhal (as we will see) himself translates as "inconvenience," itself designates a sort of brake, or *hindrance*, to the aesthetic relation—in this case to an object of nature. Here is a more complex testimony: "At that time we were without passion; we would not have been moved, as we are today [before the arc of Janus on the Forum Boarium], by the memory of Hercules making his herds pass the Tiber. There was another *drawback* (inconvenience). The education of our eyes had not been accomplished: they did not know how to distinguish in a portal the little formal differences that indicate the century of Augustin and that of Diocletian."[70] The mention of the "memory" of the herds of Hercules agrees here with a frequent piece of information of the Beylean aesthetic emotion: the historical or mythological memory attached to a certain work or place. In the Colosseum, for example, "that peaceful chirping of the birds, that resounds weakly in this vast edifice, and, from time to time, the deep silence that succeeds it, doubtless help the imagination to take flight into ancient times. One attains the most lively enjoyments that memory can provide."[71] The hindrance, if hindrance there is, can thus relate either to an affective deficit (a blockage, such as is often occasioned by a troublesome proximity) or to a cognitive deficit, which confirms the joined necessity of these two factors. And—if one forgives this naively mechanistic description—to think acts on the first by informing ("educating") the second, for example, by multiplying the modes of comparison and distinction between works or styles. I appreciate what I perceive according to my own sensibility, and I don't have to "judge my happiness" (or my displeasure): *mi piace, non mi piace* remains in any case an autonomous judgment in respect to "others" and without appeal *in respect to its object*. But this object, as an object that attracts attention, never ceases to modify itself as the field of knowledge, of analysis, and of reference in which I inscribe it refines and diversifies itself. I do not judge my feeling, but I do not stop to "think" and to rethink its object, that is to say, to construct and reconstruct it in constructing and reconstructing its context of perception. It is no doubt, though in an obviously larger way, to this cooperation of *thinking* and *feeling* that this note of the *Diary* of 1813 relates, the occasion of which is certainly not indifferent: "At ten o'clock this morning, when I saw the Duomo of Milan, I reflected that my trips in Italy caused me to become more original, more *myself*. I am learning to seek happiness with more intelligence." [72] It would be difficult, it seems to me, to imagine a more beautiful rule of life.

In this cavalier reading (but must one excuse oneself for reading Stendhal in a figurative way, as he himself boasts of reading Ariosto?) [73] I hope I have not altered the Stendhalian point of view too much, the coherence and stability of which are no doubt more problematical than I have shown here. I am nonetheless conscious of translating him into my own terms and of inscribing him in my own field. This is the inevitable fate of thoughtful works, as it is of creative works, devoted to a labor of recapturing, and sometimes of recycling, without which this fate would perhaps restrict itself to being forgotten. But I am wrong to distinguish, even a little, thoughtful works from creative works, since all creation is thoughtful, and all thoughtfulness is creation.

14

Parrot-Green

Between *Lucien Leuwen*, abandoned in November 1836, and *The Pink and the Green*, started in April and abandoned in June 1837, the presence of a country inn named *The Green Hunter* is not the only point in common. Another is that little motif, typically northern, it seems (I see none that is equivalent in the Italian work, historical or fictional, and Nancy and Königsberg are clearly for Stendhal cities of the north), that has its affective involvement in the love between Lucien and Mme de Chasteller but to which a page of *The Pink and the Green* gives a technical device of astonishing precision in the work of an author who said he detested "material description." A precision all the stranger since the use of this device will have no sequence in the unfinished novel, which gets a little involved in its relation of repetition with *Minna de Vanghel*, a novella written at the end of 1829. Thus, everything happens as though Stendhal gave himself the occasion to come back a little, for the pleasure of it, to a situation that was dear to him. Because the fictional development is in *Leuwen*, it is no doubt better, despite the chronology, to consider the version of the *Pink* first, which I allow myself to quote again *in extenso*,[1] since this abandoned work is not one of our author's best known:

> The splendid mansion built by Pierre Wanghen occupied the northern end of the Friedrichsgasse, the finest street of Königsberg, distinguished in foreign eyes by the great number of little flights of seven or eight steps jutting out into the street and leading to the entrances of houses. The polished railings of these staircases were of cast iron, produced, I believe, in Berlin and displayed all the curious intricacy of German designs. In their total effect, these elaborate structures are not disagreeable; they have the advantage of novelty and harmonize with the window-ornaments of the principal apartments which, in Königsberg, are always on the ground floor, some four or five feet above street level. The windows are fitted inside with sliding sashes covered with a metallic fabric which produces a

singular effect. The glistening materials, conveniently for the ladies inside, are impenetrable to passing eyes dazzled by the tiny sparks which leap from the metallic substance. Gentlemen cannot see into the apartments, while ladies at their needlework near the windows obtain a fine view of whoever passes.

Such entertainment—of what might be called a sedentary promenade—forms one of the notable features of social life in Prussia. From noon to four, should one choose to ride down the street and cause one's mount to make a little noise, one is certain to find all the pretty women in town doing their needlework quite close to the lower panes of their windows. There is even a style of garment which has a special name and which fashion decrees for appearing behind this pane which, in houses of pretention, is very transparent indeed.

The ladies' curiosity is assisted by an accessory resource: in every house of distinction, on either side of the groundfloor window, mirrors about a foot long are attached to a little iron rod and tilted toward the interior. By this means, ladies can see passers-by arriving from the end of the street, while as we have said, no curious eyes can penetrate the metallic screens which shield the bottom half of the windows. But if gentlemen do not see in, they know that they are seen, and the knowledge affords a special immediacy to all the little romances which enliven the society of Berlin and Königsberg. A gentleman is sure to be observed several times each morning by the lady of his choice; indeed it is not absolutely impossible for the metallic fabric to be occasionally displaced on its frame by a pure effect of chance, permitting the promenader to perceive the lady's pretty hand attempting to pull it back. One might go so far as to say that the position of these sashes can have a language all its own. Who could understand it, or be incensed by such a thing if he did?[2]

The situation here evoked is ordinarily called *to see without being seen*, and this locution clearly applies very well to the role of feminine partners, whose "curiosity" profits fully, and in all security, from a mechanism that seems to have been instituted with that end in view—and which Chateaubriand, in the course of the Hundred Days, had already noted in Gand.[3] It nonetheless seems that, contrary to the ordinary data of narrative disposition, the "point of view," in its proper sense, of the women who look through their window, in their mirror and then through their metallic fabric, does not coincide with what I will call, for lack of a better term, the affective focalization of this little iterative narrative. The fictional focus is not here as much feminine curiosity as the object of that curiosity, the "gentlemen" who lend themselves complacently to that curiosity and for whom the "entertainment" of that "sedentary prom-enade" consists, paradoxically, of *being seen without seeing*: this is for me the true meaning of that page. As for the "poetic" oxymoron *sedentary promenade*, I don't know whether it designates the studied slowness of the passage or its apparently quotidian repetitive character; we will find in *Leuwen* a more literal motivation.

As precise, even meticulous, as it is, I am not sure that the description of the device is absolutely clear and coherent: I see that the metallic fabric permits the look to pass from the interior to the exterior, without reciprocity (a simple curtain would do the same), but the "lower panes of their windows" are also qualified as "very transparent indeed" (in the two meanings?), and the preceding phrase says that "one is certain to *find* all the pretty women in town doing their needlework quite close" to that pane and putting on a special toilette to *appear* in them. This is clearly contradicted by two other indications: "These glistening materials, conveniently for the curiosity of the ladies inside, are impenetrable to passing eyes dazzled by the tiny sparks which leap from the metallic substance. Gentlemen cannot see into the apartments"; and "no curious eyes can penetrate the metallic screens"; without a doubt they could at least see, pressed to the window, the face that interests them, but the essential seems to me to be "if gentlemen do not see in, they know that they are seen," and "a gentleman is sure to be observed several times each morning by the lady of his choice." And the subsequent phrase indicates well that the most one can "perceive" of the lady who adjusts her frame is her "pretty hand." [4] No, decidedly, one does not come here to see but to be seen, knowing that one is seen. The rest of the "little novel" will depend, among other things, on the hypothetical language that can hold the position of the frames; one knows that Stendhalian fiction has no trouble with this kind of coded message.

The "matinal" exhibition (from noon to four!) of our cavaliers is thus cer-tainly not as deprived of design as it is of vision, and it may be supposed that the one of whom one perceives only the pretty hand will have been better viewed, since preferred, in a different place and will be found again at a not too distant occasion, conforming to the "singular rapidity" of "all these little novels." What remains is that the "sedentary promenade" of these gentlemen is itself a "pleasure" and not only a stage in a strategy of seduction.

We will find this point again in *Leuwen*, and in a certainly more intense climate, which is—to speak Beylean—the one of love-passion. One remembers, of course, that the point of departure of this passion is the hero's fall from a horse the day after he arrives in Nancy, under a shutter painted parrot-green that hides the window of Mme de Chasteller. Lucien had just seen this shutter "open a little way," after he had at first looked at it without indulgence ("What a taste for gaudy colors these provincials have!") and seen "a young woman with magnificent blond hair and a haughty air."[5] Since this expression of disdain and during several weeks, Lucien, who at first never meets the young woman and thinks he has forgotten her, passes "from force of habit . . . through the rue de la Pompe almost every day," without much observing the parrot-green shutters, up to the day when, these shutters being open, he remarks "a pair of charming embroidered muslin curtains" that spread apart a little bit at his passage. "Evidently someone was watching him. It was, as a matter of fact, Mme de Chasteller, who was saying to herself: 'Ah! that's my young officer about to have another fall!' She had often watched him ride past, and thought that he wore his clothes with an easy elegance quite free from all stiffness." Same cause, same effect, "his little Hungarian beast [threw him to the ground] not ten paces from the spot where he had fallen the first day. 'It must be fate,' he said. 'I am predestined to appear ridiculous in the eyes of this young woman.' "[6] This redoubled fall makes all the difference between the "gentlemen" of Königsberg and our hero, whom this exceptional clumsiness ("Yet riding a horse is perhaps the only thing I really do creditably") renders at least touching and thus interesting. On his side, and even though his relations with Mme de Chasteller progress as quickly as good manners permit, the respect of the one due to the virtue of the other, and mainly the comings and goings and the passionate banter of reciprocal "crystallization," Lucien will not cease to sacrifice to the commemorative rite of this first scene,[7] passing and passing again "through the Rue de la Pompe several times a day,"[8] at the risk of finding himself "in the not very heroic position of Saint Paul when he beheld the vision of the third heaven":[9] "It seemed to him that if he were to encounter Madame de Chasteller's eyes at that moment, he would fall from his horse for the third time."[10] But the eyes here do not meet: the young woman, very attentive, remains hidden behind her casement, and Lucien—whom "the mere idea that he might catch sight of Mme de Chasteller almost drove out of his mind. It was even a relief not to find her at her window"[11]—is able (and willing) to know only "how pleasant it would be to see those little embroidered muslin curtains lighted by the candles."[12]

But here is a variant that one does not find in the streets of Königsberg: Lucien installs himself in the evenings opposite the house with the muslin curtains, where he comes "to smoke one of his little cigars rolled in licorice paper."[13] This is where the expression *sedentary promenade* gets all its meaning, and this is where the late revelation of his state comes to him: " 'Is it possible,' he said at length half aloud, 'that I am fool enough to be in love?' and he stopped dead in the middle of the street as though a thunderbolt had struck him. Happily at midnight there was no one on the street to notice the expression of his face, and to laugh at him." Apparently, there is no one on the street, but one cannot doubt that the interested one, behind her casement, enjoys the spectacle: a few pages hence "she had been watching him ride by for such a long time now that, although he had been presented only a week ago, he seemed to her almost like an old acquaintance";[14] and still a little farther on, at the ball of Mme de Marcilly: "If M. Leuwen acts with such assurance it must be because he knows that I spend whole hours hidden behind the shutters at my window, waiting for him to ride past."[15] But it is no longer only a matter of riding past:

> he could, without being too ridiculous in his *own* eyes, pace back and forth under the parrot-green shutters, although almost immediately after his arrival the lights had gone out in the little room. Embarrassed by the sounds of his own footsteps, Lucien took advantage of the profound darkness and settled himself for a long time on a large stone directly across the street from the window, from which he never once took his eyes.
>
> His was not the only heart to be disturbed by the sound of his footsteps. Until ten o'clock Madame de Chasteller had spent the evening haunted by somber thoughts and filled with remorse. She would have been less melancholy in company, but she was afraid to risk meeting Lucien or hearing his name mentioned. At ten-thirty, seeing him appear, her deep and lonely sadness was all at once interrupted by the pounding of her heart. She hastened to blow out her candles, but, in spite of all her remonstrances with herself, did not leave the window. Her eyes were guided in the darkness by the tip of Lucien's little cigar.[16]

Lucien is clearly no longer riding a horse, and this dangerous accessory is now replaced by the more discreet—more intimate—cigar glowing in the night. The deeply obscure street from then on becomes the symbolic theater of a passion that catches fire by not declaring itself: for Leuwen the rue de la Pompe and the window with green shutters are from now on inseparable from the beloved, and he includes them in the same contradictory movements, at the will of the ebb and flow of his feeling: " 'The devil take her and her street! . . . The devil if I ever look at her windows!' . . . A few minutes later, as midnight was ringing, despite the insults he was addressing to Mme de Chasteller, he was sitting on the stone facing her window . . . Now and then, in the intense darkness, Mme de Chasteller could make out the lighted tip of Lucien's little cigar. She loved him madly at this moment."[17]

Contrary to the cavaliers at Königsberg, so certain of being seen and appreciated, Lucien does not know for sure if one looks at him, and it is understood that his "sedentary" scheme is anything but planned: he comes to the large stone because it brings him closer to the one he loves and also because this place—a scenery, in theatrical terms (street, stone, window, parrot-green shutters, muslin curtain, little cigars)—is from the start the phantasmatic emblem of this love, a little like the "little phrase" of Vinteuil will be the "national anthem" for Swann's and Odette's love, since all passion has its fetishes. As for the one her "rival," Mme d'Hocquincourt, ironically calls "the sublime Chasteller,"[18] this spectacle leads her to strange behavior:

> Days counted, and were prized by her, only because of the hours spent at night behind the shutters of her drawing room listening for his footsteps. For Lucien, little dreaming of all the success of this strategy, would remain hours on end in the Rue de la Pompe.
>
> Bathilde (the title of Madame is far too dignified for such childish behavior) spent her evenings behind the shutters, breathing through a little tube of licorice paper which she placed between her lips as Lucien did his little cigars. In the midst of the deep silence of the Rue de la Pompe (deserted even by day, but how much lonelier at eleven o'clock at night) crackling of licorice paper in Lucien's hands as he tore off a sheet from the little book to make his cigarito. It was M. de Blancet who had had the honor and the happiness of procuring for Madame de Chasteller some of these little books of licorice paper which, as everyone knows, are imported from Barcelona.[19]

I did not know, and I sometimes ask myself not, like Mme de Chasteller, "from where such horrors could come [to her]" but where Stendhal himself went, as one says, to look for these details.[20] At any rate I leave to the specialists, who must have done so already, the care of interpreting this exchange of breaths by interposed "licorice paper"—even if the excess of transparency has here, as often in Stendhal, enough to discourage the hermeneutes. This kind of object is, I think, today called a "joint," and this word, in a sense, says it all. We also know that the love of Lucien and "Bathilde" was to traverse many obstacles and contradictory emotions before knowing the happy end that the author sketches in the margin of chapter 22. But I am not sure that any of these moments would have reached the intensity of this one, a moment the happier because he does not know it is happy and because he does not know what is shared in it. I am not sure either that these hypothetical reunions, seemingly Parisian, could have held such a note: as is said sadly in another novel that has some relation to this one: "passions wilt when they are transplanted."[21] The passion of Lucien and Bathilde is doubtless more than they realize attached to this country that Nancy and its surroundings define, its Green Hunter, its Rue de la Pompe, and its shutters. Whence perhaps (I interpret in my turn) the well-known incompletion.

Being seen without seeing could thus be one of the paradoxical fantasies of Stendhalian love-passion.[22] And at the limit, the obscurity having become total and the blindness reciprocal, the two lovers could be united without ever seeing each other, which does not hinder them altogether from looking at each other. One thinks of the rather casuistic wish of Clélia in the Charterhouse that will not interdict but, rather, promote "three years of divine happiness," which, in fact, will end with its rupture. One could imagine a similar ending for Leuwen that would certainly put an end to many continuations: this phrase falling finally, in the night, from a window with parrot-green shutters: "Enter here, friend of my heart." But Nancy is decidedly not in Italy.[23]

15

Other Magic of the Faraway

Stendhal, as one perhaps knows, calls "magic of the far-away" that optical effect also called "aerial perspective" that certain painters, but not all, knew how to render. He gives as a natural example the fact that, from the Pont Royal in Paris, the close-by houses of the Pont Neuf seem

> much more colored, marked by much stronger shadow and light than the line of the quai de Grève which loses itself in a vaporous distance. In the country, as the chains of mountains distance themselves, don't they take on a more marked shade of violet blue? This lowering of all shades by distance is amusing to see in the groups of promenaders in the Tuileries, especially through the mist of autumn.
>
> Ghirlandajo made for himself an immortal name in the history of art for having perceived this effect,[1] that marble cannot convey, and that was perhaps always missing in the painting of the Classics.
>
> The magic of the far-away, this part of painting that appeals to tender imaginations, is perhaps the principal reason of its superiority over sculpture. By this it comes close to music, it engages the imagination to finish its pictures; and if, at first sight, we are more struck by the figures in the foreground, it is objects the details of which are half hidden by the air that we remember with the greatest charm; they have taken a celestial shade in our thought.

And he adds in a note, this time praising Correggio, "his art was to paint even the figures in the foreground as though they were at a distance. . . . It is music, and it is not sculpture."[2] The aerial perspective, as one can see, brings two effects together: the one is chromatic, consisting in a "lowering of the shades" toward the blue; the other is plastic, consisting in a dilution of forms, which become vague and "vaporous." By this joining of effects, painting, which in Stendhal, a little like in Hegel, always hesitates between these two firmer arts, distances itself from sculpture and draws close to music, which is a "tender painting,"[3] finding in Correggio, the favorite painter of our author, this simple means to become wholly music: to drown the entire picture in the magic of the faraway.

Such a marked bias, and so clearly overdetermined (and overmotivated), would not seem to tolerate any nuance, not to mention contradiction. But, happily, nothing is as simple as that in Stendhal, and one finds in him, without leaving "happy Italy," another effect of the "magic of the far-away," just about contrary and which painting has never depicted. It is the manner in which a mountainous background, that of the chain of the Alps, lets itself be seen from the Lombard plain, in particular from Milan, whose well-known charm, and with rather complex motifs (Scala, Corso, Dome, beauty of women, cordiality of customs, naturalness of feelings), seems inseparable from this panoramic sight, from Mount Viso at the west to the mountains of Bassano in the east, that the young soldiers of Bonaparte discover in 1796 in chapter 7 of the *Memoirs about Napoleon*,[4] which is in so many respects a sketch of the beginning of the *Charterhouse*. It is panoramic still, from a little farther away, for the voyagers, real or fictional, of *Rome, Naples and Florence*, from the convent of San Michele in Bosco, near Bologna: "Lying under large oaks, we enjoyed in silence one of the most wide-spread views of the universe. . . . In the North, we have before us the long lines of the mountains of Padua, crowned by the steep summits of the Swiss and Tyrolese Alps,"[5] and, in a manner that seems more imaginary, from the heights of the Farnese tower of the Parma prison, for Fabrice whose "delighted eyes clearly identified each of the peaks of the vast wall by which the Alps enclose northern Italy."[6] But the amplitude of the field seemingly does not in any way take away from its *depth*, a word that must now be taken in the specific meaning it has in photography and film, that is to say, the meaning in which distance does not diminish the visual clarity—lest it be better to say that the focus here favors the faraway to the detriment of the foreground. Since the human eye does not have this kind of skill, we have to look for the cause of this effect in the object itself. As a matter of fact, it is not at all mysterious, but let us first consider the fact, which Stendhal describes several times, with evident enthusiasm.

We have just seen that the "delighted eyes" of Fabrice "identified each of the peaks." The first notation of this effect is found, to my knowledge, in *Rome, Naples and Florence* (1826), at the (fictive?) date of November 5, 1816: "At the return [from a trip to Marignan], admirable sight of the Dome of Milan, with the white marble, rising above all the houses of the town, standing out against the Bergamese Alps, which it seems to touch, though a plain of thirty miles separates them. The Dome, seen from that distance, is of a perfect whiteness.

This so complicated work of men, this forest of marble needles, doubles the picturesque effect of the admirable contour of the Alps detaching themselves against the sky. I have seen nothing in the world more beautiful than the aspect of these summits covered with snow, perceived from a distance of twenty leagues, with all the lower mountains staying in the most beautiful darkness."[7] But Stendhal also attributes this observation to the soldiers of 1796 (among whom he seems to take his place here), an observation given this time an entirely physical explanation: "The closest parts, though twelve or fifteen leagues apart, seem hardly three leagues distant from each other. [. . .] By the effect of the purity of the air to which we, people from the North, were not accustomed, one perceives the country houses built on the lowest slopes of the Alps on the Italian side with such clarity that one would believe one is separated from them only by two or three leagues."[8] It is also the contrast between the actual distance and the clarity of the mountainous faraway that "delights" Fabrice in his tower: "the eye can follow the least details, although they are at more than thirty leagues from the citadel of Parma"—a citadel, let us remember, that exists only in the imaginary of the *Charterhouse*. The same Fabrice observes the same effect in a marginal sketch: "In the curves of the Italian Alps, the air is so pure and the view so easy, that one thinks at any moment one is separated by a quarter of a league at the most from those snowy peaks of which one distinguishes with clarity the least rift and the least curve and on which one could see the antelopes jump."[9] One finds it again in a fragment of 1831, in which the purity of the air is less due to altitude but doubtless still to the alpine site: "Finally, I perceived that immense lake [of Geneva] from the heights of the hills of Changy. . . . The air was so pure that I saw the smoke of the chimneys of Lausanne seven leagues away from us rise to the sky in wavy and vertical columns."[10]

I don't know for certain if this new magic of the faraway, which makes it at the same time closer and more distinct, relates to the "purity of the air" of the Lombard plain or of the Alps themselves (I suppose that both are necessary for this effect, improbable today), but it is clear that the reason for its value relates to the very quality of the mountainous horizon, which Beyle—just arrived from his native Grenoble (which he thought he detested)—had so distressingly missed in Paris and only found again in Milan.[11] The very quality, or more exactly the quality by contrast. It is precisely the opposition between the "fertile" plain, often crushed by heat, and the view of the snowy summits that strikes the soldiers of Bonaparte "with admiration," in this page from the

Memoirs about Napoleon, which I will now have to quote in its entirety, with its expressive repetitions:

> The countryside surrounding Milan, viewed from the Spanish ramparts, which, in such a unified plain, are at a considerable elevation, is so covered with trees that it looks like a thick forest, which the eye can't penetrate. Beyond this countryside, image of the most astonishing fertility, the immense chain of the Alps rises a few leagues distant, the summits of which remain covered with snow, even in the hottest months. Starting at the bastion of the Eastern Gate, the eye surveys this long chain, from Mount Viso and Mount Rose to the mountains of Bassano. The closest parts, though twelve or fifteen leagues distant, seem at most at three leagues. The contrast of the extreme fertility of a beautiful summer with mountains covered by eternal snow, struck the soldiers of the Italian army with admiration, soldiers who, during three years, had lived in the arid rocks of Liguria. They recognized with pleasure that Mount Viso, which they had seen for so long above their heads, and behind which they now saw the sun go down. The fact is that nothing can be compared to the landscapes of Lombardy. The enchanted eye surveys this admirable chain of the Alps for a space of sixty leagues, from the mountains above Turin to those of Cadore. Those acrid summits covered with snow form an admirable contrast with the voluptuous sites of the plain and the hills which are in the foreground, and seem to compensate for the extreme heat, for which one comes to be relieved on the bastion of the Eastern Gate. In the beautiful light of Italy, the foot of these mountains, the summit of which is covered with snow of such brilliant whiteness, seems dark blonde: they are absolutely the landscapes of Titian. By the effect of the purity of the air to which we, people of the North, were not accustomed, one perceives the country houses built on the lowest slopes of the Alps, on the Italian side, with such clarity that one would believe one is separated from them only by two or three leagues.

We observe in passing how Stendhal, who said he detested "material description," takes care to motivate this one by the look of the viewer—collective here—whose impressions he is evoking. He does likewise in the *Charterhouse*, in which the descriptions of the same Lombardian landscape are always focalized by a character capable of appreciating its charm: the countess of Pietranera at the lake of Como, Fabrice in his tower or on the way between Lugano and Grianta. I must still insist on these three distinct pages to try to seize the exact nuance of the "contrast" that we have already seen twice over. The Chaper page twice indicates one of its motifs, which is the sublime and even heroic severity (our preceding extract said "acridness"):

> An instant later, an unexpected detour takes away the bank of the lake that touched your soul and places you in front of those sublime rifts of the high Alps. The snow which never leaves them, even in the month of August, doubles the severity of their aspect, made to astonish the most vivid imagination. A vivid and icy air envelops you and doubles the ability you have to feel this kind of happiness. This air reminded Fabrice of all the joys of his childhood and of his promenades on the lake with his aunt. These severe aspects that raise the soul to heroism are absent from the bay of Naples, the most beautiful in the world. In the curves of the Italian Alps, the air is so pure and the view so beautiful, that at every moment one thinks one is hardly separated by a quarter of a league from those peaks of snow of which one distinguishes with clarity the least tear and the least detours and on which one could see gazelles jump.

Those "promenades on the lake with his aunt," which happen before the Waterloo episode, had been evoked in chapter 2, occasion for a new (first, in the sequence of the text) and justly famous description of the landscape of the lake of Como,[12] where the motif of "severity" comes back twice: first in the opposition between "the lake's two arms, the one toward Como so voluptuously beautiful, and the one toward Lecco so full of severity: sublime and enchanting aspects which the most celebrated site in the world, the Bay of Naples, may equal but not surpass" (again, or rather already, the comparison with the bay of Naples, which the Chaper page will reduce from its rank of equality); I suppose that the seemingly conventional "sublime and enchanting" takes up again the contrast—itself a little exaggerated by Beyle[13]—between the "voluptuous" and the severe branches that the promontory of Bellagio with the villa Melzi separates; then, à propos of the alpine background: "Beyond these hills, whose crests afford a glimpse of hermitages one longs to take refuge in, one after the next, the astonished gaze perceives the Alpine peaks, ever covered with snow and their severe austerity reminds one of life's miseries, and just how much of them it takes to increase one's present voluptuousness."

This insistence on the "severity," the "severe austerity," of the mountainous horizon seems to organize the geographic contrast around an affective opposition between the "present voluptuousness" of the countryside or (here) lakeside foreground and "life's miseries" that the "sublime rifts" of the summits recall. I believe nonetheless that the dominant theme, less heroic—less romantic, in the ordinary sense—is, rather, the one that is indicated by the contemplation of Fabrice in his Parma prison: "Beyond the left bank of this river [the Po], which formed like a sequence of immense white spots in the midst of the green landscape, his delighted eye distinctly perceived each summit of the immense wall that the Alps form in the North of Italy. These summits, always covered with snow, even in the present month of August, give something like a freshness by memory in the middle of this burning countryside." Again—as in chapter 7 of the *Memoirs* and in the Chaper sketch—the contrast is between the overwhelming heat of the summery plain and the bracing freshness of the summits, that "vivid and icy air" that "envelops you and doubles the ability you have to feel this kind of happiness" and which Fabrice breathed between Lugano and Grianta.[14] These two motifs for enhanced value are somewhat contradictory, the mountainous horizon bringing at the same time the severity needed in order to "feel" by contrast the "happiness" and the "present voluptuousness" and the tonic freshness needed to endure the weight of the heat wave. But Stendhal himself endured his contradictions quite well without feeling the need to reconcile them, and the essential for him is clearly to enhance, one way or another, this view of the "wall" of the Alps, severe but tonic, that dominates and animates the Lombard plain and the vista of the lakes. The most notable detail is certainly that "freshness by memory" that the spectacle of the snowy summits communicates to Fabrice. We must not overinterpret that strange phrase (*freshness by memory* for a freshness that one feels only at the view of its source by a reminiscent reflex, like those "impressions of [Venetian] freshness" that the Narrator of *Time Regained* will experience on the unequal paving stones of the Guermantes hotel), but its strangeness has something to do with a revealing lapsus. The action of memory is omnipresent in this textual collection, at the same time autobiographical and fictional, as though this largely dreamlike landscape, which one seems hardly ever to see for the first time, was always already the place of return: Gina, at Grianta, "began to *see again*, with Fabrice, all the enchanting places. . . . It was with delight that the countess *found again* the memories of her first youth and compared them to her present sensations"; Fabrice, in the mountains, *remembers* his promenades on the lake with his aunt; the same Fabrice, a little later, joining his mother and one of his sisters at Belgirate, on the Laggo Majore, finds there "the mountain air, the calm and majestic aspect of this splendid lake, which *reminded* him of the one on which he had spent his childhood";[15] Fabrice still, in his prison, experiences in *memory* the freshness of his past impressions. And Stendhal himself, in his apartment on rue Caumartin during the winter 1838, "begins to see again," in order to resuscitate it in writing, a landscape he loved more than anything and which he will never see again.

16

Matter of Venice

In the workshop of *Remembrance of Things Past*, and still up to the Grasset proofs that Proust probably corrected before the summer of 1913, *Swann in Love* opened with the strange page that follows:[1]

M. and Mme Verdurin were like certain squares in Venice, unknown and spacious, that the voyager comes across one evening at the chance of his walk, and which no guide book has ever mentioned. He has plunged into a network of little alleys that dissect in all directions with their furrows the chunk of Venice he has in front of him, carved out between canals and the lagoon, when suddenly, at the end of one of the "calli," as though the Venetian matter in the moment of crystallizing had experienced there an unforeseen distension, he finds himself in front of a vast campo, of which he certainly could never have guessed the scale, or even found room for it, surrounded by charming palaces in the pale facade of which the moonshine plays meditatively. This architectural whole toward which, in another town, the main street would have led us first, is hidden here by the smallest streets, like one of those palaces of Oriental tales whither one leads a character for one night, by a path he must not be able to find in the daytime, so he ends up by persuading himself that he only went there in a dream.

And in fact if the next day you want to return to this campo, you will follow alleys which are exactly like one another and refuse to give you the smallest piece of information. Sometimes an indication makes you believe that you will find and see the beautiful exiled square reappear in the confinement of its solitude and of its silence, but at that moment some evil spirit, in the form of a new calle, makes you abruptly turn back and leads you to the Grand Canal.

The anonymous reader of a fashionable newspaper is in the same situation every day; he has become familiar with the names of a lot of people that he will never know, and who were highlighted there because of a not very large fortune, a title, or a rather doubtful talent; and he never reads there the name of Verdurin. But one day, looking for a place to live at a beach, he sees several villas larger than the others and he inquires. They have all been rented by Mme Verdurin, for herself and for her friends. In Versailles the hotel is full; only the most beautiful apartment, filled with antique furniture, seems uninhabited; but it is not free, it is rented by the year to Mme Verdurin. Because Mme Verdurin has reserved them in advance for herself and her friends, one can't have the box or the table one wanted at an important concert or at a restaurant near Paris. And in those plans of social Paris that columnists work out in such minute detail and at such a grand scale that often a hundred thousand francs of income are enough to guarantee a position for the one who owns them, one notices that the necessarily vast space filled by the Verdurins, who spend about seven or eight thousand francs a year, is nowhere mentioned or foreseen.[2]

If Proust had not suppressed this page in extremis, it would have contained one of the first mentions, and certainly the first evocation, of Venice offered to the reader of Remembrance, an illustration among others of the practice of dislocation, which places, for example, the first description of the Balbec room at the head of the Parisian section "Place-Names: the Name." The reasons for this suppression are unknown to us, just like those that had at first led to envisage opening this section with a fanfare. The fanfare, the "bravura" side, might explain both gestures: Proust may have wished to open this section with a brilliant comparison, then he might have renounced it because it was too brilliant. Alden judges this page "preposterous," that is to say, absurd, but, if I believe etymology, this absurdity is like a cart put before the horse, the vehicle placed before its tenor, or, if one prefers, the thing to be compared still unknown (the societal situation of the Verdurins) badly enlightened by the thing with which it is compared (which has not yet been encountered and is thus just as unknown, unless one postulates with a Robbe-Grilletian insolence: "everyone knows Venice"). In more Proustian terms it is clearly a matter of one of those metaphors judged "unnecessary," artificial because pulled from afar, not dictated by the context and the situation, that Proust criticized in other writers and tried to avoid himself. The perfect counter-illustration is provided by this phrase from The Fugitive in which the narrator, during his sojourn in Venice, evokes "the Albertine of long ago . . . enclosed within me as in the *Piombi* of an inner Venice, the tight lid of which some incident occasionally lifted to give me a glimpse of the past."[3]

Despite this "defect" in the eyes of a (in this regard) perfectly classical aesthetics (an insufficiently metonymic metaphor being equivalent to what classical rhetoric condemned in the name of "catachresis"), the comparison between the social situation of the Verdurins and the Venetian *campo* presented the great thematic advantage of announcing right away an important trait of this situation: its unsuspected and (oxymoronically said) *secret* character. Actually, this paradoxical character is in itself not at all exceptional in Proustian society, where different milieux, and the more so different cliques, frequently ignore one another, so much so that, for example, the elevated relations of Swann are, out of ignorance or disdain, not known by the petite bourgeoisie of Combray.

But it is a matter there of relative disregard and localized ignorance, based on a sort of social provincialism, due in part to the heterogeneity of characters like Swann or Vinteuil or even Charlus, of whom the Verdurins imagine, at La Raspelière, that he is "just a baron." The "social surface" of the Verdurins is, on the contrary, here given as unknown *in general* and, as it were, in the absolute. It is not only "the anonymous reader of a fashionable newspaper" who does not know it, since this paper never mentions it—nor without a doubt any other: "a space *nowhere* mentioned or foreseen." Once crossed out from our opening page, this somewhat fantastic idea of an absolutely clandestine worldliness will never come up in *Remembrance*, neither in *Cities of the Plain*, in which Charlus, come to slum at La Raspelière for reasons that one knows, will measure its correct (i.e., minute) value, nor in *Swann in Love* itself, in which the inferiority of the Verdurins' salon is sorely felt by the "Patronne" and expressed negatively by her bitter tirades against the "boars." And when, after the death of the "Patron," his widow, become Duchesse de Duras, then Princesse de Guermantes, will continue to "participate" and to "make cliques," it will be no more than a nostalgic look at the completed past of an upstart whose least actions and gestures are henceforth public and reported by all papers. In short the hyperbolic theme (as I have formulated it) of a Verdurin space at the same time considerable and unknown does not exactly correspond to the reality of a career the evolution of which consists, rather, in the passage from a justified obscurity to a certainly considerable but by no means unknown space, whose late acquisition is one of those theatrical surprises that Proust loves so much to arrange. The only foundation of the comparison thus relates to the financial means of the Verdurins, which, perhaps from *Swann in Love* on, permit them to rent several villas at the beach, the most beautiful apartment in the "hotel" of Versailles, a box at a concert, or a table in a restaurant. The Verdurins' space, purely material since based on money alone, is thus, at the period in which the opening of *Swann in Love* is situated, an empty space, the only one that money can buy: boxes, reserved tables, apartments and villas rented by the year—it is no doubt significant that none of this is bought, still less inherited, and La Raspelière itself will be rented for the season to Mme de Cambremer, as though a fortune or, rather, such plebeian income, whatever its amplitude, could not give access to true property. A "necessarily vast" space then, but the vaster it is, the more unoccupied (though no doubt "furnished"), that is to say, in waiting, per- haps indefinite waiting, for truly frequentable—that is to say, presentable— "friends."

The theme thus corrected is not really paradoxical anymore, and it corre- sponds faithfully, and for a long time, to the situation of the Verdurins. But at the same time it stops from sustaining the flattering comparison with the vast *campo* "surrounded by charming palaces in the pale facade of which the moon- shine plays meditatively," a comparison not only pulled spatially from too far but thematically discordant: the thing with which it is compared too poetic for the altogether prosaic thing compared. A new altogether conjectural ex- plication for a crossed-out passage that, I remind the reader, will suppress at the same time the compared thing and the thing with which it is compared. Or, more exactly, that will suppress the thing compared and will *displace* the thing with which it is compared.

For the evocation of the "unknown and spacious" Venetian square is not aban- doned without recourse: we will find it again better located, disengaged of all implication with the vulgar theme of money, in the pages of *The Fugitive* devoted to the Venetian sojourn of the narrator. Reducing this auto-hypertext to its congruent parts, one can (re-)read it as follows:

> After dinner, I went out alone, into the heart of the enchanted city where I found myself in the middle of strange purlieus like a char- acter in the *Arabian Nights*. It was very seldom that, in the course of my wanderings, I did not come across some strange and spacious *piazza* of which no guidebook, no tourist, had ever told me. I had plunged into a network of little alleys, or *calli*, packed tightly together

and dissecting in all directions with their furrows a chunk of Venice carved out between a canal and the lagoon, as if it has crystallised in accordance with these innumerable, tenuous and minute patterns. Suddenly, at the end of one of these alleys, it seemed as though a distension had occurred in the crystallised matter. A vast and splendid *campo* of which, in this network of little streets, I should never have guessed the scale, or even found room for it, spread out before me surrounded by charming palaces silvery in the moonlight. It was one of those architectural ensembles toward which, in any other town, the streets converge, lead you and point the way. Here it seemed to be deliberately concealed in a labyrinth of alleys, like those palaces in Oriental tales whither mysterious agents convey by night a person who, brought back home before daybreak, can never find his way back to the magic dwelling which he ends by believing that he visited only in a dream.

The next day, I set out in quest of my beautiful nocturnal *piazza*, following *calle* after *calle* which were exactly like one another and refused to give me the smallest piece of information, except such as would lead me further astray. Sometimes a vague landmark which I seemed to recognise led me to suppose that I was about to see appear, in its seclusion, solitude and silence, the beautiful exiled *piazza*. At that moment some evil genie which had assumed the form of a new *calle* made me unwittingly retrace my steps, and I found myself suddenly brought back to the Grand Canal. And as there is no great difference between the memory of a dream and the memory of a reality, I finally wondered whether it was not during my sleep that there had occurred, in a dark patch of Venetian crystallisation, that strange mirage which offered a vast *piazza* surrounded by romantic palaces to the meditative eye of the moon.[4]

Narratively, this new (?) state presents itself like an (easy) exercise in trans-vocalization: a little like certain pages of *Jean Santeuil* taken up again in the *Remembrance*, conversion of the third (and the second) into the first person. The anonymous voyager who, in the Grasset version, discovered the secret square at the chance of a walk is now the narrator himself, in the Proustian and the technical sense of the term. One can follow the details of the grammatical transpositions made here that add to the change of person a transfer from the iterative present to an equally iterative past: "the voyager comes across" becomes "it was very seldom that . . . I did not come across"; "he has plunged into a network of little alleys," "I had plunged into a network of little alleys, or *calli*"; "a vast campo, of which he certainly should never have guessed the scale," "a vast and splendid campo of which, in this network of little streets, I should never have guessed the scale"; "you will follow alleys which are exactly like one another and refuse to give you the smallest piece of information," "following *calle* after *calle* which were exactly like one another and refused to give me the smallest piece of information," etc.

The comparison (at the second degree in the "first" version) of the Venetian adventure with a typical episode from *Arabian Nights* is now highlighted from the first sentence and stressed by what may seem a double retake. In reality the first mention provides only a preparatory indication: the narrator wanders about Venice like "the Caliph Harun al-Rachid going in search of adventures in the hidden quarters of Baghdad." [5] The "Oriental tale" comes back only a page further on in the original form of the palace furtively revealed to a character who then believes he has seen it in a dream. And it is the motif of the dream which comes back in the end, without reference to *Arabian Nights*, in the name of the confusion of real and dreamed memories.

But the most significant thematic development seems to me to be the one that relates to the contrastive evocation of the square and its surroundings. The contrast is precisely that of empty space suddenly revealed and the "crystallized Venetian matter" that surrounds it. *Venetian matter* was in the Verdurin hypotext and comes back in *The Fugitive* as "chunk of Venice" and "dark patch." *Crystallisation* is found once in the first version, three times in the "definitive" version. The complete syntagm would be something like "dark patch of crystallised Venetian matter," a sufficiently beautiful object for a substantial thematic. The motif of this unexpected characterization of the city of the Doges is evident for the person who remembers the whole episode, in which Proust insists several times over on this Venetian materiality. The Proustian Venice is not essentially the city of the palace of the Doges, of St. Mark's Square open to the lagoon, and the Grand Canal, but, rather, that of the minuscule canals and even more that of the inhabited "patches" of earth "compressed between the canals and the laguna" and of the *calli* themselves "compressed one against the other" and dividing the urban matter with its thin "furrows," as though the sparing squares of the *rios* and the alleys forced it to this extreme density that the image of crystallisation more or less illustrates. Another page of *The Fugitive*, in which the Oriental motif of the voyager guided by a genie returns, insists on the compactness of urban matter cut up by the outline of the canals seemingly open in an instant for the passage of the visitor:

> One felt that between the mean dwellings which the canal had just parted, and which otherwise would have formed a compact whole, no open space had been reserved; so that a campanile or a garden trellis vertically overhung the rio, as in a flooded city. [. . .] The belfries rose from the water in this poor and populous district like those of humble and much-frequented parish churches bearing the stamp of their necessity, of their use by crowds of simple folk. [. . .] On the ledges of the houses whose crudely cut stone was still rough as though it had only just been sawn, urchins surprised by the gondolas sat trying to keep their balance and allowing their legs to dangle vertically, like sailors seated upon a swing-bridge the two halves of which have been swung apart, allowing the sea to pass between them.[6]

A substantial compactness further accented by the essentially humble and popular, even rural, character of the Proustian Venice, the description of which opens, we remember, with a strongly emphasized comparison with . . . Combray. This paradoxical (in the etymological sense of the word) vision becomes right away the object of a typically apotropaic denial, an accusation against the anti-conformist temptation to present of this sumptuous city only "its poverty-stricken aspects, in the districts where nothing of its splendor is to be seen, and, in order to make Venice more intimate and more genuine, to give it a resemblance to Aubervilliers." But he adds in the same breath: "It was this Venice that I used often to explore in the afternoon, when I did not go out with my mother. The fact was that it was easier to find there women of the people, match-sellers, pearl-stringers, etc."—and it is in fact this Venice that he will continue to describe during almost that entire episode. One sees here that the attention given to the humble city is not without erotic resonances and motivations. With or without an Oriental genie as guide, wandering in these popular quarters, in Venice, in Paris—in Aubervilliers?—relates also to the "cruising" in search of easy and corrupt meetings, a cruising that renews in an urban setting the breathless quest for young peasant girls on the side of Roussainville. To the noble and artistic Venice visited in the dignified company of Madame Mère the proletarian Venice of outings plus riffraff would thus oppose itself. But this easy antithesis, though it is suggested by the text, excessively strains, like the two types of pictorial representations it evokes, two far more interrelated aspects of the Venetian essence. The popular and the artistic Venice coexist constantly, or, rather, they coalesce in the view of Marcel discovering that here there are "works of art, things of priceless beauty, that are entrusted with the task of giving us our impressions of everyday life"; lessons that mix Chardin and Veronese, where one sees, for example, "a little ivory temple with its Corinthian columns and an allegorical statue on its pediment, somewhat out of place among the ordinary surroundings in the midst of which the peristyle with which the canal had provided it retained the look of a landing-stage for market gardeners."[7]

It is for the grandmother of the narrator that it would have been proper to formulate this trait common to trivial objects of the most humble daily life and to the "magnificent things" that are true artworks, which is clearly their simplicity and natural quality, and here as elsewhere this Combray-like aesthetics (the most constantly and doubtless the most authentically Proustian): " 'How your poor grandmother would have loved this simple grandeur!' Mamma would say to me, pointing to the Doges' Palace. [. . .] 'How she would have loved the whole of Venice, and what informality, worthy of nature itself, she would have found in all these beauties, this plethora of objects that seem to need no formal arrangement. [. . .] Your grandmother would have had as much pleasure seeing the sun setting over the Doges' palace as over a mountain.' "[8] And still for the length of a page Marcel will feel the "truth" contained in this prosopopoeia of the dead one, all along a Grand Canal of which the dwellings make him think "of sites of nature"—before meeting for dinner, at one of those palaces transformed into hotels, this perfect symbol of a Combray transposed to Venice: Mme Sazerat.

The popular simplicity of the Venetian landscape is also illustrated, in the *Fugitive* version of our page, by a new connection, the incongruity of which is only apparent, even though the common motif of canals is nowhere invoked: that of Venice and Holland, this other emblem, famous since Hegel, of an aesthetics of daily life. This connection enlivens the few lines that I have omitted a moment ago from my quotation of this page:

> I had entered the network of little alleys, of *calli*. In the evening, with their tall, splayed chimneys to which the sun imparts the most vivid pinks, the brightest reds, it is an entire garden flowering above the houses, and flowering in such a variety of tints as to suggest the garden of a tulip fancier of Delft or Haarlem planted above the town. And then the extreme proximity of the houses made of each

casement the frame in which a cook sits looking out dreamily, a seated young girl having her hair combed by an old woman with a witch-like face distinguishable in the shadow—which resulted in an exhibition of a hundred Dutch paintings hung in a row, from each poor house quiet and close on account of the tightness of the *calli*.

The analogic motif, as one sees, is double: the splayed chimneys evoke tulips, and the compactness of the dwelling evokes at each vista the tiny courtyards and the narrow corridors of a Vermeer or a Pieter de Hoogh. But this analogy, direct as it is, evokes for the attentive reader a third term, a third urban landscape, that is, simply Paris—the Paris that is also, as we know, at the same time (and quite naturally) aristocratic and popular, of the quarter of the Hotel de Guermantes. For the lines that I have just quoted are themselves a double, reproduced without shame from one of the last pages of *Guermantes Way*, at the moment when Marcel, perched in some "observatory" to watch for his beautiful neighbor, entertains himself a moment by contemplating an urban *veduta* that evokes for him several others:

> It is not only in Venice that one has these views on several houses at once which have proved so tempting to painters; it is the same in Paris. Nor do I cite Venice at random. It is of its poorer quarters that certain poor quarters of Paris remind one, in the morning, with their tall, splayed chimneys to which the sun imparts the most vivid pinks, the brightest reds—like a garden flowering above the houses, and flowering in such a variety of tints as to suggest the garden of a tulip fancier of Delft or Haarlem planted above the town. And then the extreme proximity of the houses, with their windows looking across at one another over a common courtyard, makes of each casement the frame in which a cook sits dreamily gazing down at the ground below, or, further off, a girl having her hair combed by an old woman with a witchlike face, barely distinguishable in the shadow: thus each courtyard provides the neighbours in the adjoining house, suppressing sound by its width and framing silent gestures in a series of rectangles placed under glass by the closing of the windows, with an exhibition of a hundred Dutch paintings hung in rows. [9]

Here, again, the genetic relationship and the connection of anteriority of the two texts are not evident: one can observe at most that the *Guermantes* version is a little more developed, a little less confused, than the version in *The Fugitive*, which may be only an imperfect sketch of the former. It is nonetheless true that the analogous Venetian and Dutch types are joined by a third, the Parisian, which confirms its relative universality. The principle of this aesthetics, which would have been illustrated further in the view of Proust, if he had known it, by the Arab type of the medina, is clearly that of the heaping "without arrangement" of a beauty "full of things" and beautiful on account of its very fullness, its unplanned clutter, altogether askew, thrown together, less denied than raised by the unexpected "distension"—for the promenader who wanders without the help of a map at the chance of the *calli*—of a "vast and sumptuous campo" offered, suddenly silent, to the "prolonged meditation of the moonlight." The supreme advantage of the "beautiful nocturnal square," as one saw, is not to be "designated" by the academic and redundant perspective of a large avenue but to hide in the disordered network of alleys, thus participating by its discretion, and as though by chance, in the quite natural and (the word imposes itself in a Proustian context) involuntary aesthetics of the "popular and poor old quarter" at the bottom of which it hides. Here we are decidedly far from the Verdurins.

But not far, it seems to me, from the way Proust, seemingly, eliminates from the opening of *Swann in Love* a more or less well inspired page then borrows (without removing it) another page from the final ones of *Guermantes* in order to compose (if one can call it that) this Venetian episode that is without a doubt—at least in the state his death left it to us—one of the most heteroclite sections of *Remembrance*, obviously made from bits and pieces hastily strung together by the theme of the forgetting of Albertine and the progress of indifference. The patchwork construction, the textual makeshift, are at their height here, as though Proust had wanted faithfully to harmonize the writing with its object and imitate in a puzzling text the labyrinthine and deliciously disconcerting disorder of an emblematic, favorite city. But I have no doubt done well to write "as though . . . ." In fact, Proust undoubtedly did not *want* much here. It just happened like that, from one side as from the other, without anyone truly deciding. Between Venice and its painting—several paintings side by side—the resemblance itself is involuntary.

17

Combray-Venice-Combray

In *Remembrance of Things Past* a (the most) capital aspect of Proustian aesthetics finds its first figure in the Saint-Hilaire church of Combray, with its old porch, "black, and full of holes as a colander," "worn out of shape and deeply furrowed at the sides" by the friction of the cloaks of the peasant women, and more still its apse:[1]

> What can one say of that? It was so crude, so devoid of artistic beauty, even of religious feeling. From the outside, since the street crossing which it commanded was on a lower level, its great wall was thrust upward from a basement of unfaced ashlar, jagged with flints, in which there was nothing particularly ecclesiastical, the windows seemed to have been pierced at an abnormal height, and its whole appearance was that of a prison wall rather than of a church. And certainly in later years, when I recalled all the glorious apses that I had seen, it would never have occurred to me to compare with any one of them the apse of Combray. Only, one day, turning out of a little street in some country town, I came upon three alley-ways that converged, and facing them an old wall, rough-hewn and unusually high, with windows pierced in it far overhead and the same asymmetrical appearance as the apse of Combray. And at that moment I did say to myself, as I might have done at Chartres or at Reims, with what power the religious feeling had been expressed therein, but, instinctively, I exclaimed: "The Church!"
>
> The church! Homely and familiar, cheek by jowl in the Rue Saint-Hilaire, upon which its north door opened, with its two neighbors, Mme Loiseau's house and M. Rapin's pharmacy, against which its walls rested without interspace, a simple citizen of Combray, which might have had its number in the street had the streets of Combray borne numbers, and at whose door one felt that the postman ought to stop on his morning rounds.[2]

The essential feature of this building relates clearly here to its "familiar" character. The church of Combray tries neither to extract itself nor to distinguish itself from the countrylike village that surrounds it and with which it is rather specially and socially united, the physical commonness manifesting and symbolizing a moral citizenship that is, however, in no way a reduction to the secular state: Saint-Hilaire is not at all disaffected; it remains a church, even "the Church" par excellence; it is only, but fully, the church of the village, related to it neither by "artistic beauty" nor by "religious momentum" nor even by the "ecclesiastical" character of an entirely prosaic-looking apse. Its function is clearly religious but of a religion without "momentum," simply of a "practical" nature, daily or weekly, as proved by the wear and tear of the porch and the holy water font, on which the ancient "friction" of the peasant women cloaks has carved "grooves . . . , like those made by cart-wheels upon a stone-gate which they bump against every day."

But the most distinctive feature of Saint-Hilaire is no doubt due to its steeple, which, "from a long way off, inscribing its unforgettable form upon a horizon against which Combray had not yet appeared," signals the approach of the village to the voyagers arrived from Paris for "Easter time," whose slender silhouette "shaped and crowned and consecrated every occupation, every hour of the day, every view in the town," and whose diversely oriented and colored appearances constantly indicate to its fellow citizens the place, the moment, and the season in which they find themselves. It seems to reserve its properly aesthetic lesson for the person most capable of receiving (or creating) it, the grandmother of the narrator, charged (in the final version as apparently in all the earlier ones)[3] with presenting and explaining it to her grandson and to the whole family, who contemplate it, as it were, through her eyes. This lesson is clearly one of simple and natural distinction: "Without quite knowing why, my grandmother found in the steeple of Saint-Hilaire that absence of vulgarity, pretension, and meanness which made her love, and deem rich in beneficent influences, nature itself—when the hand of man had not, as did my great-aunt's gardener, trimmed it—and the works of genius . . . I think, too, that in a confused way my grandmother found in the steeple of Combray what she prized above anything else in the world, namely, a natural air and an air of distinction. Ignorant of architecture, she would say: 'My dears, laugh at me if you like; it is not conventionally beautiful, but there is something in its quaint old face that pleases me. If it could play the piano, I'm sure it wouldn't sound tinny.' " One of the first scenes of *Remembrance* shows the grandmother running in all kinds of weather with "her keen, jerky little step" along the alleys of the garden of Combray, "too straight and symmetrical for her liking, owing to the want of any feeling for nature in the new gardener";[4] this love of nature is accompanied, in her, by a vivid taste for art and literature but only if they stay away from vulgarity and proceed from a "strong breath of genius."[5] Later, in Balbec, Robert de Saint-Loup will make her conquest by the natural ways he has in all things. "For naturalness—doubtless because through the artifice of man it allows a feeling of nature to permeate—was the quality which my grandmother preferred to all others, whether in gardens, where she did not like there to be, as in our Combray garden, too formal flower-beds, or in cooking, where she detested those dressed-up dishes in which you can hardly detect the foodstuffs that have gone to make them, or in piano-playing, which she did not like to be too finicking, too polished, having indeed had a special weakness for the discords, the wrong notes of Rubinstein."[6] In this praise of genius as the trace of the natural in art, and in the enhanced value it implies for "natural beauty,"[7] one hears an echo of Kantian aesthetics, and in this refusal of de-natured nourishments an anticipation of the famous slogan of Curnonsky: that things have "the taste of what they are"; finally, it is not difficult to perceive some relationship between those interpretations of Rubinstein that bear the trace of their spontaneity and the not-tinny sound given to the steeple of Saint-Hilaire.

Passing from architecture to sculpture, the same advantage of nearness and familiarity is found again on the side of Méséglise, under the porch of Saint-André-des-Champs, where, on rainy days, "we would hurry to take shelter, huddled together cheek by jowl with stony saints and patriarchs."[8] By a significant accentuation of the popular character of the message, it is the servant Françoise who here acts as medium, symbolically (because she does not accompany the family on its walks), the saintly characters and the ritual scenes being "represented as they could be in the soul of Françoise," "the medieval peasant (who had survived to cook for us in the nineteenth century)," able to hold forth in her kitchen "about St. Louis as though she herself had known him"; and it is "young Théodore, the assistant in Camus's shop," the grocery of Combray, whom one recognizes in a certain little sculptured angel and who, scapegrace that he may be, spontaneously finds "the same naive and zealous mien" when he helps at the bedside of Aunt Léonie, "as though those carved stone faces, naked and grey as trees in winter, were, like them, asleep only, storing up life and waiting to flower again in countless plebeian faces, reverent and cunning as the face of Théodore, and glowing with the ruddy brilliance of ripe apples." In short "how French that church was!" joining as it does to the geographic and ethnographic faithfulness that of a historic tradition "at once ancient and direct, unbroken, oral, distorted, unrecognisable, and alive."

So great a value placed in relations of metonymic complicity between a building, perhaps a work in general, and its natural and human surroundings logically entails a refusal of anything that may disrupt or corrupt them and thus of every undertaking that could tear it from its geographic site, deprive it of its original function, or erase the marks of its historical age.[9]

The first case was nonexistent concerning architectural works in Proust's day, Western cloisters not having been transported yet to Fort Tryon Park in the north of Manhattan nor, of course, the Temple of Dendur to the Metropolitan Museum. It does not seem to me that Proust commented, retrospectively, on the transfers of sculptures and paintings, far more frequent at least since the end of the eighteenth century, but one can imagine quite easily what he might have thought of the withdrawals by Lord Elgin from the Acropolis or of the "seizures" of the Revolution, the Directory, and the Empire from the whole of Europe and what side he would have been on in the disputes occasioned by the ephemeral but memorable Museum of French monuments organized by Alexandre Lenoir at about the same period.[10] We know that the function of this museum (first a simple depository) was at its origin one of protection against revolutionary vandalism but also that it degenerated on account of the consuming ambition of its founder and that it raised the lively protests of Quatremère de Quincy, who had already courageously protested against the revolutionary seizures in Italy. In both cases the intention of Quatremère, Proustian before his time, thus was that one was not supposed to tear away a plastic work from its site of origin to exhibit it in a museum.[11]

A page of Within a Budding Grove,[12] seemingly contrary to the anti-Elginism that I attribute to Proust by pure deduction, perhaps subtly confirms this. It follows on a passage against automobile travel that has as its effect, by the insensible change in landscape, to efface the irreducible specificity of each place, which by contrast (according to Proust) the more discontinuous character of travel in a train preserves, from station to station and thus from town to town, of which each keeps its "distinct individuality." But, he adds, "in this respect, as in every other, our age is infected with the mania for showing things only in the environment that properly belongs to them, thereby suppressing the essential thing, the act of the mind that isolated them from that environment. A picture is nowadays 'presented' in the midst of furniture, ornaments, hangings of the same period, stale settings which the hostess, who but yesterday was so crassly ignorant but who now spends her time in archives and libraries, excels at composing in the houses of today and in the midst of which the masterpiece we contemplate as we dine does not give us that exhilarating delight which we can expect from it only in a public gallery, which symbolizes far better, by its bareness and by the absence of all irritating detail, those innermost spaces into which the artist withdrew to create." We could hardly imagine a more enthusiastic, a more profoundly motivated, defense of the museum, but we must observe that it is a matter here of a museum altogether opposed to what Lenoir was looking for in the Convent of the Petits-Augustins, of which the odds and ends of the "period" and the "troubadour" decorations resembled far more the artificial recreations of the hostess ridiculed earlier.[13] This ideal museum, by its nudity and its soberness, rather evokes the look of modern museography, which no doubt was not illustrated at the beginning of the century. What remains, of course, is the stress here on the "abstract" and "isolating" character of the creative act, which does not harmonize with the "commonality" and "citizenship" of the churches of Saint-Hilaire and of Saint-André-des-Champs.

Proust sometimes pleads successively for and against and elaborates freely on a given or encountered theme; we know at any rate that the one concerning the individuality of places, which the initial opposition of the "two sides" of Combray illustrated so strongly, will finally be refuted as a childish belief in the course of the sojourn in Tansonville, where Gilberte reveals to the narrator that "the nicest way to go to Guermantes is by way of Méséglise." But I don't want to play the sophist myself in attributing to rhetorical practice the developments that contradict my interpretation. It seems to me, rather, that Proust, in this case, is sensitive at the same time, and from personal experience, to the effort of "abstraction in the interior spaces" that every artistic creation supposes and to the relation of intelligence that every work entertains with its original site and milieu—the first perhaps being a paradoxical but necessary condition for the second. At any rate one of his points of obvious agreement with Ruskin—his principal initiator to Gothic architecture—is the fact that the latter "made no separation between the cathedrals and that background of rivers and valleys against which they appear to the traveller as he approaches, like in a primitive painting," that he "made no separation between the beauty of the cathedrals and the charm of the country out of which they arose, and which everyone who visits them can savour still in the particular poetry of the country and the misty or golden recollection of the afternoon he spent there. Not only is the first chapter of The Bible of Amiens called 'By the Rivers of Waters,' but the book that Ruskin planned to write on Chartres cathedral was to be entitled 'The Springs of Eure.' . . . We would be more keenly alive to the individual charm of a landscape if we did not have at our disposal those seven-league boots which are the great expresses and were obliged, as in the old days, in order to get to some remote spot, to pass through countrysides more and more like that we are making for, like zones of graduated harmony which, by making it less easily penetrable by what is different from itself, and protecting it gently and mysteriously against brotherly resemblances, not only envelop it in nature but also prepare it in our minds."[14]

We are now clearly at the antipodes of the page from *Within a Budding Grove*, with its praise of the railroad and (lacking journeys on horseback or on bicycle, reserved for Albertine, or on foot) on the verge of an inverse praise of excursions in a car, promenades about which we know how much and how gladly Proust practiced them—always ready to go back to see in its place a Romanesque church or a Gothic cathedral as well as a hawthorn bush or a blooming orchard, with or without Agostinelli and even if he had to keep the window hermetically closed on account of his asthma. A praise that is bound to appear in the neighboring text "Les églises sauvées—journées en automobile,"[15] and which one finds again in *Cities of the Plain*, in which Albertine discovers in this way "that it was easy to go in a single afternoon to Saint-Jean and La Raspelière, Douville and Quetteholme, Saint-Mars-le-Vieux and Saint-Mars-le-Vêtu, Gourville and Balbec-le-Vieux, Tourville and Féterne, prisoners hitherto as hermetically confined in the cells of distinct days as Méséglise and Guermantes were long ago, upon which the same eyes could not gaze in the course of a single afternoon, delivered now by the giant with the seven-league boots, clustered around our tea-time with their towers and steeples and their old gardens which the neighboring wood sprang back to reveal."[16] And this modification of space by speed ("Distances are only the relation of space to time and vary with it") clearly has aesthetic consequences: "Art is modified by it also, since a village which seemed to be in a different world from some other village becomes its neighbor in a landscape whose dimensions are altered." Proust comes back to this subject some pages farther on,[17] to observe that "the motor-car [which] respects no mystery" destroys the "special privilege of extra-territoriality" that once upon a time isolated each place in its specific aesthetics. Clearly conscious of the change of values that this conversion implies, he then places in the mouth of the narrator a long justifying palinode, from which I quote the essential:

It may be thought that my love of enchanted journeys by train ought to have kept me from sharing Albertine's wonder at the motor-car which takes even an invalid wherever he wishes to go and prevents one from thinking—as I had done hitherto—of the actual site as the individual mark, the irreplaceable essence of irremovable beauties. And doubtless this site was not, for the motor-car, as it had formerly been for the railway train when I came from Paris to Balbec, a goal exempt from the contingencies of ordinary life. . . . It took us backstage into the streets, stopped to ask an inhabitant the way. But as compensation for so homely a mode of progress, there are the gropings of the chauffeur himself, uncertain of his way and going back over his tracks; the "general post" of the perspective which sets a castle dancing about with a hill, a church and the sea, while one draws nearer to it however much it tries to huddle beneath its age-old foliage; those ever-narrowing circles described by the motor-car round a spellbound town which darts off in every direction to escape, and which finally it swoops straight down upon in the depths of the valley where it lies prone on the ground; so that this site, this unique point, which on the one hand the motor-car seems to have stripped of the mystery of express trains, on the other hand it gives us the impression of discovering, of pinpointing for ourselves as with a compass, and helps us to feel with a more lovingly exploring hand, with a more delicate precision, the true geometry, the beautiful "proportions of the earth." [18]

It is said that Ruskin never took the train, appreciating and using only horse-drawn carriages. Perhaps he would have ended up by tolerating, despite his hate for the mechanism, this new type of locomotion on roads that the automobile offered, and which favors, as one has just seen, an approach of towns and monuments by "commonality" and "citizenship," an approach that is obviously more in harmony with the landscapist and geographic aesthetics attached to the links in situ that Proust shares with him, perhaps judging, as Giono later judged in Italy, that "the car is nothing but a practical way of walking." [19]

After the destruction of the "territorial" context that the transfer to museums of transportable objects brings about, the second form of treason consists in tearing away buildings from their original function: here is the theme of the "assassinated churches" and the "death of Cathedrals" that, before relating to the destructions of the war, concerns the secularization, or menace of secularization, implied in the "projet Briand," which will lead in December 1905 to the law of the separation of church and state. In his article of 1904 Proust vigorously counters these menaces, [20] quoting André Hallays's earlier page against a project of secularization of Vézelay ("Anticlericalism inspires great stupidities. To secularize this basilica means to withdraw from it the bit of spirit that remains. When one will have extinguished the little lamp that shines at the end of the choir, Vézelay will be no more than an archeological curiosity. One will breathe in it the sepulchral air of museums"). And he continues in these terms (partially repeating the preface of his translation of the *Bible of Amiens*, which appeared the same year): "It is in continuing to fulfill the task for which they were originally devoted that things, even if they slowly die at it, keep their beauty and their life. Does one think that in museums of comparative sculpture the moldings of the famous stalls of sculptured wood of the cathedral of Amiens can give an idea of the stalls themselves, in their noble antiquity? Whereas in a museum a guard keeps us from approaching their moldings, the pricelessly precious stalls, so old, so famous, and so beautiful continue to work in Amiens their modest function of stalls. . . . These functions consist, even before instructing the spirits, in supporting the bodies, and this is what, worn out at every service and presenting their reverse side, they are modestly used for."[21] The inveighed-against "moldings" are, for example, those of the Museum of Comparative Sculpture created in 1882— and become in 1937 the new Museum of French Monuments. The two (successively) homonymous museums, the one founded by Lenoir and the one inspired by Viollet-le-Duc, [22] thus have, one after the other, illustrated two practices equally condemnable from Proust's point of view, but the second, if it has in principle the advantage of leaving the authentic works in situ, involves by this very fact the defect that it presents only reproductions: this is a form of what Malraux will call, but with more sympathy, the "imaginary museum." André Hallays was, like Robert de la Sizeranne (one of the first translators and commentators of Ruskin), a fierce opponent of museums; in a manuscript sketch of the preface to *La Bible d'Amiens*, Proust distanced himself from this position ("Not that I want to agree with the theory of MM. de la Sizeranne and Hallays on the disorientation and the death of the works in the museums"), [23] but it was in order to add right away: "But a work, by the fact that it belongs for ever to an individual place of the earth and that it belongs to no other (for if it were uprooted it would immediately die) holds us with ties stronger than the artwork itself, by those ties that persons and countries have to keep us." [24] There followed an antithesis, which has subsisted in the final text, between a painting like the *Mona Lisa*, whose place of origin ("without wanting to displease M. Halleys") is of little importance and which is not "uprooted" in the Louvre, and the statue called "Golden Virgin" of the southern gate of Amiens: "Emerged without a doubt from the neighboring stone quarries, having made in her youth a single voyage to come to the Saint-Honoré porch, not having budged thereafter, having been gradually tanned by that humid wind of the Venice of the North, which bent the arrow above her, watching since so many centuries the inhabitants of this town of which it is the most ancient and the most sedentary inhabitant, she is truly an *Amienoise*." [25]

It thus seems that in this question—which is tricky in theory because often insoluble in practice—the pertinent division for Proust is between, on the one hand, painting, at least easel painting, that one cannot "secularize," [26] and which can stand "disorientation" (though it is certainly difficult fully to appreciate a Carpaccio elsewhere than in Venice or a Franz Hals elsewhere than in Haarlem, but Proust will return in 1921 to see "the most beautiful place in the world," the *View of Delft* in the framework of an exhibition at the Jeu de Paume), and, on the other hand, architecture and sculpture, at least monumental sculpture, which one cannot disorient without "uprooting" nor disaffect without "assassinating." Here at any rate is the beginning of the conclusion of the article from 1904: "The protection even of the most beautiful works of French architecture and sculpture that *will die* the day when they no longer serve for the worship of the needs for which they are created, which is their function as they are its organs, which is their explanation because it is their soul, makes it a duty for the government to insist that the worship be permanently celebrated in the cathedrals, instead of the Briand project authorizing them to make of the cathedrals, at the end of a few years, the museums and conference halls (to suppose the best) that please it." [27] A strict indictment against a practice of disaffection assimilated to an act of vandalism but above all an ardent plea for an aesthetics that one might call *functionalist*, if one understands thereby an aesthetics that refuses to separate the aesthetic relation from the practical and ritual function and which judges, according to the formulation of Mikel Dufrenne, that "a church can be beautiful without being disaffected" [28]—or, rather, as Proust would no doubt say more radically, that a church cannot be truly beautiful except if it is *not* disaffected, because its "beauty" *implies* its function.

The third form of treason consists in the effacement of temporal marks that the excessive restoration of ancient works involves. When Swann qualifies as "dejections of Viollet-le-Duc" the castle of Pierrefonds, one clearly has to make room for jealousy toward a trip that Odette takes without him (and in which he would be all too ready to join her under the hypocritical pretext of "getting a more precise idea of the works of Viollet-le-Duc"),[29] but one knows that Proust shared the hostility to this kind of "work" of a historian such as Émile Mâle, from whom he draws his inspiration for different descriptions of *Remembrance*,[30] and to whom he writes in August 1907: "Restored monuments don't make the same impression on me as stones dead since the 12th century for example, and which remained for Queen Mathilde."[31] Two months later, in a letter to Mme Straus on the subject of the *Dictionnaire raisonné*, in which he nonetheless admires the "genius of architecture," he adds: "It is sad that Viollet-le-Duc has damaged France by restoring, with science but without enthusiasm, so many churches whose ruins would be more moving than their archeological patching up with new stones that do not speak to us, and with moldings that are identical to the original and have kept nothing of it."[32] In *Cities of the Plain* he mocks the "small shopkeeper" who goes on Sunday to feel "the potent sensation of the Middle Ages" in front of the vaults that "have been painted blue and sprinkled with gold stars by the pupils of Viollet-le-Duc"[33] and gives to Albertine, in front of the (fictional) church of Marcouville-l'Orgueilleuse, "half new, half restored"—which does not leave much of the original—this sentence revealing the influence of Elstir, who is her Ruskin and who has taught her "the priceless, the inimitable beauty of old stones" but also, in the eyes of the narrator, a testimony of "the sureness of the taste she had already acquired in architecture": "I don't like it, it's restored."[34] Marcel observes, however, that "this fetish of objective architectural value" here makes the impressionist painter "contradict himself," since he should take account only of the manner in which the setting sun illuminates this facade, restored or not: according to the lesson of Rembrandt (which was in fact already the lesson of Chardin), "beauty is not in objects, for surely then it would be neither as profound nor as mysterious."[35] The respect for Time, which demands that one leaves the objects in the state they have acquired gradually ("in their juice," as antique dealers say graciously), to leave them to "speak to us" from their period and by way of the "rumor of the distances traversed,"[36] is in sum only a stage toward subjectivism, of which impressionism offers a symbolic illustration and which understands that beauty is wholly in the eye of the beholder. From this point of view "what does it matter that a building is new, if it appears old; or even if it doesn't,"[37] providing that the eye knows how to place on it the "special radiance" of an aesthetic vision?

The gradation, rather than the opposition, from Chardin to Rembrandt, sketched in the famous draft of an article apparently abandoned in 1895, [38] comes back again but to be abandoned, once again, in a page of the manuscript for "Journées de pélerinage." [39] "Chardin taught you not to yawn out of boredom and disdain regarding your modest dining room, but to dream of unknown splendors. In revealing to you the life of the still life, in teaching you to admire the ray of sunshine that makes your glass of water shine, or the outline of your knife on the folds of the table cloth as one of the most beautiful things in the world, he discovered for you the beauty of everyday life. And Rembrandt succeeded in freeing you from this false belief that beauty is attached to objects, making you find beauty only in light and shadow." This double abandonment relates perhaps to the insufficiently contrastive character of these two lessons in subjectivism, which in reality are only one: beauty is not in things but in the light and shadow, which evidently represent the aesthetic power of the spirit, that power that allows Chardin and Rembrandt to "discover" the beauty of spectacles disdained until then. But, if one understands that this beauty has a purely subjective source, what follows is clearly that the privilege accorded till now (since the apse of Saint-Hilaire) to the most humble and familiar objects is only a too simple or too elementary expression of that subjectivism, which has no more reasons to neglect the objects ordinarily taken to be precious.

Another gradation sketches itself then, in the same draft, with a third term, the reference of which is here Gustave Moreau: "But if beauty lives in the most humble things, we must not disdain the things that are rare; we must believe that they can also have their beauty. Gustave Moreau arrives at just the right time to restore in you the love of jewelry and of beautiful materials." In a sketch for *Within a Budding Grove*, on the subject of the lesson of Elstir, Proust takes up again this now triple gradation and adds to the example of Moreau that of another painter, more importantly emblematic (and particularly in Proust himself) of an art devoted to luxury and to brilliance: Veronese. "When one is too much under the influence of Chardin's *La Raie*, which shows us that the simplest laws of relief and consistency suffice to render the most modest objects inestimably precious, or of Rembrandt's *Good Samaritan*, which gives all the value of matter to the lighting that makes the rope of the well and the shadow of the door divine, the view of the *Marriage at Cana* and of certain Gustave Moreaus is important to show that, if the most common things are as beautiful as the most opulent, the most opulent are not excepted and also have their beauty." [40] Although this piece does not appear in the final text, one will see the sculptor Ski amuse himself farther on with an implicit and paradoxical link between the Veronese of *Marriage* and a still life that could have inspired Chardin: "You shall fill all our glasses, and they will bring in marvellous peaches, huge nectarines; there, against the sunset, it will be as luscious as a beautiful Veronese." [41]

This name inevitably transports us to Venice, even if *Marriage of Cana*, transferred to the Louvre since Napoléon, is cruelly missing there (for reasons already mentioned, we can ask ourselves what side Proust would take in a certain present campaign for its return to the refectory of San Giorgio Maggiore) and thus from the pages of *The Fugitive* that evoke the sojourn of the narrator in the city of the Doges in the company of his mother. This is where the cardinal opposition around which the aborted or abandoned pages turned for a long time (as we have just seen) becomes explicit: "noble surfaces of marble steps continually splashed by shafts of blue-green sunlight, which, to the valuable lesson of Chardin, acquired long ago, added the lesson of Veronese." [42] One cannot say that the vision of marble steps splashed by blue-green sunlight evokes this latter artist most naturally, but this evocation exists already in (at least) two sketches for this text: "vast marble surfaces, wetted by a quick sun, of a staircase as in Veronese and which added to the lesson of Chardin—that the poorest things can become beautiful in the reflection of light—that other lesson: sumptuous things can do so as well and that they are not without beauty"; and "marine wind currents and sunlight, making vast marble extensions shine with shadow as in Veronese, thus teaching a lesson contrary to Chardin's that even opulent things can have beauty." [43] The most pertinent relation is thus clearly for him, as one has seen, between the painter of *La Raie* and the one of *Marriage*. One sees it here qualified in terms that hesitate between complementarity (*add*) and contrariness (*contrary*); it in fact illustrates what I will call in pseudo-Hegelian terms a dialectic of the humble and the luxurious, in which the attachment to humble objects constitutes a first naive degree then the acceptance, despite their price, of precious objects a second antithetical degree ("second simplicity," as Yves Bonnefoy would say), [44] leading to the final acceptance that recognizes the indifference of the object and the radical subjectivity of aesthetic appreciation. [45]

But during the sojourn in Venice this relation takes the more neutral form of an at once analogic and contrastive parallel, or, more precisely, of an *analogy with transposition* between these two symbolic poles of Combray and Venice (of which Chardin and Veronese evidently offer a pictorial version). The motif of this parallel, that we begin to know well, is clearly indicated from the beginning of this chapter: "as beauty may exist in the most precious as well as in the humblest things—I received there the impression analogous to those which I had felt so often in the past in Combray, but transposed into a wholly different and far richer key." [46] This transposition thus develops for two or three pages, the constant procedure of which consists of an "as in Combray" immediately corrected by a "but in Venice": the morning sun does not shine on the slate of Saint-Hilaire but on the golden angel on the campanile of St. Mark's; the Sunday street is here "paved with sapphire water"; the lined-up houses are here palaces of porphyry and of jasper; the blinds here are "hung between the quatrefoils and foliage of Gothic windows"; the "humble particularities" and the "asymmetries" that made the facades opening on the rue des Oiseaux so "eloquent" have their "equivalents" here, but their message is allotted "upon the ogive, still half Arab, of a facade which is reproduced in all the architectural museums and all the illustrated art books as one of the supreme achievements of the domestic architecture of the Middle Ages," etc. This complacently exploited theme necessarily implies that one abandons the part that consists in presenting only the most humble or poverty-stricken aspects of Venice, since such a presentation would reduce to nothing the contrast on which it rests in order "to make Venice more intimate and more genuine, to give it a resemblance with Aubervilliers," whereas here, for the narrator, "it is works of art, things of priceless beauty, that are entrusted with the task of giving us our impressions of everyday life."

For the narrator but also by proxy, [47] and in a completely symbolic manner, for his grandmother, uncompromising keeper and interpreter of the Combraysian aesthetics. "How your grandmother would have loved this simple grandeur!" her daughter exclaims in front of the palace of the Doges. "She would even have loved those soft tints, because they are unmawkish. How she would have loved the whole of Venice, and what informality, worthy of nature itself, she would have found in all these beauties, this plethora of objects that seem to need no formal arrangement but present themselves just as they are. [. . .] Your grandmother would have had as much pleasure seeing the sun setting over the Doges' Palace as over a mountain." The master word here is *nature*. The grandmother, of course, is already dead at this point, without ever having gone to Venice. But Proust had for a time thought of realizing this symbolic confrontation. This takes place in the Esquisse 27 of *Swann's Way*, already quoted, and precisely one of the pre-texts of the description of the steeple of Saint-Hilaire, still in the state of the steeple of Chartres: "The year she died of a sickness she knew and of which she knew the duration, she saw Venice for the first time, where she really liked only the Doges' palace."[48] The circle was closed in advance, and one thinks one hears the absent one murmur on the Piazetta, as long ago on the square of Combray: "My dears, laugh at me if you like; it is not conventionally beautiful, but there is something in its quaint old face that pleases me.[49] If it could play the piano, I'm sure it wouldn't sound tinny."

18

"One of My Favorite Authors"

In his latest book, which seems to testify to an enthusiastic conversion to the hazardous hypothetical practices and the fanatical interpretations of literary psychoanalysis, Michael Riffaterre gives (among other things) a fate to a page of *Combray* that inspires perplexity in even the least informed Proustians. [1] It is about the landscape of Guermantes and the reveries with which it is associated. The two partially quoted sentences are the following:

> I seemed to have before my eyes a fragment of that fluvial [fluviatile] country which I had longed so much to see and know since coming upon a description of it by one of my favorite authors. And it was with that story-book land, with its imagined soil intersected by a hundred bubbling water-courses, that Guermantes, changing its aspect in my mind, became identified. [2]

This fragment contains an allusive mention ("one of my favorite authors") that is bound to raise the curiosity of the reader: who can that author be, one of his favorites, in whom the young Narrator has seen described the fluvial region that evokes for him the landscape of Guermantes? (And, in addition, where is that region?) For Riffaterre the answer leaves no doubt, and this a priori certitude permits him to move on immediately: " 'one of my favorite authors' is, in fact, Virgil himself."

For reasons I will not consider in detail, the supposed reference to Virgil partakes here of an interpretive network of Freudian inspiration, in which the other point of support is a mention (this time real) of the narrative from the fourth *Georgic* about the visit of Aristaeus to the aquatic kingdom of his mother Cyrene (in connection with Swann's worldly relations). [3] But Riffaterre additionally sees in this narrative the "subtext" of the famous episode of the evening at the Opera, [4] where the members of the aristocracy appear to the Narrator, in their boxes, like divinities in their submarine caverns. This is not impossible, but nothing indicates it, and I continue to think another hypothesis more pertinent and more motivated (and more Riffaterrian in his former manner): this entire metaphor is nothing but the development of the two meanings of the word that textually results in it—the word *baignoire*.[5] As for the value of the theme of the aquarium wall, not psychological (separation from the mother) but sociological (exclusion of the simple spectators), it is strange that Riffaterre does not think of the parallel with the no less famous page of *Within a Budding Grove* on the dining room–aquarium of the Grand Hôtel, illuminated in the evening for the frustrated contemplation of the Balbec populace.[6]

But let us return to Guermantes and to "one of the favorite authors" of the Narrator. The only textual justification put forward for his identification with Virgil is the "hyper-Latin form" of the adjective *fluviatile*,[7] of which Riffaterre knows and mentions another Proustian use, apparently without Virgilian allusion or Oedipal connotation.[8] *Fluviatile* does not seem to me in the least "hyper-Latin": it is an adjective of which the Latin form *fluviatilis* is found, if I believe my Latin dictionary, in Cicero and Livy (but not in Virgil, who only uses *fluvialis*) and of which the Latin meaning concerning vegetables and animals is: "which lives in or near a body of water." Proust turns it around twice for sites or landscapes embellished by modest bodies of water: brooks, torrents, or little rivers like the Couesnon or the "Vivonne"; it clearly contrasts, as a true *diminutive*, with *fluvial*, which evokes a larger river. The simple presence of this word cannot therefore in any case suffice to suggest a Virgilian subtext, with the pseudo-Freudian associations that Riffaterre complacently finds in it.[9] The less so since the use of the word *author* (*écrivain*) to designate the creator of the *Georgics* would be less than idiomatic: it seems to me that, for a writer of the beginning of the century and of the culture of Marcel Proust, Virgil is not an *author* but a *poet*. Linguistic feeling thus opposes such an identification with great force.[10]

In other respects, and above all, the interpretive trail is far more cluttered than Riffaterre seems to believe. In fact, the mention here of a "favorite author" who describes a fluvial country is only the recall of one or two other anterior occurrences in the narrative of the reading afternoons in the garden. We know the theme: the young reader lives more intensely in the landscape evoked by the book than in the one where he finds himself during the reading. Here is the specific illustration of this theme:

> Thus for two consecutive summers I sat in the heat of our Combray
> garden, sick with a longing inspired by the book I was then reading
> for a land of mountains and rivers, where I could see innumerable

sawmills, where beneath the limpid currents fragments of wood lay mouldering in beds of watercress; and near by, rambling and clustering along low walls, purple and red flowers. And since there was always lurking in my mind the dream of a woman who would enrich me with her love, that dream in those two summers was quickened with the fresh coolness of running water; and whoever she might be, the woman whose image I called to mind, flowers, purple and red, would at once spring up on either side of her like complementary colours. [11]

It is clearly these indeterminate erotic-landscapist reveries ("a woman") that, in the course of promenades Guermantes's way, link up with the more precise phantasm of fluvial and poetic loves with the duchess:

> I used to dream that Mme de Guermantes, taking a sudden capricious fancy to me, invited me there, that all day long she stood fishing for trout by my side. And when evening came, holding my hand in hers, as we passed by the little gardens of her vassals she would point out to me the flowers that leaned their red and purple spikes along the tops of the low walls, and would teach me all their names. [12]

The landscape is of the same type, except that the initial reverie dealt with a mountainous region with sawmills, of which the park of Guermantes is only a very calm replica. The taste for landscapes embellished by fresh and rapid courses of water is a constant of Proustian sensibility, and the evocation of purple and reddish (elsewhere yellow or blue) flowers in clusters or cattails is a veritable tic, the "phallic" connotation of which will escape no one and the frequency of which has been pointed up, to my knowledge for the first time, by Jean Milly in his study of the *Pastiches*. [13] He quotes the two pages that have detained us and a sentence from *The Guermantes Way* that recalls "that land of bubbling streams where the Duchess taught me to fish for trout and to know the names of the flowers whose red and purple clusters adorned the walls of the neighboring gardens." [14] These mentions (and others, to which I will return in a moment) are clearly justified in the study of Milly by the presence of another occurrence (the first to be published), in the pastiche of Flaubert: "and they ended up by seeing only two clusters of purple flowers, descending to the rapid water that they almost touched, in the crude light of an afternoon without sun, the length of a reddish wall that was crumbling." [15]

Starting from this rather insistent micro-corpus, curiosity can only orient itself toward two inquiries: that of bookish "sources" and other "subtexts" and that of rough drafts, or pre-texts. Milly explored both trails with the means at his disposal at the time. On the side of the subtext the pastiche of Flaubert shows the track that leads to this page of Sentimental Education: "Clumps of reeds and of rushes lined it unequally; all sorts of plants, which had taken root there, were flaunting golden buds, trailing yellow clusters, pointing spindly purple flowers or darting out random spikes of green."[16]

One could consider that this quotation closes the inquiry and gives the key to the allusion: "one of my favorite authors" would be quite simply Flaubert, and several commentators have held to this. But this evocation of the banks of the Seine at Nogent is not likely to prompt the vision of a mountainous land, and in any case Milly quoted two fragments of pre-texts, of which one contributes to mixing up the cards:

> On the other hand certain novels that I read then, perhaps Le Lys dans la vallée, but I am not sure of this, gave me a great love for certain cattails, whose dark colored clusters grew beyond a flowered path. How many times I looked for them on Guermantes' way, stopping in front of some foxglove, letting my parents go past me, disappearing around some curve of the Vivette, so that nothing would trouble my thoughts, reciting to myself the beloved sentences, asking myself if this was indeed what the novelist had described, trying to identify with the read landscape the landscape I contemplated in order to give it the dignity that literature already conferred for me on reality, in manifesting its essence and teaching me its beauty.[17]

Here, then, is Flaubert in competition with Balzac, but the Indre of Le Lys dans la vallée is no more mountainous nor provided with sawmills than the Seine of Sentimental Education, and there are neither clusters nor cattails in the Balzacian flora. The newly published pre-texts, of the reading afternoons as well as of the promenades to Guermantes, will perhaps tell us a little more.

Much more, in fact, but I fear that they tell us nothing that draws near to Virgil or his generating penis. I follow this track by going back through the sketches of the Pléiade edition, which seem roughly chronological (to the extent that it is possible to establish a chronology for the Proustian pre-text). Esquisse 26 is still about the days of reading. I extract the sentences that concern our subject most directly:

> The book also provided the landscape that was the one of the day in which I read, and the book I was then reading raised high hump-backed hills, all wet with frothy currents and covered with green

lentils, that make the sawmills work and from the height of which one sees in the valley the silver bubble of a steep-sided river [. . .]. The fact is that I desired to see only a land where there were sawmills, natural sources, a silver river seen from high up. I informed myself about the regions of France where I would see these precious things and I asked my parents to send me, rather than to Reims, to Laon, or to Chartres, to spend a few days near Avallon, in the region called Little Switzerland, or in the Vosges. The book that introduced these imaginary sites into my days in Combray and projected desire onto my entire future, wasn't it the one that I figured so much according to the site where it took place, and according to the year I wrote on its cover? Or did it come off one of its pages by an association of ideas because I made myself reconstitute an image it did not contain? In any case, this landscape of brisk waters and aquatic industries that I wanted so much to visit was inseparable for me from some enclosure, at the foot of which grew reddish cobs, clusters of purple and yellow flowers. [18]

Here we thus have again the mountainous landscape, the torrents, and the sawmills, and here is a new referential location: the Vosges or the region of Avallon. But these desired places are not necessarily the "landscape" of the book that communicated the desire, or, rather, they certainly are not: if it were a matter of visiting this landscape itself, there would be no choice between sites as different as the Vosges and the region of Avallon. It is a matter, then, of landscapes *similar* to the one of the book, themselves apparently inaccessible.

Esquisse 31 is probably the oldest. It is also the most revealing. Here is its essential:

When I was reading a book by Bergotte that took place in the Jura [. . .] the landscape of the novel rose in the middle of the real landscape, and the images that it evoked constantly of boiling water, of rivers with trouts like silver ribbons seen from the height of wooded hills, of mechanical sawmills walking in the water, of green plants growing in the ramblings of these so fresh edges, of natural sources, of boats descending the rapids, which gave me the desire to ask my parents to let me spend a summer in this or that watering place where I knew there were mechanical sawmills, wooded heights, sources with a fresh and salubrious taste, and where mainly one canoed and fished for trout in agitated rivers.

In rereading today this book by Bergotte I cannot find anywhere a sentence dealing with reddish cobs, clusters of purple and yellow flowers falling the length of a wall oozing water. Nonetheless this idea of running water, of bubbling water, of silver brooks seen from the height of wooded hills, of wood from the sawmills half decayed by water, that I had all the time before my eyes, dining, taking walks in the garden, which during a year, at least at certain hours, for at others I rather thought of cathedrals and *The Bible of Amiens*, was linked to reddish cobs, to clusters of purple and yellow flowers, that I would have liked to know and that I nonetheless figured out very well for myself, the image of which clearly came from a book, always colored my landscape of mountains and sprightly rivers. I despised the flowers of the garden, and stopped hopefully only on a path along the humid wall of which I saw something that vaguely resembled my purple and yellow clusters. When I had heard the pastor say that Guermantes was a little Switzerland, I saw there the silver brooks, the woods decayed by water, the purple and yellow clusters along a wall spotted by humidity. Now Mme de Guermantes was not only for me the girl of her name, born of her sonority and of her legend. Sometimes I saw her firing a rifle at the trouts along the waterfalls, looking from the height of a hill at rivers which from this high were nothing but a silver bubble, and toward evening going with a slow step to look at the little enclosures of her farms where reddish cobs and yellow and purple clusters were stuck.[19]

There are numerous revelations in this page, fascinating on account of its compulsive repetition. The first relates to the site of the book, this time unhesitatingly the Jura, the apparent origin of all ulterior reveries. The qualificative *mountainous* and the evocation of sawmills clearly applies without difficulty to this region. The second relates to the author, the famous and mysterious "favorite author": here it is quite simply Bergotte. But this identification is only provisional—it will disappear long before the final version; and, moreover, it brings no referential "key," since Bergotte is a fictional author. But there is more to say on each of these two points.

It seems that Proust renounced very quickly attributing the "novel" (since there is a novel in this version) to Bergotte; a note facing this page indicates, "It would be better if this book were not by Bergotte so that the flowers are not associated with Mlle Swann." A note waiting for a new writing that will not be long delayed and that will remove Bergotte from the paternity of the novel with the "mountainous and fluvial landscape" to make him the author of another. Proust decides, in fact, that Bergotte will be linked to Mlle Swann, as a friend of the family, and associated with more artistic images of visits to cathedrals in the company of Gilberte. There will thus be more than one example of bookish influence in the reveries of Marcel; there will be two successive ones: the one of the fluvial landscape and the one of the visits to the cathedrals—and Bergotte will be linked only to the second, in a temporal substitution clearly marked by the already quoted final text.[20] The fluvial landscape will nonetheless come back in the course of the promenades around Guermantes, at a moment evidently contemporaneous of the first series of readings, which the anachronic disposition of Combray permits. We thus have, starting from that moment (not precisely dated in the genetic chronology), two favorite authors the first of which is no longer Bergotte but an anonymous author, imaginary or not. In the Esquisse 31 there were, however, already two, but two that came to conjoin their influences in the same synthetic reverie: the mountainous land came from "Bergotte," and the cattail flowers came "clearly out of a book," that is to say, certainly out of another book. We know the extradiegetic "model" for this one since the 1908 pastiche of Flaubert: it is Sentimental Education.

What would remain to be identified is the other, the one whose plot "develops in the Jura," unless there is no model for what would be an invention ex nihilo. But it seems that this is not the case. A note on this sketch by Jo Yoshida in fact indicates:

> Proust is perhaps thinking of Ruskin's Seven Lamps of Architecture, of which a passage, extracted by Robert de La Sizeranne in his Pages choisies, bears the title: "Spring in the Jura." Ruskin there describes a twilight landscape that he saw on the hills towering over the run of the Ain, above the village of Champagnole. The description of the landscape evoked by Bergotte's book has a striking resemblance with Ruskin's text. Not only does one find the "wooded hills" and the "green plants growing in the ramblings of those so fresh edges" in this passage of the English writer, but there is a whole page devoted to the description of the "clusters of flowers."[21]

Another note, to the final text, confirms this hypothesis by relativizing it, since it mentions both the Flaubert pastiche and the Renan pastiche for its evocations of transparent waters and trout fishing. But this page of the pseudo-Renan,[22] devoted to a fluvial landscape in the north of France, itself refs us explicitly to Ruskin, who vaunted (in the *Bible of Amiens* translated by Proust in 1901) "the grace of its poplars, the icy freshness of its sources." We are thus left with two "sources"—the right word: Flaubert and Ruskin for the flowers in clusters and in cattails; and Ruskin once again, and he alone (?) for the mountainous landscapes, originally from the Jura, and other evocations of fluvial sites, for which his taste seems as constant as Proust's—it being understood here as elsewhere that one comes under the "influence" of someone only if one calls for it, that is to say, when it meets and confirms an autonomous tendency: a reader indifferent to this type of landscape would not emphasize these descriptions, whoever their author.

A detail of Esquisse 31 seems to me to confirm the Ruskin hypothesis—that is to say, Ruskin here as a model for Bergotte. The dissociation between the two authors having not yet been accomplished, the mention of a reverie on the cathedrals, which later will refer to Bergotte alone, refers also explicitly to Ruskin: "at other [moments] I thought rather of the cathedrals and of *The Bible of Amiens.*" This *rather* and this explicit mention seem to me to establish an opposition between two Ruskins, the one of *Amiens* and of the cathedrals and the one of the *Seven Lamps* and (among others) of the landscape of the Jura. In this case (a simple hypothesis but made very plausible by the ramblings and the accents of the text) the two Bergottes—the first of which, for reasons already mentioned, will become an anonymous favorite author—would have as their common model the sole Ruskin, but considered from two different sides of his abundant and many-sided work.

Ruskin has long been considered as one of the models of Bergotte. The most pertinent feature of this connection is at least that Ruskin has had an analogous influence on Proust's aesthetic and writing as the one of Bergotte on Marcel[23]—and which is perhaps attested by the evolution from *Jean Santeuil* to *Remembrance.* But the little genetic course that we have just followed in reverse is perhaps its most precise, and its most striking, illustration.[24]

But it is understood that a genetic trail is no more than a genetic trail. It is not a matter of drawing from this one an excluding hypothesis of the kind "The 'favorite author' of the Narrator of *Combray* is, *in fact,* Ruskin + Flaubert"— readings that are not very plausible for a boy who reads *François le Champi.* In *Swann's Way* such as Proust wanted it and ended it in 1913, this author is anonymous and imaginary and on the point of being supplanted, in relation to Gilberte, by the no less imaginary Bergotte. What genetic study does give us is not a key for what is not a roman à clef but only a trace of the process of transformation by which different elements of reality became elements of fiction. The materials given by reality in no case say the "truth" about a fiction that is exactly what it pretends to be—this is its privilege and its definition. On the other hand, they can tell us a part (even if it is infinitely small) of the truth about the progressive elaboration of that fiction, for this elaboration belongs to reality: a reality that can be called, in this instance, Proustian *bricolage*.

The debate, or rather the division, between genesis and structure always evokes for me the famous page where Saussure compares the evolution of language to a chess game:[25] at any moment of the game the synchronic system of the positions is "totally independent of any previous state of the board. It does not matter at all whether the state in question has been reached by one sequence of moves or another sequence. Anyone who has followed the whole game has not the least advantage over a passer-by who happens to look at the game at that particular moment. In order to describe the position on the board, it is quite useless to refer to what has happened ten seconds ago." This remark is not only valid for the "inspection" of the state of the game but ultimately for the continuation of the game by two players who would come at that moment to take the place of the two earlier ones: the state of the game is such and such, and one can pursue it without paying any attention to its antecedents. On the other hand, if one wants to know and to appreciate the technique of the two first players, it is very useful to know "how they got there." The "state of the game" is an autonomous fictional system that one has to take as it is if one wants to enter into it and participate in it, but the talent of each player is an element of reality (outside the game), the total comprehension of which escapes us, no doubt, but the partial knowledge of which presumes as close a diachronic observation as possible of the stages of the game.

My reader will have seen where I am going: the reading of a text, and especially a fictional text, supposes nothing but a consideration of the state of the game and linguistic competence (to know the meaning of *fluvial* or of *author*) and encyclopedic competence (to know where one finds torrents) that permit one to decipher and to interpret it; the knowledge and comprehension of the author's work are of a different order, for which no information on the diachronic series of antecedents, or what an aesthetician calls the "heuristic path" of the work,[26] can be neglected.

These two points seem to me reasonable, and the exploration of our corpus illustrates them quite well: the immanent interpretation of the object "favorite author—fluvial landscape" demands no knowledge of the genetic course, and its only condition of validity is the taking into account and the integration of the context: for example, to compare page 188 of *Swann's Way* with page 92, to which it obviously sends the reader, and to page 7 of *The Guermantes Way*, which is its obvious echo, and to infer from it that the author in question is the one the Narrator reads before discovering Bergotte and that the evoked landscape is not only fluvial but mountainous and torrential. By contrast, the comprehension of Proust's work demands a diachronic perspective (when it is possible) on all the elements, bookish and other, of which the genetic record bears the trace.

It is thus appropriate to distinguish these two activities as clearly as possible a priori. But this does not mean that they have no relationship: after all, the literary work is not a practice as autonomous, and exhaustively defined by its "constitutive rules," as a chess (or other) game. First of all, it goes without saying that the reading of a pre-text supposes the same aesthetic appreciations as the one of a "final" text, for the simple reason that a pre-text is also a text. Moreover, it happens that certain anomalies of a text, as there are so many in *Remembrance*, are explained by the consultation of pre-texts, if any exist, and in this case the genesis contributes to enlightening the structure. In situations of an unfinished work (like the one of *Remembrance* after *The Captive*) the distinction even between final text and pre-text becomes problematic, and we know at least since Valéry that the very notion of completion is hazardous. Finally, between the purely aesthetic appreciation (of the kind "This painting is fuzzy") of a work as an autonomous object and its *artistic* appreciation ("This work is Impressionist), which supposes a consideration of its historical context, and thus of its "heuristic path," there can be no watertight divider; there are many interactions. [27] Or, rather, outside the artificial situation à la Condillac, and specifically in literature, the art of signification par excellence, there can be no purely aesthetic appreciation (or completely innocent reading of an absolutely naked text), to which no extratextual datum would associate itself. But, if we begin to integrate this kind of data (e.g., the fact that Proust had read Virgil), it would without a doubt be better to integrate as many as possible (e.g., take into account that Proust has read Flaubert and Ruskin as well), for nothing leads more astray than an incomplete, or truncated, information.

And, above all, it seems to me indispensable to know (and to say) at each moment what one is speaking about. Too often interpretation does not say if it is structural or genetic, if it relates to the rough text or to its process of elaboration, setting aside for itself the ease of jumping onto one terrain as soon as the other resists, and, for example, invoking a reading of Virgil without specifying if the reader is called Proust, Marcel—or Riffaterre. I know that the night of the Unconscious, where all cows are crazy—especially since we have collectivized it into the "Unconscious of the text" or the "Unconscious of fiction"—legitimates all kinds of dogma and glibness and responds to every unstoppable objection, "All the more reason"; but, as my reader will have understood, that is a little of what I reproach it with.

Notes

CHAPTER 1. FROM TEXT TO WORK

1. An expanded version of a lecture given at the Maison Française, New York University, October 1997.

2. Who declares—with a revelatory precision that could or should seem superfluous today—to have himself represented a form of criticism "turned more toward the works than toward the persons" (*Histoire de la littérature française* [Paris: Stock, 1936], 528).

3. Translator's note: "First year of preliminary art studies prior to the competitive examination for entry to the École Normale Supérieure" (Larousse, *Grand dictionnaire*, 447).

4. VIe section, which was to become in 1975 the École des Hautes Études en Sciences Sociales.

5. Which was joined, after 1965, by Greimas's seminar, more "scientist" in appearance and with a larger multidisciplinary opening, marvelously complementing the Barthes seminar for the apprentice "structuralists" that we were.

6. Translator's note: *por linhas tortas* is Portuguese for "by crooked lines." A Portuguese proverb reads: "Deus escreve direito por linhas tortas."

7. Paris: Seuil, 1966 (later become *Figures I* on account of the volumes that followed). Despite the insistence of Philippe Sollers, who had accepted several of them for *Tel Quel*, I hesitated to publish so disparate a volume; curiously or not, it is Georges Poulet who persuaded me, with a somewhat enigmatic but all the more convincing phrase: "Do it, you won't regret it." As a matter of fact, I have never known whether I regretted it, nor even if I should have (known it).

8. One of them, "L'Or tombe sous le fer," was first entitled "A 'Structural' Poetics?" Under the cover of a quotation and a question mark it was, of course, a matter of the poetics of the baroque but apparently not without premonition of something else. Rapidly disturbed by the too oblique effect of the announcement, I wanted to change the title when I saw the proofs of the journal, but Sollers, whose theoretical libido was stronger than mine on that day, firmly objected.

9. The respective translations into French of *Ficciones* (1944, trans. 1952); and *Otras Inquisiciones* (1952, trans. 1957).

10. Albert Thibaudet, *Reflexions sur la critique* (Paris: Gallimard, 1939), 136.

11. First published in 1962 in *L'Homme*.

12. During a few months I think I liked the idea of a study on the work of Corneille that would have treated his world as one of those strange (distant from our own) "samples of civilization" that Ruth Benedict had described. Various obstacles rather quickly turned me away from this project, which was without doubt a little too metaphorical, applied, or transposed, anthropology; witness, a very allusive sentence in *Figures I* (160). I'll perhaps end up writing this book, in one or two centuries.

13. Clearly prepared several months earlier, the first issue of the magazine and the first volume of the collection (Todorov, *Introduction à la littérature fantastique*) appeared together at Éditions du Seuil in February 1970. Our subject, which the first summary and the explicit subtitle "Revue de théorie et d'analyse littéraires" bear witness to and which was firmly maintained since then, was in fact more complex, or more strategic: it was to bring about and to put to work a defensive and offensive alliance between poetics and the "nouvelle critique."

14. Reprinted in *Figures II* (Paris: Éditions du Seuil, 1969). Translator's note: English: "Principles of Pure Criticism," in *Figures of Literary Discourse*, trans. Alan Sheridan (New York: Columbia University Press, 1982).

15. Wölfflin designates in this fashion after the fact the thesis of his *Fundamental Principles* of 1915, adding, "I don't know where this expression came from: it was in the air" ("Pro domo," 1920, French trans. by R. Rochlitz in *Réflexions sur l'histoire de l'art* [Paris: Flammarion, collection "Champs," 1997], 43).

16. *Cours de philosophie positive*, 4th ed. (Paris, 1877), 5:12, quoted in connection with Wölfflin by Germain Bazin, *Histoire de l'histoire de l'art* (Paris: Albin Michel, 1986), 177.

17. Tocqueville, *L'Ancien Régime et la Révolution*, bk. 2, chap. 12.

18. "Conclusions sur Flaubert" (August 1934), in *Réflexions sur la littérature* (Paris: n.p., 1940), 2:251.

19. See Paul Veyne *L'Inventaire des différences* (Paris: Seuil, 1976), 18–33, on the presence "at the very center of historical practice" of what he calls the "transhistorical invariant."

20. "Poétique et histoire" (Cerisy, July 1969), printed in *Figures III* (Paris: Seuil, 1972).

21. See Lucien Febvre, "Littérature et vie sociale. De Lanson à Daniel Mornet: Un Renoncement?" (1941), in *Combats pour l'histoire* (Paris: Colin, 1953).

22. "Figures," first entitled "La rhétorique et l'espace du langage" (*Tel Quel* 19 [Fall 1964]).

23. "La Rhétorique restreinte" (*Communications* 16 [December 1970]), reprinted in *Figures III*. Translator's note: English: "Rhetoric Restrained," in *Figures of Literary Discourse*.

24. No. 8, November 1966.

25. Translator's note: English: "Flaubert's Silences," in *Figures of Literary Discourse*.

26. Translator's note: English: "Frontiers of Narrative," in *Figures of Literary Discourse*.

27. Translator's note: published separately in English under the title *Narrative Discourse: An Essay in Method*, trans. Jane E. Lewin (Ithaca, NY: Cornell University Press, 1980).

28. Paris, Seuil, 1983. Translator's note: English: *Narrative Discourse Revisited*, trans. Jane E. Lewin (Ithaca, NY: Cornell University Press, 1988).

29. Paris, Seuil, 1991.

30. Paris, Seuil, 1976. Translator's note: English: *Mimologics*, trans. Thais E. Morgan (Lincoln: University of Nebraska Press, 1995).

31. Gaston Bachelard, *The Psychoanalysis of Fire* (1949) (Boston: Beacon Press, 1968), 5, in which he links precisely this work of "making explicit"—which he will later extend, as we know, to reveries on water, earth, air, etc.—to the effort of a "psychoanalysis of objective knowledge" that constituted in 1947 *The Formation of the Scientific Mind*. Making explicit ("psychoanalyzing" in this sense) the seductions, this is the means not certainly of dismissing them (which is not the design) but perhaps of keeping them from becoming an *epistemological obstacle* (by "falsifying the inductions"). It seems to me that this is the function that unites the two sides of the Bachelardian enterprise, and it is the one that I have tried, in my way, to apply to the mimological reverie, a seductive reverie to which Bachelard himself contributed, no doubt in the spirit of an at once critical and sympathetic explication; whence, among other things in *Mimologics*, a chapter ("The Genre and Gender of Revery") that concerns him twice over.

32. Paris: Seuil, 1979. Translator's note: English: *The Architext: An Introduction*, trans. Jane E. Lewin (Berkeley: University of California Press, 1992).

33. Paris: Seuil, 1982. Translator's note: English: *Palimpsests: Literature in the Second Degree*, trans. Channa Newman and Claude Doubinsky (Lincoln: University of Nebraska Press, 1997).

34. Translator's note: Giraudoux is here parodying Lamartine.

35. Paris: Seuil, 1987. Translator's note: English: *Paratexts: Thresholds of Interpretation*, trans. Jane E. Lewin (Cambridge: Cambridge University Press, 1997).

36. Paris, Seuil, 1991. Translator's note: English: *Fiction and Diction*, trans. Catherine Porter (Ithaca, NY: Cornell University Press, 1993).

37. This distinction is superbly illustrated by a page of *Jean Santeuil* that I reproach myself for not having quoted in this connection—but it is never too late to do things well: on the eve of New Year's Day Jean's tutor, to whom Jean had given as a gift a "little bust," brings him also "a present. It was a book by Joubert. During two hours M. Beulier read it with Jean; when they had finished [. . .], at the moment Jean looking at the book said: 'No present has given me more pleasure,' M. Beulier took the book, put it into his briefcase and never brought it back. Having given its entire meaning, its soul, its moral help to Jean, he had given him all of it" ([Paris: Gallimard, Pléiade, 1971], 269).

38. I spoke then rather imprudently of aesthetic *appreciation*, and even of aesthetic *satisfaction* (*Fiction and Diction*, 17), without regard for the distinction, established later on, between *appreciation* and *attention*. It is certainly excessive to make of aesthetic *satisfaction* the criterion for conditional literarities, because a negative appreciation ("This text is not beautiful") is quite as much the indication of an aesthetic relationship (that is to say, first of all of an attention) to a text. The most prudent formula thus consists in defining conditional literature by the fact of according a text, whatever it is, an aesthetic *attention*, itself defined by the question "Does this text please me (aesthetically)?" The response—that is to say, the appreciation—can then be positive or negative; the relation to the text will be no less of an aesthetic order. One can thus define conditional (or attentional) literarities by the necessity of a personal appreciation but with the condition of not identifying appreciation and satisfaction.

39. Kant, *Critique of Judgement*, para. 58.

40. Jacques Lecarme and Éliane Lecarme-Tabone, *L'Autobiographie* (Paris: Armand Colin, 1997), 269–73.

41. See "Vraisemblance et motivation," in *Figures II*.

42. See "A Logic of Literature," in this collection.

43. Jean Prévost, *La Création chez Stendhal* (Paris: Mercure de France, 1951), 92. This remark concerns retrospective autobiography and not the journal of immediate notation, which (as Prévost says of the one Stendhal wrote in 1804) is precisely lacking "the use of memory." But one could possibly find in the act of writing a journal *other* impulses of seduction.

44. Jacques Lecarme, "L'Hydre anti-autobiographique," in *L'Autobiographie en procès*, under the direction of Philippe Lejeune (Paris: Université Paris X, 1997), 36.

45. Preface to *Spirit of the Laws*.

46. Philippe Lejeune, *Pour l'autobiographie* (Paris: Seuil, 1998), 11–25.

47. See "What Aesthetic Values?" in this collection.

48. *Palimpsests*, 250; I came back to this at greater length in "Le Paratexte prou-stien," lecture to the colloquium "A la recherche du texte," New York, December 1984, published in *Études proustiennes* (Paris: Gallimard, 1987), 6:29–32; and again in *Paratexts*, 302–3. That is a lot but apparently not enough.

49. See, for example, Marie Darrieussecq, "L'Autofiction, un genre pas sérieux," *Poétique* 107 (September 1996).

50. See *Paratexts*, 94–103. Translator's note: English: *The Aesthetic Relation*, trans. G. M. Goshgarian (Ithaca, NY: Cornell University Press, 1999), 158–80.

51. See Dorrit Cohn, "L'Ambiguité générique de Proust," *Poétique* 109 (February 1997).

52. The question mark is due to the fact, clear to everyone, that all fiction con-tains, and feeds on, innumerable elements of "reality"—autobiographical ones, among others, as critics who want to fill their copy and still more interviewers who try to think of questions don't tire of suspecting.

53. *L'Oeuvre de l'art, I: Immanence et transcendance* (Paris, Seuil, 1994). Translator's note: English: *The Work of Art*, trans. G. M. Goshgarian (Ithaca, NY: Cornell Uni-versity Press, 1997).

54. Already suggested by James Edie, "La Pertinence actuelle de la conception husserlienne du langage," in the collection *Sens et existence. En hommage à Paul Ricoeur* (Paris: Seuil, 1975).

55. "I do not believe in things, only in their relationship" (quoted by Jakobson, *Selected Writings* [The Hague: Mouton, 1971], 1:632).

56. The formulation of Eco is, in fact, reciprocal: "A work is *open* as long as it re-mains a *work*" (*The Open Work*, trans. Anna Cancogni [Cambridge, Mass.: Harvard University Press, 1989], 104).

57. Paris: Seuil, 1997.

58. Chapters 6 and 7 for the first part; chapters 11, 12, and 13 for the second.

59. What makes this recuperation sometimes more difficult today is not the conceptual detour, which was quite pleasant at its start, but the repetitive char-acter of a practice that, nearly a century after Malevich and Duchamp, really has nothing much to transgress. Unless it affects, by an aesthetic value of the second (or third) degree, the feeling of despondency that it procures. On this complex set of actions and reactions, see Nathalie Heinich, *Le Triple jeu de l'art contemporain: sociologie des arts plastiques* (Paris: Minuit, 1998).

60. Once again, I do not present the specification that this adjective comprises

as being without problems, since it is today contested by many artists, critics, and theoreticians: it expressed on my part a choice, which I think necessary, of a necessity that I have attempted to demonstrate but about which I must admit that it is not to be recognized by all.

61. "The concept of the work of art implies that of success. Works of art that have not succeeded are not works of art" (Adorno, Théorie esthétique [1970] [Paris: Klincksieck, 1989], 241).

62. Adorno, Théorie esthétique, 333—unless, of course, one gives to aesthetic the current meaning of individual or collective "taste," as when I speak, in a good or bad sense, of the aesthetic of my neighbor, attested by the color of his shades. But aesthetic in the sense (of "meta-aesthetic") in which I understand it here, as all activity of knowledge and of description, owes itself to respect the "axiological neutrality" dear to Max Weber.

63. See "Style and Signification," in Fiction and Diction.

64. In this paragraph I answer a little, without much hope of convincing him, the objections formulated by Henri Mitterand in "A la recherche du style," Poétique 90 (April 1992); and in "Un 'Bel artiste': Balzac," in Le Roman à l'oeuvre (Paris: PUF, 1998). But I have to specify that in these two articles Mitterand proposes, as a concession, to dissociate two notions that I, for my part, conjoin, since I define the first by the second: style and aspect. He allows me the second as a purely descriptive notion and advocates that the first is necessarily and legitimately axiological— and, according to myself, of an axiology with a strong objectivist, or universalist, connotation: "Balzac has a style by the very fact that he is recognized as great." Definitions, quite clearly, are free, and I can't refuse them to my contradictor and friend, who is free to call "aspect" what I nonetheless will continue to call style and "style" what I would rather call "positively valued style"; what I would, by contrast, refuse is that his axiological definition apply surreptitiously to my descriptive notion. It goes without saying that I think as he does that "Balzac has a style"—on which, universal recognition or not, I apply diverse, fluctuating, varied appreciations. I even think that he has several styles, but I would not want to complicate things too much.

65. "De l'oeuvre au texte," Revue d'esthétique (Oeuvres complètes [Paris: Seuil, 1994], 2:1211).

CHAPTER 2. WHAT AESTHETIC VALUES?

1. An expanded version of a communication to the forum Le Monde–Le Mans, October 1997.

2. Durkheim, "Jugements de valeur et jugements de réalité," *Revue de Métaphysique et de Morale*, 1911.

3. See "Axiological Relations," in this collection.

4. See Nathalie Heinich, *Le Triple jeu de l'art contemporain* (Paris: Minuit, 1998).

5. *Critique of Judgement*, para. 42.

6. Hegel, *Aesthetics* (Oxford: Oxford University Press, 1975), 1:2.

7. Oscar Wilde, "The Decay of Lying," in *Complete Works* (London: Collins, 1997), 985–86; Marcel Proust, *Remembrance of Things Past* (London: Chatto and Windus, 1981), 2:338. Proust refers explicitly to Wilde on a different page of *Against Sainte-Beuve* (*Against Sainte-Beuve and Other Essays* [London: Penguin Books, 1988], 65) under a perhaps apocryphal form: "It is only since the Lake Poets that there have been fogs on the Thames"; the influence of Turner would no doubt be more pertinent here than that of the Lake Poets. I had myself compared the propositions of Wilde and Proust in *The Aesthetic Relation* but without reference to the text of "The Decay of Lying," which I found afterward in Alain Roger's book *Court traité du paysage* (Paris: Gallimard, 1997).

8. Roger, *Court traité du paysage*, 12–14.

9. Charles Lalo, *Introduction à l'esthétique* (Paris: Armand Colin, 1912), 133 and 128, quoted by Roger, *Court traité du paysage*, 16.

10. *Against Sainte-Beuve* (London: Penguin, 1988), 123.

11. I borrow this notion—stronger than that of *aesthetic attention*, or underlining more the active side that it involves—from Jean Marie Schaeffer, *Les Célibataires de l'art* (Paris: Gallimard, 1996).

12. Georg Simmel, "Philosophie du paysage," in *La Tragédie de la culture*, French trans. (Paris: Rivages-Poche, 1988), 233.

13. Simmel, "Philosophie du paysage," 235.

14. Simmel, "Philosophie du paysage, 239, 239–40; my emph.

15. "A 'piece of nature' is actually a self-contradiction; nature has no pieces; it is the unity of a whole, and as soon as one detaches a fragment from it, the latter is no longer entirely nature" (Simmel, "Philosophie du paysage," 232).

16. I perhaps strain the comparison I propose between Simmel (and Croce) and the "artialist" thesis of Roger, who continues in these terms: "This idea of a nature aestheticized by the eye of the artist." This is a formulation that suits me perfectly and that I believe to conform to the thought of Simmel. I add that Simmel's reflection on the aesthetics of landscapes leads to the notion of *Stimmung*, decisive for him. Like Roger, I shall leave it aside.

17. Hegel, *Aesthetics*, 1:43.

18. Translator's note: "Le Petit vin blanc" is a French popular song.

19. Translator's note: *La Fontaine de Cuivre* is a still life by Chardin.

20. I say "no objective criterion," which clearly does not exclude *subjective opinions*; the latter are as intense in private as they are impossible to (legitimately) objectify as public criteria.

21. See again the investigations of Nathalie Heinich mentioned earlier.

22. Nikolaus Harnoncourt, *Le Dialogue musical*, French trans. (Paris: Gallimard, 1985), 130–31.

CHAPTER 3. AXIOLOGICAL RELATIONS

1. I paraphrase, or rather condense, a page from Kant here, a rather pleasant page (there are some), which ends in this definition: "We wish only to know if this mere representation of the object is accompanied in me with the satisfaction, however indifferent I may be as regards the existence of the object of this representation" (*Critique of Judgement*, trans. J. H. Bernard [New York: Hafner Press, 1931], 39).

2. I understand here by artistic failure the fact that the artist fails in his "candidacy" for positive aesthetic appreciation, rather than the fact that he misses the goal that he personally envisioned (a failure that the public may very well miss). The two effects are often independent from each other: a work can disappoint its author and please the public or, conversely, satisfy its author and displease the public. Ridicule (by definition a fact of intersubjective relation) is exclusively relevant for the second case, even if it can happen that (if I back up a little and thus redouble myself somewhat) I judge myself to be ridiculous.

3. I nonetheless suppose that all occasions for ridicule have in common the fact of a pretense, or of a postulation, that misses its effect: the most obvious of them is the refused and disdained amorous demand, like Arnophe's to Agnès or Alceste's to Célimène. These situations go back on the whole to what Stendhal called "to exhibit an *inferior self*" (*Love*, chap. 41) or, voiced by Prince Korasoff, "*to show an inferior self*" (*The Red and the Black*, pt. 2, chap. 24).

4. Kant, *Critique of Judgement*, 126.

5. The word is clearly a little too strong to qualify most of the relations of this kind, but I use it because I can't think of a weaker one, counting on the reader to make the mental adjustment that is demanded here.

6. Kant, *Critique of Judgement*, 125.

7. Kant, *Critique of Judgement*, 145.

8. I borrow this example from Beardsley, *Aesthetics: Problems in the Philosophy of Criticism* (1958) (Indianapolis: Hackett, 1981), 51.

9. Or, as in the example of the false nightingale or of the artificial flower, à

propos of objects of uncertain or deceptive status—at first taken as natural, sub-sequently revealed to be artificial; for obvious reasons the error can work in the other direction as well (I take an authentic nightingale for an adroit imitator), but this does not hold for the deception; Oscar Wilde was able to say, paradoxically (metaphorically), that nature "imitates" art, but one can't literally say that nature *apes* it.

10. *Remembrance of Things Past* (London: Chatto and Windus, 1981), 2:603.

11. See the "case studies" assembled by Nathalie Heinich in *L'Art contemporain exposé aux rejets* (Nimes: Jacqueline Chambon, 1997); and, by the same author, *Le Triple jeu de l'art contemporain* (Paris: Minuit, 1998).

12. "One will say that *good* taste imposes itself against *bad* taste. But this changes nothing, since it is good taste that qualifies the other one as bad" (Jean-Marie Schaeffer, *Les Célibataires de l'art* [Paris: Gallimard, 1996], 198).

13. See "Egotism and Aesthetic Disposition," in this collection.

14. It is difficult, in connection with the subject of psychocultural relations evoked here, not to refer to Yasmina Réza's play *Art*, which, however, mixes—in a register midway between Nathalie Sarraute and Jean-Loup Dabadie—the prob-lematics specific to "contemporary" art, in a today perfectly classical vein, with a white monochrome à la Ryman.

CHAPTER 4. THE TWO KINDS OF ABSTRACTION

1. The most conceptual, in this (as in other) business, is in the title: it is enough to mention it in the absence of the picture to produce an effect (of surprise, provo-cation, amusement, etc.). One says, "Malevich has painted a white square on a white surface," as one says, "Duchamp has exhibited a bottle drainer." It's a good one, but the painting, taken naively and in itself, in no way leads to smiling—assuming that one can today take such a famous work "naively and in itself."

2. The truth is that every one, or almost, of these artists has his own registered designation (neoplasticism for Mondrian and Van Doesburg, orphism for Delau-nay, etc.), and I don't think Mondrian himself ever used the term *abstract geometric* for his own pictures; his work is nevertheless emblematic for what it designates.

3. 1936, Guggenheim Museum, New York.

4. This is the original German title (Munich, 1927) of the fundamental theo-retical work by Malevich, published at the Bauhaus, of which Kandinsky was a member.

5. The title of the English translation (Chicago: P. Theobald, 1959) of his book is *The Non-Objective World*, and it seems to me that one sometimes calls abstract painting "nonobjective."

6. Clement Greenberg, "Surrealist Painting," in *The Collected Essays* (Chicago: University of Chicago Press, 1986), 1:231.

7. *Album de l'exposition Kandinsky* (Paris: Centre Pompidou, November 1984–January 1985), 83.

8. Collection Adrien Maeght, Paris; *Album de l'exposition* Kandinsky, 87.

9. Meyer Schapiro, "Recent Abstract Painting" and "On the Humanity of Abstract Painting," in *Modern Art: Selected Papers* (New York: George Braziller, 1978), 221–22 and 228–29. The last sentence, which I underline, seems highly pertinent to our discussion.

10. On this moment of Kandinsky's "critical fortune," see Christian Derouet, "*Parties diverses, en attente de commentaire*," *Album cit.*, 94–100.

11. The *Album* already quoted contains a text by Frank Stella, "Commentaire du tableau *Complexité simple-Ambiguité*," that evokes Pollock in connection with the canvas of 1939.

12. 1950, Metropolitan Museum, New York.

13. I am clearly speaking here of the "early" canvases (or watercolors), the only ones present in New York in the 1930s and 1940s; their reception owes much to the teaching of Hans Hoffmann.

14. Arthur Danto, *After the End of Art: Contemporary Art and the Pale of History* (Princeton University Press, 1997), 75.

15. I allow myself to refer here to my *The Work of Art* (Ithaca, NY: Cornell University Press, 1997), 168; and especially to the commentary that I mention there by Irving Sandler in *The New York School: The Painters and Sculptors of the Fifties* (New York: Harper and Row, 1978), 180–81.

16. Rauschenberg, at any rate, did not stop, after 1957, practicing the manner he seems here to overthrow; he and Jasper Johns seem to me to continue on a grand scale, in a period when pop art ruled supreme, the technique (if not the intention) of abstract expressionism; and it is Rauschenberg, if I believe Sandler (*New York School*, 181), who said, as modern painting since Maurice Denis has never stopped saying: "I don't want a picture to resemble anything else than what it is."

17. Quoted in *Nicolas de Stael: Rétrospective de l'oeuvre peint* (Saint-Paul: Fondation Maeght, 1991), 104.

18. 65 x 81, 1952, Musée National d'Art Moderne.

19. 161.5 x 128.5, 1952, Kunstsammlung Nordrhein-Westfalen, Düsseldorf.

20. Letter of September 1950, quoted in Kunstsammlung Nordrhein-Westfalen, Düsseldorf, 56.

21. Danto, *After the End of Art*, 72.

22. *Journal romain* (Paris: POL, 1987), 33. The passage concerns *Nature morte*

avec gravure d'après Delacroix (Musée des Beaux-Arts de Strasbourg); and *Paysage* (Collection Picasso).

23. Painted bronze, 1960, collection of the artist.

24. Painted wood, 1964, private collection.

25. Autumn 1913, Picasso Museum, Paris.

26. 1914, Guggenheim Collection, Venice.

27. 1928, Hirschhorn Collection, New York. It goes without saying that here, as in painting, the appreciation of the degree of figurativity of each work is largely up to attentional interpretation.

28. This trompe l'oeil illusion can be present in sculpture only in a quite momentary and purely visual manner, as with the personages of George Segal and others, when one places them on purpose in a position and environment favorable to mistakes: for example, seated on a public bench.

29. 1961–62, Barbara Hepworth Museum and Sculpture Garden, St. Ives.

30. This genetic reference is just as, and even more, present in the figurative sculptures produced by the assemblage of preexistent manufactured objects, as in Picasso's famous *Tête de taureau* (saddle and handlebars of a bicycle, 1942, Picasso Museum, Paris), but there it competes with the figurative reference itself.

31. "Abstract, Representational, and so forth" and "The New Sculpture," *Art and Culture* (Boston: Beacon Press, 1961), 137 and 140.

32. There is a little of this in Picasso's *Mandolin*, to which I referred earlier, and in other "constructions" of the cubist period (and style) and in many "flat reliefs" that can, with the help of tri-dimensional materials, give the paradoxical illusion of an abstract canvas; see Max Ernst's *Fruit of a Long Experience* (1919), Musée National d'Art Moderne. But it is no doubt more reasonable (more "literal" in any case) to assign this last type of work to an intermediary category between painting and sculpture, which begins with the first collages.

33. See his *Obélisque brisé* (1963–67), Ménil Foundation, Houston.

CHAPTER 5. THE STONEMASON'S YARD

1. National Gallery, London. Its precise date is not certain, but it is necessarily anterior to the fall of the belfry of la Carità (1741); historians prefer to go back to the years 1726–30—rather early in the career of the painter, who lived from 1697 to 1768. If this painting is a masterpiece, it comes rather typically from what one has called (à propos of the *Cid*, I think) "the hour of the first masterpiece."

2. See K. Baerjer and J. G. Links, *Canaletto* (New York: Metropolitan Museum of Art, 1989), 144.

3. For example, the *Rio dei Mendicanti*, Cà Rezzonico (c. 1723), for the shambles

of the shed (doubtless a *squero*, a workshop where one repaired gondolas) and the hanging linen that occupies the right side; we know, more generally, the painter's taste for effects of color and of matter, from walls to degraded roughcasts.

4. 1830, Louvre Museum.

5. 1878, Cambridge, Fitzwilliam Museum.

6. And that one finds from the other angle in another, just about contemporary canvas, *The Grand Canal, from Santa Maria della Carità toward the Basin of San Marco* (collection Windsor Castle; there exist several replicas, autographs and others), which shows the church from the front, with, on the left, the house still stuck to the campanile and revealing its entrance door on the square.

7. See "What Aesthetic Values?" and "Axiological Relations," in this collection.

8. *Pensées*, ed. L. Brunschwicg, 327–37.

9. Nathalie Heinich, *Le Triple jeu de l'art contemporain* (Paris: Minuit, 1998).

10. *Remembrance of Things Past* (London: Chatto and Windus, 1981), 3:640. This criticism seems to address specifically a painting like *The Stonemason's Court*, but Proust apparently never mentions Canaletto, or, rather, he mentions him only in an early version of the pastiche of the Goncourts, in which his name, cited in favor of an analogy between the dome of the Institute and that of the Salute, is crossed out in favor of Guardi's—a substitution now in the final text. Canaletto, as I said, in fact illustrates as well, and alternatively, the two styles of Venetian "vedute" that Proust contrasts here.

CHAPTER 6. THE GAZE OF OLYMPIA

1. First published in *Mimesis et semiosis: Miscellanies offertes à Henri Mitterand* (Paris: Nathan, 1992).

2. February 1868, Musée d'Orsay. On this painting in general, see T. Reff, "Manet's Portrait of Zola," *Burlington Magazine* 117 (1975); and F. Cachin, note in the catalog of the Manet exhibition (Paris: Grand-Palais, 1983), Édition de la Réunion des Musées Nationaux.

3. See, among others, A. Chastel, "Le Tableau dans le tableau" (1964), in *Fables, formes, figures* (Paris: Flammarion, 1978); J. Lipman and R. Marshall, *Art about Art* (New York: Dutton, 1978); and P. Georgel and A. M. Lecoq, *La Peinture dans la peinture* (Paris: A. Biro, 1987).

4. Incorrectly, because *mise en abyme* in the strict sense of the word supposes that the contained image be a (more or less exact) reduction of the containing picture—and so on, in principle to infinity.

5. Roy Lichtenstein has perhaps given up on this emblematic object, as some

others, with his *Stretcher Frame with Cross Bars* of 1968, in which he represents it in his usual technique of false typographical threads.

6. This term will henceforth designate the contained picture, of whatever kind, whereas the term *first picture* will designate the containing picture.

7. I do not forget that an "imaginary" picture can represent a real object (which is perhaps the case of the landscape of Franche-Comté in *L'Atelier*), a subject I will take up when I discuss second pictures that are "real." It can also represent Venus, the Virgin, a unicorn, an imaginary landscape.

8. "Some Questions concerning Quotation," *Ways of Worldmaking* (Indianapolis: Hackett, 1985), 41–56.

9. I have no idea if this case is more or less frequent than the previous one, but, as to all pointless questions, there will be an answer to this one someday.

10. Luca Cambiaso, *Autoportrait de l'artiste peignant le portrait de son père*; see Chastel, "Le Tableau dans le tableau," 74; I don't know whether this portrait is preexistent or not.

11. The status of these two examples is not identical: the first constitutes a far more motivated "series." There is, as it happens, no rule that forbids a painter from producing a *remake* of the work of another painter, such as (if one wants) the *Moderne Olympia* by Cézanne, nor is there a rule that forbids two or more painters from working at the same time on the same motif, such as Monet and Renoir at the Grenouillère in (if I dare say so) double-make. It is clearly necessary (but this is not the place for it) to relativize and gradualize the opposition between response and *remake*.

12. Even if it is "imaginary": the ad hoc "super-Courbet" of *L'Atelier* can function as a faithful representation of a landscape of the Franche Compté.

13. To abbreviate, I neglect the fact that *Olympia* is moreover and in its own way a variational remake of the *Venus of Urbino*.

14. To simplify everything, there exists a photograph made by Zola himself of his portrait by Manet, or, rather, of a part of his apartment in the rue de Bruxelles where this picture hangs, naturally with its frame; the reproduction of the *Olympia* is almost imperceptible here; see F. Émile-Zola and Massin, *Zola photographe* (Paris: Denoel, 1979), 180.

15. The personage can also face the viewer even as he turns away his face in (quasi) profile: see, among others, Titian's *Portrait of a Man* at the National Gallery in London.

16. I recall in passing that the location of the first picture is uncertain; what is certain is that it isn't Zola's home.

17. This would be roughly the case of Jan van Eyck's *Madonna with the Canon*

Van der Paele, if one took its Virgin-with-child for a (polychrome) statue, but this hypothesis has no (other) justification.

CHAPTER 7. PISSARRO AT L'HERMITAGE

1. Besides a few childhood memories, I base myself largely on the very attentive study by Richard Brettell, *Pissarro et Pontoise. Un Peintre et son paysage*, French trans. by Solange Schnall (Paris: Du Valhermeil, 1991) (abbr.: Br.); the most complete reference is still the *catalogue raisonné* by Ludovic-Rodo Pissarro and Lionello Venturi, *Camille Pissarro, son art, son oeuvre*, 2 vols. (Paris, 1939) (abbr. PV). I refer as much as possible to these two works and to the catalog of the Pissarro exhibition of 1981, Paris, RMN (abbr. cat.) and to that of the exhibition *L'Impressionisme et le paysage français* (Paris: RMN, 1985) (abbr. IPF).

2. In 1881 he moves to the quai du Pothuis, his last quarters in Pontoise, which he will leave for Osny, at the northwestern borderline of Pontoise, in December 1882, which he will leave in turn and definitively in 1884 for Éragny-sur-Epte, near Gisors.

3. One finds an exceptionally comparable effect, but with the interposition of an arm of the river, in *Au bord de l'eau, Bennecourt*, 1868, by Monet (who does not generally like steep-sided views): the eponymous village, on the right bank of the Seine upstream from Vernon and seen from a facing island, is depicted at the foot of a slope that overhangs it, as happens even more frequently on the banks of the Seine than on those of the Oise.

4. PV 56, Cologne.

5. A later canvas, *Paysage à Chaponval* (1880, PV 509, Br. 167, Orsay), even though it is painted on the same level, avoids this effect but with a large backward stand that, as in the *Bennecourt* of Monet, hinders the line of the houses from hiding that of the hill, at the foot of which, by contrast, the village seems to be stuck.

6. 1867–68, PV 57, private collection.

7. 1867, PV 55, Br. 95, MMA.

8. PV, I:20.

9. 1868, PV 61, Br. 130, private collection.

10. The word is not to be taken in its strict sense here, as for Monet's cathedrals of Rouen: Pissarro never exhibited nor, to my knowledge, planned to exhibit this group of canvases together, which nothing but a certain unity of motif (but not of point of view) unites, like Cézanne's Sainte-Victoires later on.

11. 1867–68, 1.51 x 2, PV 58, cat. 11, Guggenheim Museum, New York.

12. *The Poetics of Revery* (Boston: Beacon Press, 1960), 55; and already *La Terre et les rêveries du repos* (Paris: Corti, 1948), chap. 1, "Les Rêveries de l'intimité matérielle."

13. The slopes of L'Hermitage contained a few, apparently rather miserable, troglodytic habitations, but their easy picturesqueness does not seem to have attracted the attention of our painter (see Br., 44–45).

14. Salon of 1866, in *Écrits sur l'art* (Paris: Gallimard, collection "Tel," 1991), 133.

15. C.J.F. Le Carpentier, *Essai sur le paysage* (Paris, 1817).

16. Letter to Pissarro, December 6, 1873, quoted by F. Cachin, cat. 1981, 38.

17. 1835–40, Louvre.

18. "Cézanne", *L'Occident*, September 1907, quoted in Rewald, *Histoire de l'impressionisme*, rev. ed. (Paris: Albin Michel, 1986), 361.

19. PV 183–86, private collection, Madrid. These four canvases have a very panoramic format (55 x 130).

20. 1872, PV 172, Br. 39, Orsay.

21. Around 1872, absent from PV, Br. 40, Memphis.

22. 1874, PV 257, Br. 41, private collection.

23. *Journal*, 20-7-56 (Paris: Gallimard, Pléiade, n.d.), 5:41.

24. 1878, PV 442, Br. 38, Reeves Collection, New York.

25. 1884, PV 628, Br. 171, private collection.

26. 1873, PV 209, cat. 27, collection Durand-Ruel.

27. 1875, PV 310, Br. 97, Basel.

28. 1878, PV 447, Br. 98, Basel.

29. 1879, PV 489, Br. 166, Cleveland.

30. 1875, PV 308, cat. 41, IPF 32, Brooklyn.

31. Note to this painting in IPF.

32. "A propos of *La Côte des Boeufs*, one can quote the allusion of Pissarro to 'autumn and its sadness' in a letter of October 13 1877 to Eugène Murer" (note for this picture in the 1981 catalog). A somewhat later canvas, *Le Jardin potager à L'Hermitage, Pontoise* (1878, PV 437, Br. 22, Tokyo), in which the painter once again manifests his well-known (and sometimes mocked) taste for cabbage squares, nonetheless dissipates all uneasiness in a rather joyous wintry or early springlike light.

33. 1877, PV 380, Br. 154, National Gallery, London.

34. 1877, PV 384, Br. 155, Orsay.

35. Venturi 138, National Gallery, Washington, DC.

36. Venturi 145, Orsay.

37. Venturi 1833, Orsay.

38. PV, I:21.

CHAPTER 8. SONGS WITHOUT WORDS

1. See *Paratexts: Thresholds of Interpretation* (Cambridge: Cambridge University Press, 1997); and Françoise Escal, "Le Titre de l'oeuvre musicale," *Poétique* 69 (February 1987).

2. Romanze. Translator's note: Genette's interest in the usage of this term is motivated by the fact that the initial French publication of Mendelssohn's "Lieder ohne Worte" translated *Lieder* as "romances."

3. Symphonische Dichtung.

4. Between the two extremes of the piano piece and the orchestral "poem," chamber music seems more resistant to thematic investment, but there are exceptions, such as Schönberg's *Verklärte Nacht* for string sextet (if I am not mistaken, this at first referred to a literary text, the mention of which finally disappeared) or (by its adjective) Berg's *Lyric Suite* for quartet; I don't know what was the intention of Boulez's *Livre pour quatuor*, which does not lack a subtly (ambiguously) literary effect.

5. See "Fantasy Landscape," in this collection.

6. Bertrand Tavernier, *Autour de minuit*.

CHAPTER 9. THE OTHER OF THE SAME

1. A. Kilito came close to it in *L'Auteur et ses doubles* (Paris: Seuil, 1985), 19: "At the origin, there is repetition." Kilito here paraphrases (that is to say, repeats and varies) a traditional topos of classical Arabic poetics, so that my question remains without an answer, as is more appropriate to it than to any other. Someone in addition signaled to me Henri Michaux, *Déplacement dégagements* (Paris: Gallimard, n.d.), 56: "In the beginning is REPETITION."

2. New York: McGraw-Hill, 1966.

3. Or the Goldberg Variations, which are in fact a sequence of pieces with a common bass. André Boucourechliev recently found the same principle at work in the *Diabellis*, which is certainly not an absence of relationship: a jazz musician who preserves "only" the harmonic framework of the theme, rather, has the impression of preserving its *essential*. The analogy between the jazz improvisation and those forms of variation with *obligato* bass seems to me reinforced by the analogy of their origins: music for popular dances and even (passacaglia from *pasar calle*) for ambulant brass band (Lope de Vega even believes that the *chaconne* comes . . . from America). But, since I have not found it mentioned by specialists of any kind, I have come to doubt my ears, or my readings.

4. I am not suggesting by this a superiority on principle of the free variation over the "simple" paraphrase: certain expositions of themes, almost literal ones

(but everything rests on this *almost*), in Armstrong, for example, or (in an entirely different spirit) in Monk, are worth all the elaborations, whether or not they are improvised.

CHAPTER 10. A LOGIC OF LITERATURE

1. First published as preface to Käte Hamburger, *Logique des genres littéraires*, French trans. by Pierre Cadiot (Paris: Seuil, 1986). This translation was first published as preface to Käte Hamburger, *The Logic of Literature*, English trans. by Marilynn J. Rose (Bloomington: Indiana University Press, 1993).

2. See the following studies for a sampling of reactions—positive, negative, perplexed: Franz Stanzel, "Episches Präteritum, erlebte Rede, historisches Präsens," *Deutsche Vierteljahrsschrift* 33 (1959); Roy Pascal, "Tense and Novel," *Modern Language Review* 57 (1962); Harald Weinrich, *Tempus* (1964); R. Wellek, "Genre Theory, the Lyric and Erlebnis," in *Discriminations* (1967); Roy Pascal, *The Dual Voice* (Manchester: Manchester University Press, 1977); Dorrit Cohn, *Transparent Minds* (Princeton, NJ: Princeton University Press, 1978); Franz Stanzel, *A Theory of Narrative* (Cambridge: Cambridge University Press, 1984); Ann Banfield, *Unspeakable Sentences* (London: Routledge and Kegan Paul, 1982).

3. *Theory of Narrative*, 14 ff.

CHAPTER 11. THE DIARY, THE ANTI-DIARY

1. First published in *Roland Barthes*, special number of *Poétique* 47 (September 1981).

2. *Oeuvres complètes* (Paris: Éditions du Seuil. 1993–95), 3:1004–14.

3. Translator's note: CNRS stands for Centre National de Recherche Scientifique.

4. *Oeuvres complètes*, 1:23–33.

CHAPTER 12. FANTASY LANDSCAPE

1. This employment of the word *poem*, capable, for example, of designating a simple sonnet, is in fact relatively recent: for the classics a poem consisted necessarily of an extended text, in a genre most often narrative or didactic. "Poem in prose" (an expression Boileau applied to novels) answered the same demand, and this is the reason for the Baudelairean title *Petits poèmes en prose* (posthumous, 1869), which still testifies to the ancient usage, by its adjective of modesty.

2. According to Antoine Adam, these collections or anthologies appeared in large numbers at the beginning of the seventeenth century, fluctuated between 1627 and 1662, and almost disappeared after 1673 (*Histoire de la littérature française au XVIIe siècle* [Paris: Domat, 1949–56], 1:333, 2:47, 3:157).

3. 1798–1802.

4. Letter to Vigny of December 16, 1861, *Correspondance* (Paris: Gallimard, Pléiade, 1973), 2:196. One also knows the importance that an article had for Baudelaire, solicited by him (and finally censored), where Barbey praised the "secret architecture" of the collection: "*Les Fleurs du mal* don't follow each other like so many lyric pieces, dispersed by inspiration and assembled in a volume for no other reasons than publishing them together. They are less poems than a *strongly unified* poetic work" (Baudelaire, *Oeuvres complètes* [Paris: Gallimard, Pléiade, 1975], 1:1196), an article that he made his lawyer quote during the trial. The fact is that the overall organization was for him a defensive argument, since he had to avoid a condemnation incurred for the only pieces judged the most "daring" and of which the structure of the book contradicted, according to him, the apparent immorality. He noted for his lawyer: "The book has to be judged *as a whole*, and then a terrible morality emerges from it" (1:193). Barbey had prepared the way: "From the point of view of art and aesthetic sensation, they would lose a lot not to be read *in the order* in which the poet, who knows what he is doing, has arranged them. But they would lose a lot more *from the point of view of the moral effect*." Meaning that unity is not only an aesthetic value; it is an aesthetic value with ethical connotations: diversity is always suspected of dispersion and futility.

5. I leave the field initially circumscribed a little in mentioning narrative texts (tales and novellas), but it goes without saying that our question, mutatis mutandis, can be found in them; it can also be found in collections of essays: *Poésie et profondeur* clearly claims more thematic unity than *Essais critiques*.

6. *L'Olive* is a homogeneous collection of decasyllabic sonnets, even though the volume that contains it in 1549, and then, increased, in 1550, contains "a few other poetic works"; the *Antiquités* (1558) systematically alternates sonnets in decasyllables and alexandrines, a meter that Ronsard made fashionable around 1555; the *Regrets* (also from 1558) is a collection of sonnets all in alexandrines.

7. This one is actually ambiguous, since *méditation* could be received as the name of a new genre, which the volume could well have inaugurated; on all these questions of titles and generic indications, see *Paratexts: Thresholds of Interpretation*, trans. Jane E. Lewin (Cambridge: Cambridge University Press, 1997), chap. 4.

8. With this display of skepticism, I do not target thematic interpretation generally, which is quite pertinent at the level of the complete work of an author, in which it reveals constant traits or the evolution of a traceable, more or less conscious personality; what I do target is the interpretation that amounts to motivating in depth a grouping that is often arbitrary or inspired by a purely editorial opportunity. Of course, collections that are equivalent with complete poetic

works, such as *Les Fleurs du mal*, *Leaves of Grass*, or Pound's *Cantos*, eliminate, or at least weaken, this distinction.

9. See *Oeuvres poétiques* (Paris: Gallimard, Pléiade, 1967), 2:1359.

10. This chronological division around the drama of 1843 takes precedence over a strongly thematic arrangement; such a two-stage structure is found again in *Chansons* ("Jeunesse"/"Sagesse"); the *Légende* in its final state contains no less than sixty-one parts; the *Quatre vents* will have four books that follow a generic division: "satirique," "dramatique," "lyrique," "épique."

11. See Claudel's *(Five Great) Odes* or Rilke's *Duineser Elegien* and *Sonette an Orpheus*.

12. One encounters at least in Supervielle an openly chronological title: the collection of 1939–45, but these two dates make a clear reference to a historical period, capable of suggesting a meaning, a sort of counterpart to *L'Année terrible* of Hugo. Explicitly chronological titles more frequently head collections of collections, such as Borges's *Poemas, 1922–1943*, which regroups three collections of the 1920s (*Fervor de Buenos Aires, Luna de Enfrente, Cuaderno San Martin*) or Eluard's *La Jarre peut-elle être plus belle que l'eau (1930–1938)* (the parenthesis is in the title), which regroups four anterior collections (*La Vie immédiate, La Rose publique, Les Yeux fertiles, Cours naturel*).

13. *Remembrance of Things Past*, trans. C. K. Scott Moncrief and Terence Kilmartin (London: Chatto and Windus, 1981), 3:157–58.

14. I owe my knowledge mainly to Jacques Bornecque, *Lumières sur les "Fêtes galantes,"* with commentary (Paris: Nizet, 1959); and mainly to Jacques Robichez, edition of *Oeuvres poétiques* (Paris: Classiques Garnier, 1969). Bornecque adopts the text of the last anthumous edition (1891), Robichez the one of the original edition of 1869.

15. See Robichez, *Oeuvres poétiques*, 545.

16. The late character is attested by an announcement of November 1865 at Lemerre under the purely generic title *Poèmes et sonnets*; see Robichez, *Oeuvres poétiques*, 12.

17. The "manuscript" published in facsimile by Messein in 1920 has nothing of a rough draft; it is, in fact, a mosaic of autographs, of clean copies, and of corrected proofs (Robichez, *Oeuvres poétiques*, 713).

18. In order: "Clair de lune," "L'Allée," "Sur l'herbe," "Mandoline," "Pantomime," "Le Faune."

19. "A la promenade," "Dans la grotte," "Les Ingénus," "A Clymène," "En sourdine," "Colloque sentimental."

20. "Cortège" and "L'Amour par terre."

21. It is impossible to date this moment with precision, but the fact is that the second group, with its transference of the title, appears ten months after the first.

22. Bornecque, *Lumières sur les "Fêtes galantes*," 49–50. But it seems that Bornecque did not notice the prepublication of the six pieces of January 1868 and that he forgets here the publication of the two last pieces of March 1869 (that he will however signal [148]), which strongly distorts his statistics: it is not twenty-one diverse pieces compared to eight *fêtes galantes* but twenty-one compared to fourteen and even, if one counts only the poems, fourteen as compared to fourteen: equality. The strange omission of Bornecque is confirmed by this sentence: "Between the first two *fêtes galantes* and the publication of a second series, seventeen months will pass" (50), but the "second" series appears, as I said, ten months after the first, and it is a third that appears not seventeen but sixteen months after the first (if I believe the indications of Robichez).

23. Bornecque, *Lumières sur les "Fêtes galantes*," 10.

24. Bornecque reminds us that this poem was first entitled "Trumeau" (later "Dessus de porte") on the manuscript (which Verlaine naturally could not have known), like the actual "Mandoline" of the *Fêtes galantes*. The term is abandoned in both cases, perhaps because it too openly admits the trans-artistic procedure.

25. An elegant pastiche of this style, "Lettre" literally borrows its first hemistich ("Éloigné de vos yeux . . .") from Théophile's "Désespoirs amoureux," and the grotto of "Coquillages," willfully or not, evokes the one of Tristan's "Promenoir des deux amants."

26. Translator's note: There follows a long paragraph, "only to verify this assertion," which I consider too specialized to render into English.

27. Variable depending on the authors and the periods: the creator of the genre, Froberger, framed the two rapid movements by the two slow movements, but even during his lifetime the alternate structure imposed itself, from Louis Couperin to Bach, without counting the occasional optional or supplementary (and sometimes redoubled) movements.

28. I cheat a little in this reference, since in the Suites, as already in the Brandenburg Concertos, Bach does not change the size movement by movement but only suite by suite (or concerto by concerto); the principle of instrumental variation in reality acts only in the series formed by the four suites (or the six concertos), and I don't know whether other suites, by other composers, present a variation movement by movement (too bad for my purpose that this is not the case in Schönberg's *Pierrot lunaire*, but it is not, after all, too late to apply this principle to a sequence of melodies, which are left to be composed, based on the entire collection of *Fêtes galantes*). I would thus say that the principle of variation is more

active in Verlaine than in Bach, and no doubt than in most composers, but this would be to abuse an already approximate analogy.

29. Bornecque and Robichez partially agree with each other in insisting on the movement that leads "toward sadness," a movement that Robichez (better informed than his predecessor, as we have seen à propos the prepublication chronology) finds again in the intermediary groupings. Without denying the nuance of "cruelty" that in any case marks "Colloque sentimental," I have a little trouble in seeing in this effect something else than artistry.

30. The only important variant of this poem is in the ninth verse, which read, "Au calme clair de lune de Watteau," in 1867, clearly indicating its artistic "source." As a result of an ironic remark by Anatole France, who asked him "where he saw moonlight in Watteau, the sunny painter," Verlaine ended by replacing *de Watteau* in 1869 by the poor cheville *triste en beau*, which at least has the advantage of blurring the pictorial reference, correctly or not.

31. Robichez, *Oeuvres poétiques*, 550.

32. "As for the fantasy landscape, which is the expression of human reverie [. . .] this singular genre, for which Rembrandt, Rubens, Watteau and some English books of Christmas presents offer the best examples, and which is, in a small frame, the analogue of beautiful decorations in the Opera" ("Salon de 1846," XV, "Du paysage," in *Oeuvres complètes* [Paris: Gallimard, Pléiade, n.d.], 2:480).

CHAPTER 13. EGOTISM AND AESTHETIC DISPOSITION

1. *The Private Diaries of Stendhal*, trans. Robert Sage (London: Victor Gollancz, 1955), 417. A little farther on, this complementary observation: "They have *sensibility* and the naturalness which is a result of it. This country is therefore eminently that of the arts" (460). Or, again, in "The Abbess of Castro" (1839), in *Three Italian Chronicles*, trans. C. K. Scott-Moncrieff (New York: New Directions, 1991): "Then [in the sixteenth century] was born [in France] the *spirit of galantery*, which led to the destruction, one after another, of all passions, including love, in the interests of that cruel tyrant whom we all obey: namely vanity [. . .] Then one saw [in Italy] passions, and not the habit of gallantry. That is the great difference between Italy and France, that is why Italy has given birth to a Raphael, a Giorgione, a Titian, a Correggio" (46).

2. "Vanity, unique passion of the French of the 18th and 19th centuries" (*Journal*, December 14, 1829, *Oeuvres intimes* 2:109). One remembers among other things that the *love of vanity* is especially strong with the French (*Love*, chap. 1) and "that there is always one thing that a Frenchman respects more than his mistress,

namely vanity" (chap. 41). We might note that this denunciation is one of the themes common to Stendhal and Chateaubriand ("In France, land of vanity . . . ," *Mémoires d'outre-tombe*, L. 36, chap. 23), even if the first willingly, and not without reasons, suspected the second of illustrating the denounced flaw quite well.

3. *Rome, Naples et Florence* (1826), in *Voyages en Italie* (Paris: Gallimard, Pléiade, 1973), 501.

4. *Histoire de la peinture en Italie* (Paris: Gallimard, collection "Folio-Essais," 1996), 52.

5. *Promenades dans Rome*, in *Voyages en Italie*, 755.

6. *Stendhal et l'italianité* (Paris: Corti, 1982).

7. I quote here the Petit Robert, adding the adjective *excessive* for greater precision because I suppose one does not call vanity a justified self-satisfaction—if indeed such a thing exists.

8. *Rome, Naples et Florence en 1817*, in *Voyages en Italie*, 79.

9. We will meet it very soon in an antithesis that I do not want to introduce right away.

10. Paris: Garnier-Flammarion, 1970, 209.

11. In Paris, Mr. Hiéky explains in *The Pink and the Green*, "the unique passion that moves all these Parisian hearts is the *desire* to *appear* a little more than they are." In Italy, on the contrary, "one wants true pleasures, and *appearance* is nothing" (*Promenades dans Rome*, 625).

12. Stendhal, *Promenades dans Rome*, 152. One could add, following another suggestion of the same critic, as a *rival*: "Equality is inherent to a society without a model, without rivalry." I will not follow this track, which would gradually distance us from our subject, but I see it as very close to ours: every model is also a rival, in regards to whom the mimetic submission can always tip toward resentment. This is also called "killing the father."

13. "Cautious vanity anxiously eyes a neighboring vanity that borders on it" (*Life of Rossini*, trans. Richard N. Coe [New York: Orion Press, 1970], 118).

14. *Life of Rossini*, 201.

15. *Rome, Naples et Florence* (1826), 357. Cf. *Histoire de la peinture en Italie*, 346: the "*what will one say*, an unknown thing in this country with little vanity."

16. Or sometimes the Spaniard, "never concerned with others" (*Love* [London: Penguin, 1975], 153).

17. *Rome, Naples et Florence* (1826), 586. "In Spain and in Italy, each person despises his neighbor, and has the savage pride to be of his own opinion" (*Life of Rossini*, 317).

18. *Life of Rossini*, 337.

19. *Life of Rossini*, 348.

20. *Love*, 159.

21. *Rome, Naples et Florence en 1817*, 149.

22. *Rome, Naples et Florence* (1826), 380.

23. *Rome, Naples et Florence* (1826), 384.

24. The Romantic dramatist that *Racine et Shakespeare* calls for will gain "the votes of the people who think by themselves" (108).

25. *Life of Rossini*, 348.

26. "It answers objections in the Italian manner, that is by repeating, and shouting a little louder, the sentence which one has just answered" (*Rome, Naples et Florence en 1817*, 50).

27. *Rome, Naples et Florence en 1817*, 98.

28. *Rome, Naples et Florence* (1826), 321.

29. He honors him nonetheless in *Lucien Leuwen* (chap. 22) with a quotation, of which the intention, doubtless ironic, escapes me.

30. *Life of Rossini*, 409.

31. *Racine et Shakespeare*, 103–6.

32. *Life of Rossini*, 71.

33. *Life of Rossini*, 45.

34. This restrictive definition is evidently not shared by those who charge with hedonism every aesthetic (starting with Kant's) that sees (correctly, I think) an affective reaction in aesthetic appreciation, but the term is so inevitably pejorative that I prefer to reserve if for what I actually regard as an error, or an excess— though Kant himself accords to Epicurus that "pleasure and pain are in the last analysis [i.e., without doubt, in their effects] of a corporeal order" (*Critique of Judgement*, para. 29).

35. *Rome, Naples et Florence en 1817*, 39. "The German, who makes a doctrine of everything, deals with music knowledgeably; the voluptuous Italian looks for lively and passing enjoyment in it; the Frenchman, more vain than sensible, manages to speak about it with wit; the Englishman pays for it and does not bother with it" (*Life of Rossini*, 204).

36. *Mémoires d'un touriste*, in *Voyages en France* (Paris: Gallimard, Pléiade, 1992), 312, 307; it is the supposed iron dealer who speaks, but the reference to Milan certainly has nothing fictional about it.

37. *Oeuvres intimes*, 2:172. Cf. "The more likeable a Frenchman is, the less he feels the arts" (*Rome, Naples et Florence en 1817*, 164). These two hindrances (wit and sociability) are not the same, but they converge in aesthetic insensibility.

38. Although we will find it in the phrase "feeling of the arts."

"The Italian peasant has received from heaven infinitely more sensitivity [than the Frenchman] to feel with force and depth, in other words, infinitely more energy of passion" (Rome, Naples et Florence [1826], 500).

39. Rome, Naples et Florence en 1817, 9. It is a matter here of love but narrowly (and abruptly) linked to music: "Music alone lives in Italy, and one must make only love in this beautiful country."

40. Life of Rossini, 51.

41. Rome, Naples et Florence en 1817, 38.

42. Life of Rossini, 331–32.

43. Promenades dans Rome, 1053.

44. Life of Rossini, 137.

45. Rome, Naples et Florence (1826), 320; Promenades dans Rome, 610.

46. Promenades dans Rome, 482.

47. "Love of art struggles with sociability, which is the national character in France" (Salon de 1827, Mélanges [Paris: Cercle du Bibliophile, 1972], 3:107).

48. Rome, Naples et Florence (1826), 507.

49. Promenades dans Rome, 611.

50. Life of Rossini, 242–43.

51. Histoire de la peinture en Italie, 162.

52. Life of Rossini, 315. The force Stendhal gives to the word extinguisher (éteignoir) is known; it designates in his eyes all forms of moral and political repression or regression.

53. Racine et Shakespeare, 210.

54. Life of Rossini, 333.

55. Life of Rossini, 471.

56. Racine et Shakespeare, 183. Voltaire's text was, in fact, of a racism without scruples and not at all "politically correct," but our scrupulousness in this regard has progressed farther since 1825.

57. Promenades dans Rome, 888.

58. Racine et Shakespeare, 182–84, 191.

59. Stendhal, Histoire de la peinture en Italie, 238. This very brief chapter is today entitled "Philosophy of the Greeks," but the original edition obligingly specified: "Philosophy of the Greeks who did not feel that everything is relative"; and it is not indifferent that this defense, attributed (legitimately or not) to Voltaire in a note, sort of opens a book (the fourth) devoted to the "classical ideal Beautiful."

60. Stendhal, Histoire de la peinture en Italie, 71.

61. Léon Blum, Stendhal et le beylisme (1914) (Paris: Albin Michel, 1947), 192. The political aspect that this last clause designates is by no means secondary: one

knows all that the history of Italian art owes, according to Stendhal, good and bad, to events such as the victory of Charles V or the passage of the bridge of Lodi; and that he never ceases asking if the "budget" and "the two Chambers" would be favorable or unfavorable to his future fate.

62. *Vies de Haydn, de Mozart et de Metastase* (Paris: Divan, n.d.), 72.

63. *Histoire de la peinture en Italie*, 164–65.

64. *Life of Rossini*, 7.

65. *Promenades dans Rome*, 771. One sees that Voltaire is here sometimes a positive reference (for his relativism), sometimes a negative one (for his supposed intellectualism and for the manner in which he illustrates the "wit" of the salon).

66. *Love*, chap. 42.

67. *Rome, Naples et Florence* (1826), 446; *L'Italie en 1818*, 241.

68. *Life of Rossini*, 35.

69. *Mémoires d'un touriste*, in *Voyages en France*, 163.

70. *Promenades dans Rome*, 921.

71. *Promenades dans Rome*, 618. This participation of historical memory in aesthetic appreciation is another motif that, despite his declared aversion, brings Stendhal closer to Chateaubriand: "The historical memories are very important for the pleasure or displeasure of the traveller" (Chateaubriand, *Voyage en Italie*, *oeuvres romanesques et voyages* [Paris: Gallimard, Pléiade, 1969], 2:1429).

72. *Private Diaries*, 513. The following sentence is still important for our purposes and leads us back to our point of departure: "All the characteristics of the Italians I meet are pleasing to me: first, I believe because I see a man who feels and not a man who calculates the interests of his vanity."

73. "I read Ariosto while riding, accompanying my general" (*Diary of 1811*, complementary pages from March 20), a perhaps apocryphal memory from the voyage of 1801, as assistant to General Michaud).

CHAPTER 14. PARROT-GREEN

1. I already quoted it in an essay in *Figures II* ("Stendhal"), in which this page was meant to illustrate Stendhalian semiotics; I don't tire of it. Translator's note: This essay was published in English in *Figures of Literary Discourse* (New York: Columbia University Press, 1982).

2. *The Pink and the Green*, trans. Richard Howard (New York: New Directions, 1988), 12–13.

3. "We, the emigrants, were in the town of Charles V. like the women of that town: seated behind their windows, they see the soldiers passing in the street in a bent little mirror" (*Mémoires d'outre-tombe*, bk. 23, chap. 15).

4. One could eliminate the contradiction by supposing that this deviant paragraph relates to Prussian towns, with the exception of Königsberg and Berlin, which would be the only ones whose windows were armed with "impenetrable" frames. I tend to think that Stendhal displays his usual negligence here.

5. *Lucien Leuwen*, trans. Louise Varèse (New York: New Directions, 1950), 1:36.

6. *Lucien Leuwen*, 1:149.

7. "I only began to live and to know myself the day when my horse fell under the windows with the green shutters" (Lucien to Mme Chasteller in *Lucien Leuwen*, vol. 2).

8. *Lucien Leuwen*, 1:165.

9. It is his friend Mlle Théodelinde who evokes his initial, or initiating, accident in those terms (*Lucien Leuwen*, 1:168).

10. *Lucien Leuwen*, 1:205.

11. *Lucien Leuwen*, 1:204.

12. *Lucien Leuwen*, 1:207.

13. *Lucien Leuwen*, 1:162.

14. *Lucien Leuwen*, 1:181.

15. *Lucien Leuwen*, 1:195.

16. *Lucien Leuwen*, 1:208.

17. *Lucien Leuwen*, 1:164, 212.

18. "But how do you manage not to be at the feet of the sublime Chasteller? Is there discord in the family?" (*Lucien Leuwen*, vol. 2). In reality Leuwen is never so much "at the feet" of his beloved as when he stations himself under the window of that Juliet without a balcony.

19. *Lucien Leuwen*, 1:219–20.

20. *Lucien Leuwen*, vol. 2.

21. "Frederic had expected to feel paroxysms of joy;—but passions wilt when they are transplanted, and, finding Madame Arnoux in a setting which was unfamiliar to him, he had the impression that she had somehow lost something, that she had suffered a vague degradation, in short that she had changed. The calm of his heart astounded him" (Flaubert, *Sentimental Education*, trans. Robert Baldick [London: Penguin, 1964], 116).

22. Cf. Jean Rousset, "Aimer de loin: *Lucien Leuwen*," in *Passages. Échanges et transpositions* (Paris: Corti, 1990).

23. No more than in Spain: "If, as in Spain, I saw him through a gate, myself on the ground floor of my house, and he in the street, at midnight, I could say dangerous things to him" (Rousset, "Aimer de loin," vol. 2); it is Mme Chasteller who

speaks (to herself), of course. Since the writing of this essay, Jacques Tournier's nice book *Des persiennes vert perroquet* has appeared (Paris: Calmann-Lévy, 1998), which, as its title indicates, also takes for its subject the situation that has just occupied us and which has never escaped the love of *Leuwen* devotees. I should perhaps change mine, but I prefer, in conserving it, to add to it the oblique value of a sign of Beylean complicity.

CHAPTER 15. OTHER MAGIC OF THE FARAWAY

1. Stendhal has just specified that this painter "knew how to distribute his figures in groups, and distinguishing by a just degradation of light and of color the planes in which the groups were placed, the surprised viewers found that his compositions had *depth*."

2. *Histoire de la peinture en Italie* (Paris: Gallimard, collection "Folio-Essais," 1996), chap. 28, 147–49. Panofsky has since then attributed the discovery of this perspective, which he calls "atmospheric," to a miniaturist of the beginning of the fifteenth century: "In observing that when it approaches the earth the sky loses some of its substance and color, he observed that objects also lost their substance and their color when they became distant: trees, heights and the furthest constructions took on fantastic airs, their outlines dissolved in the atmosphere, and their local color drowned in a bluish or grayish haze. In short, the Master of Boucicaut discovered the atmospheric perspective, and one can appreciate what that meant at the beginning of the fifteenth century, if one remembers that Leonardo da Vinci still had to combat the erroneous belief according to which a landscape darkens, rather than lightens, in proportion to its distance from the spectator" (*Les Primitifs flamands*, French trans. [Paris: Hazan, 1992], 115). Stendhal seems to share this "belief" in speaking of a lowering of the shades; they are, at any rate, in agreement about the effect of "dissolution."

3. *Les Primitifs flamands*, 333; cf. *Rome, Naples et Florence, Voyages en Italie* (Paris: Gallimard, Pléiade, 1973), 127.

4. *Mémoires sur Napoléon* (Paris: Divan, 1930), 180. Stendhal himself, we must remember, will arrive in Milan only in June 1800.

5. Stendhal, *Mémoires sur Napoléon*, 82.

6. *Charterhouse of Parma* (New York: Modern Library, 1999), 298–99.

7. Stendhal, *Rome, Naples et Florence* (1826), 319.

8. *Mémoires sur Napoléon*, 180–82.

9. *La Chartreuse de Parme* (Paris: Gallimard, Folio, 1972), 551. This page, added to the Crozet exemplar, tells with greater detail of the return of Fabrice to Grianta,

after Waterloo, which the published text evoked only in one sentence in chapter 5. It was part of the attempts at correction more or less inspired by the criticisms of Balzac; they never reached their goal, for lack of a second anthumous edition (among other reasons).

10. *Le Rose et le vert, Mina de Vanghel, et autres nouvelles* (Paris: Gallimard, Folio, 1982), 179. According to the editor Del Litto, this sketch goes back to a memory of the first Italian journey.

11. *Life of Henry Brulard*, chap. 36.

12. *Charterhouse of Parma*, 23.

13. Or by Gina: this page is given from her point of view, in free indirect style.

14. I do not forget that this last page is not in the published text of the *Charterhouse*, but I note that it develops one of the sentences of that text, and it seems to me that this development was not at all called for by the revisions that Balzac wished for (to begin the novel in medias res by the Waterloo episode and then to return briefly to Fabrice's childhood); one can thus suppose that Stendhal spontaneously felt the need for it or at least the desire.

15. *Charterhouse of Parma*, 148; he will come back to it after his escape (Belgirate is on the Piedmont side of the lake), and Stendhal notes in the margin of the Chaper exemplar that the addition of ten lines of description would be suitable here.

CHAPTER 16. MATTER OF VENICE

1. First published in *Territoires de l'imaginaire. Pour Jean-Pierre Richard* (Paris: Seuil, 1986).

2. Douglas Alden, *Marcel Proust's Grasset Proofs* (Chapel Hill: University of North Carolina Press, 1978), 267–68. The same page is contained, with some minute differences, in the variants of the Pléiade edition of *A la Recherche*, 1:1193.

3. *Remembrance of Things Past*, trans. C. K. Scott Moncrieff and Terence Kilmartin (London: Chatto and Windus, 1981), 3:654.

4. *Remembrance*, 3:665–66.

5. I borrow this from a page of *Time Regained, Remembrance*, 3:837, in which this image comes to the mind of the narrator changing gradually into another "network of black streets," the one of Paris during the war.

6. *Remembrance*, 3:641–42.

7. *Remembrance*, 3:640–42.

8. *Remembrance*, 3:643.

9. *Remembrance*, 2:594. What follows orchestrates for two pages a new comparison between the "oblique plans" of the roofs close to the Hotel de Guermantes and some alpine landscape painted by Turner or the inevitable Elstir.

1. *Remembrance of Things Past*, trans. C. K. Scott Moncrieff and Terence Kilmartin (London: Chatto and Windus, 1981), 1:63.

2. *Remembrance*, 1:66–67.

3. See Esquisse 28, in *A la recherche du temps perdu* (Paris: Gallimard, Pléiade, 1987–89), 1:738–43; and Esquisse 27, 736–38, apparently anterior, in which the role of the steeple of Combray is still played by the steeple of Chartres, which already "wouldn't sound tinny."

4. *Remembrance*, 1:12.

5. *Remembrance*, 1:42.

6. *Remembrance*, 1:789. He means Anton Rubinstein, of course.

7. The accounts of aesthetic relationship with natural objects and spectacles are too frequent in Proust for one to undertake making a list of them. I'll merely remind the reader that he attributes to Bergotte, in front of several paintings of a Dutch exhibition and before finding the View of Delft, "the aridity and pointlessness of such an artificial kind of art, which was greatly inferior to the sunshine of a windswept Venetian Palazzo, or of an ordinary house by the sea" (*Remembrance*, 3:185)—an impression that clearly makes of nature a standard of "value" in respect to which art does not always measure up.

8. *Remembrance*, 1:164.

9. See "Métonymie chez Proust," *Figures III* (Paris: Seuil, 1972), on the effect of contagion that these relations have on metaphorical description, in particular of different steeples. Let us remember in passing that the intimate relation between a being and the "ground" of which he is the "product" and of which "one tastes in him the particular charm" animates as much the erotics of Proust as his aesthetics: see the peasant woman of Roussainville (*Remembrance*, 1:164, 170), the merchant woman who sells coffee along the train to Balbec (1:705), or the Maria of Esquisse 70 of *Within a Budding Grove* (*A la recherche du temps perdu* [Paris: Gallimard, Pléiade, 1987–89], 2:1005). We also know the strength and the duration of the links that according to him attach a literary work to the place, the circumstances, and the support of its first reading (*Against Sainte-Beuve and Other Essays*, trans. John Sturrock [London: Penguin, 1988], 205–6; *Remembrance*, 3:923: "I should seek out original editions, those, that is to say, in which I once received an original impression of a book").

10. Between October 1795, the date of its opening to the public, and April 1816, the date of its closure by law (see Francis Haskell, *L'Historien et les images* [Paris: Gallimard, 1995], chap. 9; Dominique Poulot, "Alexandre Lenoir et les Musées des Monuments français," in *Les Lieux de mémoire*, ed. Pierre Nora, vol. 2:

La Nation [Paris: Gallimard, 1986], 497, 531; and *Musée, nation, patrimoine, 1789–1815* [Paris: Gallimard, 1997], chaps. 10–12). One knows that there Michelet, in his childhood, had "first received a vivid impression of history. I filled these graves with my imagination, I felt those dead through the marble, and it was not without some terror that I entered under the low vaults where Dagobert, Chilpéric, and Frédegonde were sleeping" (Dedication of *Peuple* to Edgard Quinet [1846]; cf. *Cours au Collège de France* [1843] [Paris: Gallimard, 1995], vol. 1).

11. See Antoine Quatremère de Quincy, *Lettres à Miranda sur le déplacement des monuments de l'art de l'Italie* (1796) (Paris: Macula, 1989); and *Considérations morales sur la destination des ouvrages de l'art* (1815) (Paris: Fayard, 1989).

12. *Remembrance*, 1:693–94.

13. See plate 18 of the Album Lenoir, reproduced by Haskell, *L'Historien et les images*, 328.

14. *Against Sainte Beuve*, 174, 176.

15. *Against Sainte Beuve*, 63–69.

16. *Remembrance*, 2:1029. We see that the "seven league boots" have changed sides in the antithesis train/automobile.

17. *Remembrance*, 2:1037.

18. *Remembrance*, 2:1038.

19. Jean Giono, *Voyage en Italie* (1953), in *Journal, poèmes, essais* (Paris: Gallimard, Pléiade, 1995), 643.

20. "La Mort des cathédrales," *Le Figaro*, August 16, 1904, reprinted in the collection *Pastiches et mélanges*; now in the volume *Contre Saint-Beuve* of the Pléiade edition, which gives the passages suppressed in 1919 in a note. The whole of the writing relative to this theme, and/or the work of Ruskin, is a rather trying bibliographic labyrinth.

21. *Contre Sainte-Beuve*, 777.

22. And which Lenoir envisaged already in 1816, as a second-best, when the return in situ of the works kept in his museum and its closure began to be contemplated (see Poulot, "Alexandre Lenoir," 296).

23. The French word *dépaysement* is already used by Quatremère, whose opposition to the museum was, like La Sizeranne's and Hallays's, far stricter than Proust's: "It is to kill art to make its history; it is not to make history of it, but to make its epitaph" (*Considérations*, 48). If one wanted to push the comparison farther, one would have to add that Quatremère, by contrast, does not seem to be hostile to restorations (he approves at any rate of those of Roman antique dealers) and also that, between 1791 and 1793, when he was in charge of the

"pantheonization" of Sainte Geneviève, he can be regarded as a (virtual) precursor of the secularizations feared by Proust.

24. *Contre Sainte Beuve*, 735.

25. *Contre Sainte Beuve*, 85. Her homely look even inspired the name of "soubrette picarde."

26. The painting on an altar (e.g.) transported into a museum loses one of its functions, but that of representing what it represents stays with it.

27. *Contre Sainte-Beuve*, 780.

28. *Esthétique et philosophie* (Paris: Klincksieck, 1980), 1:29.

29. *Remembrance*, 1:219.

30. Thus for the one of the church of Balbec, *Remembrance*, 1:898–901.

31. *Correspondance*, ed. Ph. Kolb (Paris: Plon, VII, 1981), 250.

32. *Correspondance*, 8 October 1907; it is during the summer of 1907 that Proust visits in a car several churches and castles of Normandy, between Cabourg and Paris.

33. *Remembrance*, 2:911.

34. *Remembrance*, 2:1046–47.

35. *Against Sainte-Beuve*, 129.

36. As Marcel says à propos of the memory of the madeleine; it is certainly a matter of temporal distances.

37. *Remembrance*, 3:165.

38. *Against Sainte-Beuve*, 122–31.

39. Pre-text in manuscript, printed in *Contre Sainte-Beuve*, 724–25.

40. *A la recherche du temps perdu*, 2:975.

41. *Remembrance*, 2:971.

42. *A la recherche du temps perdu*, 4:205.

43. *A la recherche du temps perdu*, Esquisse 15–1, 4, p. 693, Esquisse 15–3, p. 694.

44. The title of an essay on the baroque in *Un Rêve fait à Mantoue* (Paris: Mercure, 1967).

45. I say "indifference of," and not to, the object because the aesthetic relation is certainly not a relation of indifference, but it invests, as passionately as one would wish, an object of which the election, and the "beauty," depend on it.

46. I mean chapter 3, "Sojourn in Venice," of *The Fugitive, Remembrance*, 3:637–71, in which the parallel fills the main parts of 637–44. Different pre-texts are presented under the title Esquisse 15, *A la recherche du temps perdu*, 4:689–98.

47. The proxy is double here, or rather triple: the grandmother expresses by way of her daughter an aesthetics shared by her grandson, the narrator, and their "father," the author Marcel Proust, who often defended it outside the novel.

48. *A la recherche du temps perdu*, 1:737. One must remember that the two characters of the mother and the grandmother have their root in a common figure and that Proust really did visit Venice in 1900 in the company of his mother.

49. Proust certainly knows Ruskin's commentaries on the asymmetry of the great facade of the Doges' Palace.

CHAPTER 18. "ONE OF MY FAVORITE AUTHORS"

1. Michael Riffaterre, *Fictional Truth* (Baltimore: Johns Hopkins University Press, 1990).

2. *Remembrance of Things Past*, trans. C. K. Scott Moncrieff and Terence Kilmartin (London: Chatto and Windus, 1981), 1:188.

3. *Remembrance*, 1:19. By a mistake already present in *Jean Santeuil*, Proust substitutes Thetys, Achilles' mother, for Cyrene.

4. *Remembrance*, 2:31–55.

5. Cf. *Figures III* (Paris: Seuil, 1972), 54.

6. *Remembrance*, 1:731–32.

7. Translator's note: This is the original word used by Proust, translated as *fluvial* in the passage quoted earlier.

8. "Questembert, Pontorson . . . lieux fluviatiles et poétiques" (*A la recherche du temps perdu*, 1:382).

9. "*Penei genitoris ad undam*, where the name of the river Peneus in the genitive (*Penei genitoris*) is almost identical to the Latin term that designates the generative penis (*penis genitoris*)" (Riffaterre, *Fictional Truth*, 103).

10. It is true that on this same page the Narrator evokes the *poems* that he dreams of composing and continues: "And these dreams warned me that, since I wanted some day to be an *author*." But it is one thing to begin, according to the custom of the period, a career as an author by the composition of juvenile poems, a different thing to qualify as an author the whole of a poet like Virgil. Marcel distinguishes the two notions clearly in speaking a little farther on of "the hope I had lost of succeeding one day in becoming an author and poet" (*Remembrance*, 1:195).

11. *Remembrance*, 1:92. Four pages farther on comes another, this time negative, mention of this motif: "But the interruption and the commentary which a visit from Swann once occasioned in the course of my reading, which had brought me to the work of an author quite new to me, Bergotte, resulted in the consequence that for a long time afterwards it was not against a wall gay with spikes of purple blossom, but against a wholly different background, the porch of a gothic cathedral, that I saw the figure of one of the women of whom I dreamed" (1:97). I will come back to this substitution.

12. *Remembrance*, 1:188.

13. *Les Pastiches de Proust. Édition critique et commentée* (Paris: Colin, 1970), 83–91.

14. *Remembrance*, 2:7.

15. *Contre Sainte-Beuve* (Paris: Gallimard, Pléiade, 1971).15. This pastiche was published in *Le Figaro*, March 1908.

16. *Sentimental Education*, trans. Robert Baldick (London: Penguin, 1964), 250.

17. Milly quotes this passage from a publication made in *La Table ronde* in April 1945 under the title "Un des premiers états de Swann." The other pre-text quoted by Milly comes from the *Contre Sainte-Beuve*, ed. Fallois (Paris: Gallimard, 1954): "Thus each of my summers had the face, the form of a being and the form of a country, or rather the form of a dream that was the desire of a being and of a country that I quickly mixed up; cattails with red and blue flowers surpassing a sunny wall, with leaves shining from humidity, were one year the signature that marked all my desires for nature" (84). This fragment does not seem to have been reprinted in the sketches of the Pléiade edition.

18. *A la recherche du temps perdu*, 1:761–62; see also the note on 1454. The place called Little Switzerland must be the valley of the Cousin, in the southwest of Avallon, where, in fact, one sees more mills than sawmills.

19. *A la recherche du temps perdu*, 1:753–54.

20. See n. 11.

21. *A la recherche du temps perdu*, 1:1451. The anthology of La Sizeranne appeared in 1909, and Proust certainly read it and read even the original text of *Seven Lamps* or its translation by G. Elwall (1900), in which this page opens chapter 6, "The Lamp of Memory." The description by Yoshida of these few pages is faithful, but we must notice that they mention no sawmill.

22. *Contre Sainte-Beuve*, 32.

23. This influence is too well known for us to insist on it, but it is necessary to note a double mention (*Remembrance*, 3:660 and 862) that the Narrator works on a translation of *Sesame and the Lilies*, a mention that makes of the active taste for Ruskin, common to Proust and to Marcel, one of the autobiographical traits of *Remembrance*.

24. I have stayed with the data given by specialists for mere readers, to which I belong. The Bibliothèque Nationale no doubt has other "versions" and other surprises. I admit my disappointment at having found no trace of *The Mill on the Floss*, one of the "cult books" of Proust and of which I long imagined that it contributed its part to the landscape of Guermantes.

25. *Course in General Linguistics*, trans. Roy Harris (London: G. Duckworth, 1983), 87–88.

26. See Gregory Currie, *An Ontology of Art* (New York: Macmillan, 1989).

27. See the commentaries when, in spring 1990, the Whitney version of the *Moulin de la galette* was sold, which turned around the idea: "This painting is fuzzier than the one in the Musée d'Orsay, thus in a sense more Impressionist." One could as well say, in an inverse sense and at the same level, that the Orsay version is not very fuzzy "*for* an Impressionist painting." On these interactions between the aesthetic and the historical, and thus in a sense between structure and genesis, see Kendall L. Walton, "Categories of Art," *Philosophical Review* 79 (1970): 334–67.

In the Stages Series